QuickBooks®
Online

Australian Edition

by Priscilla Meli
Elaine Marmel

for
dummies®
A Wiley Brand

QuickBooks® Online For Dummies®

Australian Edition published by

Wiley Publishing Australia Pty Ltd
42 McDougall Street
Milton, Qld 4064
www.dummies.com

Copyright © 2017 Wiley Publishing Australia Pty Ltd

The moral rights of the author have been asserted.

National Library of Australia
Cataloguing-in-Publication data:

Creator:	Meli, Priscilla Jo, author.
Title:	QuickBooks Online For Dummies / Priscilla Jo Meli, Elaine Marmel.
ISBN:	9780730344971 (pbk.)
	9780730344995 (ebook)
Edition:	Australian edition.
Series:	For Dummies.
Notes:	Includes index.
Subjects:	QuickBooks Online (Computer program)
	Accounting — Computer Programs —
	Handbooks, manuals, etc.
Other Creators/	
Contributors:	Marmel, Elaine

Cover image: © Intuit Australia Pty Ltd 2017. QuickBooks® and the QuickBooks logo are registered trademarks of Intuit Australia Pty Ltd.

Typeset by SPi

Printed in Singapore by C.O.S. Printers Pte Ltd

10 9 8 7 6 5 4 3 2 1

Contents at a Glance

Table of Contents

Foreword

Dear reader,

Welcome to Intuit QuickBooks Online! I'm delighted that you're taking a closer look.

You're actually in great company, with the world's leading cloud accounting solution for small businesses *and* their financial advisors. Each day, more than 50 000 Aussies — together with more than 1.6 million global customers — rely on our financial management solution to fuel business success.

Whether you're new to cloud accounting software, switching from another program, or just checking us out, this book will give you plenty of tips and shortcuts to help make you a QuickBooks Online pro in next to no time.

In case you wondered, Intuit offers a localised, cloud-based QuickBooks Online version specifically made for Australia, backed by more than 30 years of leading innovation.

Our Aussie small business customers tell us that using QuickBooks Online is easy and frees up their time to focus on growing their business or doing what they love. What's more, QuickBooks Online was designed mobile first, and customers can access and manage their finances anytime, anywhere and on any device.

A *For Dummies* book suggests the topic might be complex, so let me assure you, cloud accounting is pretty simple. For a start, it automates many business processes and removes time consuming tasks like data entry. QuickBooks Online can even help you get paid twice as fast thanks to our growing ecosystem and product innovation.

Around the world, we spend more than 10 000 hours with small business owners each year gathering insights to understand their experience with QuickBooks Online. The information we gather is then shared with our product development team so we can continually enhance our products, services and support. This is our innovation process and one that ensures we're continuously working to improve how we fuel your success.

The move to the cloud is well underway with rapid changes taking place. I'm so excited about the emerging trends and their impact on cloud accounting. In fact, I look forward to the next edition of this book because I anticipate highlighting our continued innovation, such as artificial intelligence and machine learning.

I wish you the best of everything with your small business. Based on what our customers tell us, we know that managing a small business presents challenges, yet the rewards can be great.

I'd also like to thank you for picking up this book. Your commitment to building a strong financial foundation by using QuickBooks Online helps ensure your business is more resilient to market forces. In turn, this helps build a prosperous economy and nation. That's great news for all.

Be sure to visit our community of customers at the following sites. I know they'd love to have you onboard and join the conversation.

You can find us on Facebook at www.facebook.com/QuickBooksAU.

Engage with us on Twitter at @QuickBooksAU.

If you are looking for more resources, please visit our Small Business Centre at www.intuit.com.au/r/.

And lastly, should you need an accountant or bookkeeper to help you get set up or to provide training, please find your perfect match at https://proadvisor.intuit.com.

Until next time,

Nicolette Maury

VP and Country Manager, QuickBooks Australia

Find me on Twitter or LinkedIn

Introduction

Have you been thinking about moving your accounting into a web-based product? Are you a QuickBooks desktop user who wants to stick with something you know but wants the flexibility of a web-based product? Are you interested in finding out more about Intuit's web-based product, QuickBooks Online (QBO)? Are you an accountant who is considering beginning to support your QuickBooks clients via QuickBooks Online Accountant (QBOA)? If you answered yes to any of these questions, this book is for you.

QuickBooks Online and QuickBooks Online Accountant are web-based accounting solutions from Intuit. Don't be fooled; they are *not* the desktop product migrated to the web. They've been built from the ground up to function on the Internet and can be used on multiple devices such as PC, Mac, iOS and Android. No matter which device, QBO will instantaneously synchronise data between users and devices.

About This Book

Intuit's web-based accounting product is really almost two products: Business users who want to do their accounting on the web use QBO, whereas accountants use QBOA, which enables the accountant to log in to a client's books and make changes and queries as needed. Although much of QBO and QBOA look and behave alike, QBOA incorporates tools that an accountant needs while working on a client's books. And accountants need to manage multiple client companies, whereas business user clients typically do not.

This book has been divided into three parts. In the first part of the book, we examine what QBO and QBOA are — and what they aren't — and we describe what you need to be able to use QBO and QBOA. We explain the various editions and features available. And in Chapter 1, you'll find some information about the available interfaces for QBO and QBOA (you can work with the products using a browser or using an app).

The second part of the book focuses on using QBO and is aimed at the business user; however, the accountant who opens a client's company via QBOA will be able to use the same tools that the business user uses to manage lists, enter transactions and print reports.

The third part of the book is aimed at the accountant and covers using QBOA.

We don't pretend to cover every detail of every feature in QBO or QBOA. Instead, we focus on covering the tools we think most users will need as they navigate QBO and QBOA.

REMEMBER

As we discuss in Chapter 2, different versions of QBO are available; we used QBO Plus as we wrote this book because it contains the most features. Users of other versions might find references in this book to features they don't have because they aren't using the Plus version.

Before we dive in, let's get a few technical convention details out of the way:

>> Text that you're meant to type as it appears in the book is **bold.** The exception is when you're working through a list of steps: Because each step is bold, the text to type is not bold.

>> Web addresses and programming code appear in monofont. If you're reading a digital version of this book on a device connected to the Internet, note that you can tap or click a web address to visit that website, like this: www.dummies.com.

>> In our experience, QBO and QBOA function best in Chrome. For that reason, we've devoted The Part of Tens chapters in this book to Chrome so that, if you aren't familiar with Chrome, you can get up and running more quickly.

>> When we discuss a command to choose, we separate the elements of the sequence with a command arrow that looks like this: ⇨. For example, when you see Chrome Menu ⇨ Settings, that means you should click the Chrome Menu button and, from the drop-down menu that appears, click Settings.

Foolish Assumptions

We had to assume some things about you to write this book. Here are the assumptions we made:

>> You know that you need to manage the accounts for your business, and you might even have some sort of setup in place to record this information. We *don't* assume that you know how to do all that on a computer.

>> You have some interest in managing the accounts for your business using a web-based product.

>> You are probably but not necessarily a QuickBooks desktop edition user.

>> You have a personal computer (that you know how to turn on) running Microsoft Windows Vista, Windows 7, Windows 8.1 or Windows 10. We wrote this book using Windows 10.

>> You might have purchased an edition of QuickBooks Online, but not necessarily.

>> You have some basic accounting or bookkeeping knowledge.

Icons Used in This Book

TIP

Think of these icons as the fodder of advice columns. They offer (hopefully) wise advice or a bit more information about a topic under discussion.

REMEMBER

This icon points out juicy tidbits that are likely to be repeatedly useful to you — so please don't forget them.

WARNING

Danger, Will Robinson, danger! Well, okay, it's really not life-threatening. In this book, you see this icon when we're trying to help you avoid mistakes that can cost money.

Beyond the Book

In addition to the content in this book, this product also comes with a free access-anywhere cheat sheet that gives you keyboard shortcuts for QBO and QBOA and some handy tool buttons in QBO. To get this cheat sheet, simply go to www.dummies.com and search for 'QuickBooks Online For Dummies Cheat Sheet' in the Search box.

Where to Go from Here

Simply turn the page. Seriously. You can dive in anywhere you want and come back as often as you like. You don't have to read through this book cover to cover, because each section stands alone and provides step-by-step instructions for common tasks. You should consider this book a reference that you use when you need it.

That said, if you're just getting started with QBO or QBOA, you might want to turn the page and follow, in order, the chapters in Part 1. Then feel free to explore any topic you like, using the table of contents or the index to help you find a topic.

1

Getting Started with QBO and QBOA

IN THIS PART . . .

Compare the differences between QBO products.

Learn the requirements to use QBO.

Meet the QBO interface.

Chapter **1**

Introducing QBO and QBOA

QuickBooks Online (QBO) and QuickBooks Online Accountant (QBOA) are web-based products you can use to manage your business's accounting. This chapter introduces these products and discusses whether you should move into the cloud to manage your accounting. It also examines the system requirements for these products.

QBO for the Business User and QBOA for the Accountant

QuickBooks Online offers you the ability to manage your business's accounting in the cloud. The software is divided into two products: One for the business user and the other for accountants. QBO and QBOA work on multiple devices, such as PC, Mac, smartphone, tablet and mobile devices.

QuickBooks Online (QBO) is the cloud-based product for business users who need to perform typical accounting tasks.

QuickBooks Online Accountant (QBOA) is the cloud-based portal that accountants use to access their clients' QBO companies, work in them, and communicate with clients and other members of their accounting team. QBOA also comes with one free company that accountants can use to track their own businesses.

Comparing interfaces

QBO and QBOA were initially written and optimised to be used in the major web browsers — Chrome, Safari and Firefox. Later, Intuit added QBO apps that you can use for Windows, Mac and Android mobile devices. In this section, you explore what QBO and QBOA look like in a browser and in the Windows app.

In a browser, an open company in QBO looks similar to the one shown in Figure 1-1. We cover the interface in more detail in Chapter 3 but, for the time being, the most important thing to notice is the Navigation bar that runs down the left side of the screen. If you've been a QuickBooks desktop user and you've used the Left Icon bar in that product, you might find the Navigation bar a familiar tool. The Left Icon bar and the Navigation bar work the same way; you click a link in either of them to navigate to a portion of the program.

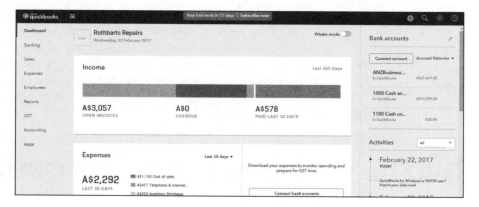

FIGURE 1-1:
An open
company in QBO.

When you collapse the Navigation bar, you have more screen real estate to view the right side of the QBO interface.

At the top of the screen on the far right side, you see tools that help QBO users create transactions, search for existing transactions and view recent transactions. These tools are marked by icons as follows:

Quick Create Tool: Shortcut to frequently used transactions

Search Function: Including basic and advanced search options

Settings Menu (Gear icon): Links to advanced settings and more complex functions

Help Menu: Shortcut to support feature, including Online Chat and Forums

Figure 1-2 shows what an accountant sees immediately upon logging in to QBOA. The Navigation bar changes to support an accountant's needs; you can read more about the QBOA interface in Chapter 13.

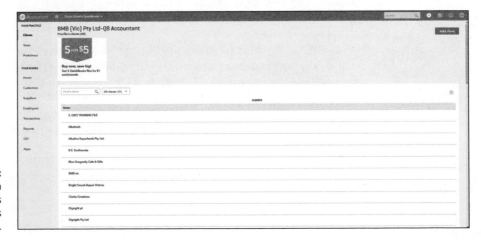

FIGURE 1-2:
The first view an accountant sees when he opens QBOA.

When an accountant opens a client's company from within QBOA (see Figure 1-3), the interface resembles what a client sees, with some minor differences — compare, for example, Figure 1-1 with Figure 1-3. First, you know you're using QBOA because the top of the Navigation bar shows QuickBooks Accountant. Second, the tools used to search for a transaction, go to a report and view recent transactions are combined into one Search box near the right side of the screen. And third, the Accountant Tools menu (the briefcase icon) displays tools not found in QBO that help accountants manage client companies.

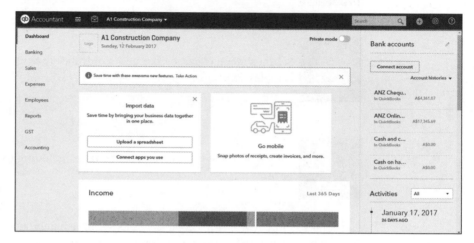

FIGURE 1-3: An open company in QBOA.

Even though an open company looks a bit different depending on whether it is opened using QBO or QBOA, the basic functionality doesn't really change, other than accountants having more options than business users have.

REMEMBER

Because QBOA contains functionality that QBO doesn't have, we've organised this book so that QBO users can focus on Part 2 when using the product, and QBOA users can use the information in both Parts 2 and 3 to work with a company file.

To browse or not to browse . . .

In addition to working in a browser, you also can work in mobile apps. To find the app that works best for you, visit the Intuit Mobile App website (`www.intuit.com. au/mobile`).

TIP

Mobile apps are also available for Macs and iPhone, iPad and Android devices. You'll find Pinch and Zoom functionality is now available in the mobile apps and in browsers on mobile devices.

So take your choice: Work in a browser, work in a mobile app or work in both, depending on your needs at the moment! You're not limited; you don't have to choose between an app and a browser. Work in one or the other, or both. The free app is a great resource for businesses with people on the road or offsite. They can have their customers sign off on orders via the tablet app, issue invoices, input expenses and receipts while all the time collaborating instantly with their teammates in the office.

TIP

An example Priscilla uses all the time to highlight the benefits of the free app is that when she wakes up, she checks her bank accounts via her mobile phone to see what has gone out and what has come in overnight (hopefully more has come in that what has gone out!). After she closes her bank app, she opens the QuickBooks app on her phone and cashes off the customer payments. In a matter of seconds, her books are updated before she even gets into the office and turns on a computer! Just keep in mind that the browser provides a full experience (that is, full functionality), whereas a mobile app includes only certain functions. See Figure 1-4 for an idea of how the mobile app looks.

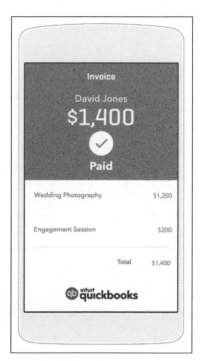

FIGURE 1-4:
QBO on a smartphone.

REMEMBER

QBO and QBOA come with free smartphone and tablet apps that sync automatically with your PC or Mac; however, QBO also has Self Employed — a standalone app separate to the other software that can only be used on a smartphone (see Figure 1-5). At the time of writing, QBO Self Employed does not support GST but does have a great feature that enables you to track mileage, which the other QBO programs don't have.

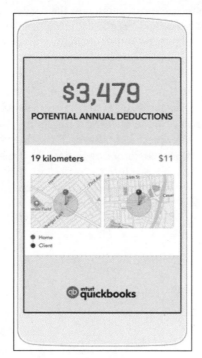

Understanding the Cloud

Just to make sure we're on the same page here, we're defining the *cloud* as software and data housed securely in remote data centres (not on your office premises) and accessed securely using the Internet. Working in the cloud can increase your efficiency by offering you the opportunity to work anywhere, communicate easily with others and collaborate in real time.

REMEMBER

Regardless of whether you use QBO or QBOA in a browser or in an app, both the software and the data are housed on servers controlled by Intuit and accessible via the Internet.

In the traditional model of software use, you buy software and install it on your computer. Or you might buy the software and install it on a vendor's server. QBO and QBOA fall into the category of Software as a Service (SaaS). You typically don't buy SaaS software; instead, you rent it (that is, you purchase a subscription).

Because SaaS software is typically web-based software, you access SaaS software over the Internet using a browser. A *browser* is software installed on your local computer or mobile device that you use to, well, browse the Internet, looking up cool stuff like what the stock market is doing today, what kind of weather you can expect on Friday when your vacation starts, how to get to your boss's house for the party she's having, and — oh, yes — to work with web-based software such as QBO and QBOA. In the case of QBO and QBOA, you can work with these web-based SaaS products using either a browser or an app you download to your computer.

Using web-based software can be attractive for a number of reasons. For example, using web-based software, you have access to that software's information anywhere, anytime, from any device — stationary or mobile.

REMEMBER

Some people see the 'anywhere, anytime' feature as a potential disadvantage because it makes information too readily available — and therefore a target for hackers. Intuit stores your data on servers that use bank-level security and encryption, and Intuit automatically backs up your data for you. Others see the 'anywhere, anytime' feature as a disadvantage for exactly the reason that they have access to the software's information anywhere, anytime and from any device, offering the opportunity to work more than they'd like. You are in charge of your life, so . . . no comment on this 'disadvantage'.

In addition to the 'anywhere, anytime' advantage, web-based software like QBO and QBOA promotes collaboration and can help you save time. Using QBO and QBOA, accountants, bookkeepers and business users can communicate about issues that arise, as described in Chapter 16.

Then there's the issue of keeping software up to date. Desktop software such as QuickBooks is updated typically once each year. Unlike their desktop cousin, QBO and QBOA are updated (automatically by Intuit without your time and effort) every two to four weeks.

REMEMBER

Because updating occurs so frequently to QBO and QBOA, by the time this book is published, things (and screens) might have changed. Actually, make that 'probably have changed'.

Should You Move to the Cloud?

Before you make the move to the cloud, you should consider the needs of your business in the following areas:

» Invoicing, point of sale, electronic payment and customer relationship management

» Financial and tax reporting

» Budgeting

» Time-tracking and payroll

» Inventory, job costing and job scheduling

» Managing company expenses and vendor bills

Beyond the advantages described in the preceding section, the particular needs of a business might dictate whether you can use QBO. For example, QBO may not work for you if your business has industry-specific needs for which add-on applications are not currently available. In addition, QBO won't work for you if you need to track your balances by class.

System Requirements

Using a web-based software product typically doesn't require a lot of hardware and software; in fact, the demands of QBO and QBOA aren't extensive. In particular, you need

» An Internet connection — Intuit recommends a high-speed connection

» One of the four supported Internet browsers:

- Chrome

- Firefox

- Internet Explorer 10 or higher

- Safari 6.1 if your operating system is iOS 7 or higher

Although QBO and QBOA work in all the major browsers, they work best, in our experience, in Chrome, with Firefox coming in a close second. Therefore, we use Chrome throughout this book, and the Part of Tens chapters cover using Chrome so that you can get comfortable with that browser. If you're a Firefox user, give QBO and QBOA a try in Firefox.

You also can use the QuickBooks Online mobile app, which works with Windows phones and tablets, the iPhone and the iPad, and Android phones and tablets. The requirements for the QuickBooks Online mobile app are the same as those outlined for the non-mobile versions: You need a browser on your device and an Internet connection. Be aware that mobile devices do not support all features of QBO and QBOA (see Figure 1-6 for an example of this).

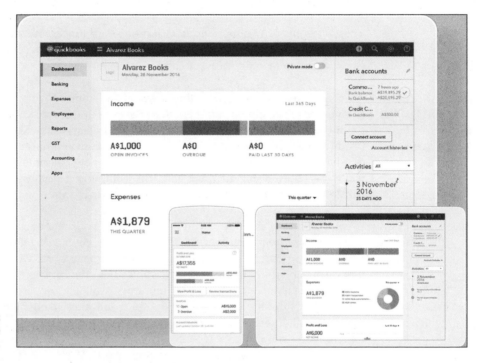

FIGURE 1-6:
QBO using the mobile app.

REMEMBER

In this book, we use a Windows 10 desktop computer and the Chrome browser.

Whether you work on a desktop computer or on a mobile device, the computer or device should meet the basic requirements of the operating system you use on that computer or device. For example, if you're using a Windows desktop computer, you need the amount of RAM (random access memory) specified by Microsoft to load Windows on the computer before you can even launch your browser. If you don't have sufficient RAM to run the operating system, you certainly won't be happy with the behaviour of QBO and QBOA. You won't be happy with the behaviour of the computer, either.

Basic requirements (and we stress the word *basic*) for a Windows 7, 8.1, and 10 computer, as specified by Microsoft, are

>> 1-gigahertz (GHz) or faster 32-bit (x86) or 64-bit (x64) processor

>> 1 gigabyte (GB) of RAM (32 bit) or 2GB of RAM (64 bit)

>> 16GB of available hard disk space (32 bit) or 20GB (64 bit)

>> A display that supports at least 800 x 600 dpi

>> DirectX 9 graphics device with WDDM 1.0 or higher driver

These versions of Windows work with multi-core processors, and all 32-bit versions of Windows can support up to 32 processor cores, whereas 64-bit versions can support up to 256 processor cores.

REMEMBER

A word on the word *basic*. You'll be a whole lot happier if your desktop computer components have higher numbers than the ones in the preceding list. If you have a computer that's fairly new — say, three to four years old — you might need only to add some RAM or possibly hard disk space. If your computer is older than three or four years, you should consider purchasing new equipment, simply because you'll be unbelievably happier with the computer's performance. Technology continues to improve dramatically in short spurts of time.

If you buy a new computer, you don't need to worry about much to meet more than the basic requirements. We're pretty sure you can't buy a new computer containing a 1GHz processor; most computers today come with at least 2.5GHz processors and they support better graphics than the DirectX 9 graphics listed in the basic requirements. And most monitors available for purchase today don't support low resolutions such as 800 x 600; you most likely own a monitor that supports higher resolution. In our opinion, 1GB of RAM is insufficient; your desktop computer should have at least 4GB of RAM, and you'll be much happier if it has 8GB of RAM. On the hard drive requirement, if you don't have the 16GB or 20GB of available space specified, you probably should be considering a hard drive replacement for your computer.

The amount of RAM your computer can successfully use depends on the computer's architecture — in particular, if your computer uses a 32-bit processor, as older computers often do, your computer might not be able to 'see' more than 4GB of RAM. So, you could put 16GB of RAM in the computer and only be able to use 4GB. And part of that 4GB goes to other stuff, like your video card; so, with most 32-bit processors (there are a few exceptions), your computer can use only 3GB of RAM. Bottom line here: Newer computers use 64-bit processors and can take advantage of much more RAM, which makes them much faster.

Chapter **2**

Embracing the QBO/QBOA Format

QBO and QBOA are not traditional software that you buy and install on your local computer. In this chapter, we explore the QBO/QBOA software format. If you need more help evaluating whether QBO can meet your needs, head back to Chapter 1.

It's All about Subscriptions

QBO and QBOA fall into the category of Software as a Service (SaaS). As such, you don't buy the software. Instead, you rent it; that is, you buy a subscription to use the software for a time period specified by the seller.

REMEMBER

Traditionally, you buy a *licence* to use software that you install on your computer and, typically, that licence permits you to install the software on only one computer.

Of course, a QBO user can pay varying amounts for a subscription, depending on the subscription level purchased.

QBO is available at four different subscription levels, and each subsequent subscription level costs more and contains more functionality. The QBO subscriptions available at the time of writing are

>> Self-Employed

>> Simple Start

>> Essentials

>> Plus

REMEMBER

All versions of QBO share three attributes in common. First, you can use a tablet, smartphone or desktop computer to access your data (except for Self-Employed, because it is app-based only). Second, your data is automatically backed up online. And third, all versions of QBO use 128-bit Secure Sockets Layer (SSL), the same security and encryption used by banks to secure data sent over the Internet.

After you assess your needs as described in Chapter 1, use the following information to identify the subscription level that will meet your requirements. You can also later upgrade subscriptions to a higher level, but you cannot downgrade to a lower level.

The Self-Employed version

This version of QBO is aimed at freelancers and self-employed individuals who do not track GST. Using the Self-Employed version, you can

>> Separate business from personal spending

>> Calculate and pay estimated quarterly taxes

>> Track mileage

>> Track income and expenses

>> Take snapshots of your expense receipts

>> Download transactions from your bank and credit card accounts

Like the other versions of QBO, you can use a tablet or smartphone to access your data. In addition, the Self-Employed version uses the same security and encryption as banks, and your data is automatically backed up online. As you might expect, this version has the fewest reports available — only three — and only permits one user.

REMEMBER

Be aware that, at the time of writing, the Self-Employed version of QBO didn't link with QBOA.

The Simple Start version

The Simple Start version of QBO is great for a new business with basic bookkeeping needs. With Simple Start, you can

- » Track your income and expenses
- » Download transactions from your bank and credit card accounts
- » Create an unlimited number of customers
- » Send unlimited estimates and invoices
- » Print cheques and record transactions to track expenses
- » Import data from Microsoft Excel or QuickBooks desktop
- » Invite up to two accountants to access your data
- » Integrate with available apps

Although the Simple Start version supports Accounts Receivable functions, you can't track bills due in the future in the Simple Start version because it doesn't include any Accounts Payable functions. And one other important consideration: The Simple Start version also has no general ledger.

Although the Simple Start version allows two accountants to work in the client's company (or an accountant and a bookkeeper), Simple Start is still designed for a single user. Therefore, the accountant cannot create the client's company for the client. At the time the company is created in QBO, whoever creates the company becomes, in QBO language, the Master Administrator.

Although QBO Simple Start has a single-user restriction, it offers more than 20 reports. And Simple Start users can memorise report settings and produce memorised reports.

REMEMBER

For subscription levels that support multiple users, the accountant can create the company for the client and then assign the Master Administrator role to the client. And, if the accountant doesn't make the client the Master Administrator when creating the company, the accountant can, later on, transfer the Master Administrator role to the client.

The Essentials version

The Essentials version of QBO includes all the features found in Simple Start. In addition, you can

>> Set up invoices to automatically bill on a recurring schedule

>> Take advantage of Accounts Payable functions, including entering vendor bills and scheduling their payment for later

>> Compare your sales and profitability with industry trends

>> Create and post recurring transactions

>> Control what your users can access

The Essentials version permits three simultaneous users and two accountant users. In addition, the Essentials version contains the reports found in Simple Start and 20 additional reports.

The Plus version

The Plus version of QBO is the most full-featured version of QBO. It contains all the features found in the Essentials version. In addition, you can

>> Create, send and track purchase orders.

>> Create budgets to estimate future income and expenses, and create multiple budgets per year, location, class or customer.

>> Track inventory using the first in, first out (FIFO) inventory valuation method.

TIP

QBO supports light inventory needs: If you sell finished goods, QBO should be able to manage your needs. But if you need to assemble finished goods to sell, QBO won't meet your needs on its own. You can look for an app to supplement your inventory needs; we talk about apps at the end of this chapter.

>> Categorise income and expenses using class or location tracking.

>> Track sales and profitability by business location. **Note:** You can assign only one location to a transaction, but you can assign multiple classes to a transaction.

>> Give employees and subcontractors limited access to the QBO company to enter time worked.

>> Track billable hours by customer.

QBO supports light job-costing needs, but it does not allow you to automatically cost labour.

REMEMBER

REMEMBER

We use QBO Plus for this book because it contains the most features, which means users of other versions might find references in this book to features they don't have. If you're an accounting professional using QBOA, note that the company that comes with QBOA is a Plus company.

The Plus version supports five simultaneous users and two accountant users. The Plus version also contains more than 65 reports: All the reports found in both the Simple Start and the Essentials versions, and some additional reports.

When purchasing your subscription through an accountant or bookkeeper, the subscription will come with unlimited users.

What Does QBO Cost?

The big question: What does it cost? The price is dependent primarily on the QBO version you choose.

If you're a business user who signs up on your own for a QBO subscription, the price per month at the time of writing appears in Figure 2-1. You should check the Intuit QuickBooks Online website for regular specials and the option of a free trial.

REMEMBER

The prices shown in Figure 2-1 are monthly subscription prices and, at the time of writing, the sale price was good for six months.

REMEMBER

If you opt for a 30-day free trial, you won't get the sale price for the subscription. But, if you 'buy now', Intuit gives you a 60-day, money-back guarantee on your purchase.

If you are an accounting professional, you can sign up for the Wholesale Pricing program and use QBOA for free. If you create a client's company as part of the Wholesale Pricing program and you manage the client's subscription, Intuit sends you the bill for the client's subscription. It is then your responsibility to bill the client for the QBO subscription. The bill you receive from Intuit is a single consolidated bill for all the QBO subscriptions you manage. For a little more information on the Wholesale Pricing program, see Chapter 13. But for the complete skinny on the Wholesale Pricing program, contact Intuit. Note that accounting professionals might be able to get QBO for their clients at a reduced price.

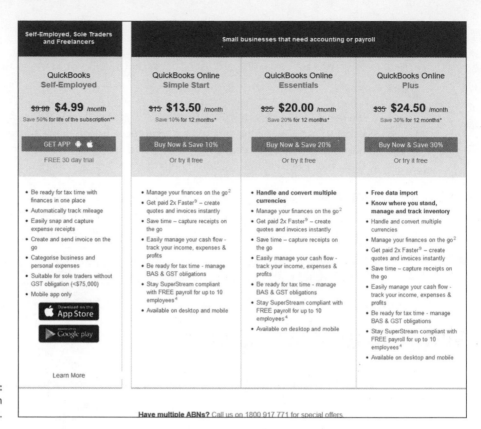

QuickBooks Self-Employed	QuickBooks Online Simple Start	QuickBooks Online Essentials	QuickBooks Online Plus
Self-Employed, Sole Traders and Freelancers	**Small businesses that need accounting or payroll**		
~~$9.99~~ **$4.99** /month	~~$15~~ **$13.50** /month	~~$25~~ **$20.00** /month	~~$35~~ **$24.50** /month
Save 50% for life of the subscription**	Save 10% for 12 months*	Save 20% for 12 months*	Save 30% for 12 months*
GET APP	Buy Now & Save 10%	Buy Now & Save 20%	Buy Now & Save 30%
FREE 30 day trial	Or try it free	Or try it free	Or try it free

QuickBooks Self-Employed:
- Be ready for tax time with finances in one place
- Automatically track mileage
- Easily snap and capture expense receipts
- Create and send invoice on the go
- Categorise business and personal expenses
- Suitable for sole traders without GST obligation (<$75,000)
- Mobile app only

App Store · Google play

Learn More

QuickBooks Online Simple Start:
- Manage your finances on the go[2]
- Get paid 2x Faster[9] – create quotes and invoices instantly
- Save time – capture receipts on the go
- Easily manage your cash flow - track your income, expenses & profits
- Be ready for tax time - manage BAS & GST obligations
- Stay SuperStream compliant with FREE payroll for up to 10 employees[4]
- Available on desktop and mobile

QuickBooks Online Essentials:
- **Handle and convert multiple currencies**
- Manage your finances on the go[2]
- Get paid 2x Faster[9] – create quotes and invoices instantly
- Save time – capture receipts on the go
- Easily manage your cash flow - track your income, expenses & profits
- Be ready for tax time - manage BAS & GST obligations
- Stay SuperStream compliant with FREE payroll for up to 10 employees[4]
- Available on desktop and mobile

QuickBooks Online Plus:
- **Free data import**
- **Know where you stand, manage and track inventory**
- Handle and convert multiple currencies
- Manage your finances on the go[2]
- Get paid 2x Faster[9] – create quotes and invoices instantly
- Save time – capture receipts on the go
- Easily manage your cash flow - track your income, expenses & profits
- Be ready for tax time - manage BAS & GST obligations
- Stay SuperStream compliant with FREE payroll for up to 10 employees[4]
- Available on desktop and mobile

Have multiple ABNs? Call us on 1800 917 771 for special offers.

FIGURE 2-1:
QBO subscription pricing.

REMEMBER

If an accounting professional creates a company through QBOA, the company does not come with a 30-day free trial. Instead, at the time the accounting professional creates the company, she must provide a payment method to ensure uninterrupted service.

If your client initially sets up QBO with his or her own subscription, you can move that existing QBO subscription to your consolidated bill at the discounted rate. And, if your arrangement with your client doesn't work out, you can remove the client from your consolidated bill, and the client can begin paying for his own subscription.

Addressing Payroll Needs

When you sign up for QBO Simple Start, Essentials or Plus subscriptions (or your accountant/bookkeeper creates a file for you), you will automatically have access to payroll features via KeyPay, a third-party provider with software that is fully integrated into the QBO program. At the time of writing, payroll is free for up to 10 employees per month — if you have more employees than this, an additional cost of $4 per additional employee is charged via a separate billing method. This means KeyPay will prompt you to enter payment details and will bill you directly. For details on paying employees, see Chapter 9.

To turn on the Payroll feature, go to the Employees section of the Navigation bar and click the Turn on Payroll button (see Figure 2-2).

FIGURE 2-2:
Turning on the
Payroll feature.

Switching from QuickBooks Desktop

At this point (or maybe earlier than now), you might be wondering if you can easily switch to QBO if you have been a QuickBooks desktop program user. The answer is yes. The Appendix provides details on importing QuickBooks desktop data into QBO. And the import process doesn't affect your original desktop company; it's still available via the desktop product.

TIP

After you import your desktop data into QBO, you should run the Profit & Loss report and the Balance Sheet using the Accrual method for all dates from both QBO and QuickBooks desktop to ensure both versions show the same information. You should also reconcile any bank accounts.

And if you want some reassurance that you'll get the same accurate information from QBO that you got from QuickBooks desktop, you can 'run in parallel' for a time period you specify. For example, you might decide to enter all your transactions in both versions of the software for one month; at the end of that time, you can run reports from both products and make sure you see the same information.

WARNING

Although you can continue to use the QuickBooks desktop while using QBO, once you make the switch to QBO, be aware that no synchronisation occurs between QuickBooks desktop and QBO. So changes you make in one are not reflected in the other. Unless you're temporarily running in parallel, continuing to use both products could really mess up your books, because you might accidentally enter transactions into one product and not the other.

Where Add-On Apps Fit In

QBO doesn't operate as a complete, standalone accounting solution. It does have functional limitations. To achieve more functionality in QBO, you can use apps (available via Intuit add-ons).

Many third-party developers have been creating apps to enhance the functionality of QBO and, over time, you can expect more apps to be developed.

In QBO, you can click the Apps link in the Navigation bar that runs down the left side of QBO to visit the App Centre and explore available apps. In QBOA, this won't appear, so you need to go directly to the QuickBooks App Store (apps.intuit.com) to research and connect apps to your file. Figure 2-3 shows the QBO App Centre and some of the available apps.

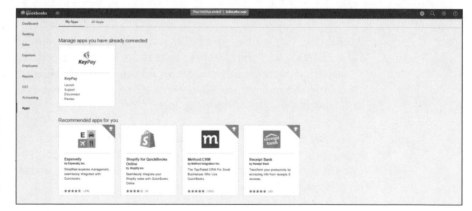

FIGURE 2-3: Take a trip to the QuickBooks App Centre to search for additional functionality for QBO.

Click any app to navigate to a page that describes the app, provides pricing information and often provides a video about the app (see Figure 2-4).

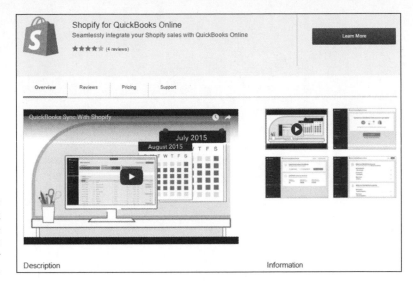

Apps are making inroads towards eliminating any possible software limitations. For example, Lettuce, an app that provides advanced inventory management features for QBO, did such a fine job of handling inventory functions that Intuit acquired Lettuce for the purpose of integrating it into QBO.

2
Managing the Books for the Business User

Chapter **3**

Setting Up a Business in QBO

After you sign up for QBO, you log in. QBO then prompts you to set up your business. You may choose to have your data imported from another software program to your QBO file, and we quickly look at this option towards the start of this chapter. Or, you can use the QBO set-up wizard, as shown through the remainder of this chapter.

Signing Up for QBO

After you complete the sign-up process for a QBO account, Intuit, by default, logs you in to your account and walks you through the process of setting up your QBO file. The process is relatively quick — you're asked for just enough information to allow you to set up your file, so make sure you enter additional information and fine-tune your settings as soon as it's convenient to do so.

You'll need the following information to complete the set-up process:

>> Your company's name and address

>> The industry in which your company operates

>> Your company's legal structure (such as sole trader, company or partnership)

>> The types of payments you accept from your customers (that is, cash, cheques and/or credit cards)

To sign up for a QBO account, follow these steps:

1. **Visit www.intuit.com.au/pricing.**

2. **Find the four boxes describing each version of QBO.**

3. **In the version of QBO that you want to try, click the Free 30-Day Trial link.**

   The Free 30-Day Trial link appears below the Buy Now button.

REMEMBER

   Be aware that the price you pay for QBO depends on whether you choose the Buy Now option or the Free 30-Day Trial. If you opt to 'buy now', you pay less for your subscription because discounts don't apply to the Free 30-Day Trial.

4. **Fill in your email address and name, and create a password (see Figure 3-1).**

   If you already have an Intuit user ID, supply that user ID and password.

   Your password must be between 6 and 32 characters and consist of a mix of letters and numbers. The password can also contain some special characters — for example, you can include an exclamation point (!) in your password and it will be accepted. The user ID and password you supply are the ones you use each time you log in to QBO.

5. **Click the Start Free Trial button below the boxes you completed in Step 4.**

   At the time that we wrote this, a window appeared that offered the option to skip the free trial and buy the product at a discounted rate. You can buy, but we opted to click the Continue to Trial button.

QBO sets up your free trial, logs you in to QBO, and displays the set-up wizard . . . read on.

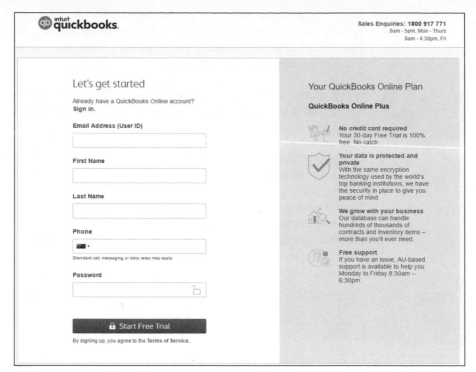

FIGURE 3-1:
Fill in the
information
needed to start
the free trial.

Setting Up a New Business

When you first sign up for a QBO account, Intuit logs you in to your QBO account and, by default, displays the set-up wizard. The first screen of the wizard, shown in Figure 3-2, asks for basic company information.

FIGURE 3-2:
Provide basic
company
information.

As you supply address information, QBO automatically prepares an invoice form that contains the information; you'll use this form (or a variant of it) to prepare the invoices you send to customers.

TIP

If you have a basically square company logo in JPG, GIF, BMP or PNG format, you can upload it to include on your invoice. Just click the Logo button to navigate to your logo.

When you finish providing address information, click the Next button in the lower left corner of the screen.

On the next screen, shown in Figure 3-3, you provide more information about your company so that Intuit can customise QBO to suit your needs: Supply your industry, the type of things you sell and, if you have the information handy, your business type and age. Then click Next.

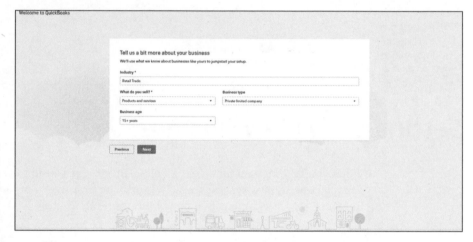

FIGURE 3-3:
Provide information about the stuff you sell and your company's industry.

REMEMBER

Only your industry and the type of stuff you sell are required. Supplying your business type helps QBO set up your Chart of Accounts more accurately.

If you're keeping track of your business information now, supply the method you currently use on the next screen. You can choose from the following:

>> Excel

>> Google

>> Pen and paper

- >> Online banking

- >> Other software

The answer you provide determines the screen you see next. For this book, we chose 'pen and paper', which assumes you have nothing in electronic form to import. (See the following section if you do have data to import.)

When you click Next, the wizard then asks you to select the elements that matter to you most; you can choose any of the following that apply to you:

- >> Invoicing

- >> Expense tracking

- >> My accountant

- >> Mobile

- >> Point of sale

- >> E-commerce

- >> GST

- >> My employees

For our trial company, we chose invoicing, expense tracking, my accountant, mobile and GST. If something matters to you later (like working with an accountant), you can set that up in your company when it suits you. So don't worry if you don't select something that you later determine you should have selected.

Click Next and QBO searches online for businesses similar to yours and establishes appropriate options and settings; when QBO finishes the search, you see a message that your QuickBooks is ready and you can click the Let's Dive In button to get started.

When you click Next, QBO displays your company's Dashboard and displays links to options you might want to set up to get started. In this case, we see boxes containing options to Set Up GST, Get Set Up by a Pro and Go Mobile (see Figure 3-4).

We examine the Dashboard in the section 'Understanding the Dashboard', later in this chapter, but essentially you've just completed most of the initial set-up work; other program settings are covered later in this chapter.

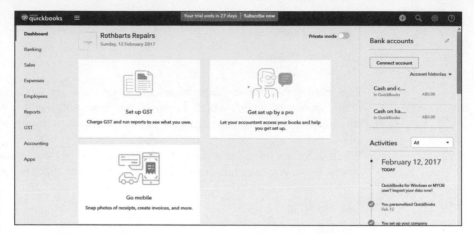

FIGURE 3-4:
Your QBO
Dashboard just
after creating
your company.

Importing Company Data into QBO

At the time of writing, importing data into QBO from another source is free for up to two years of data. *Note:* This covers importing data for the current financial year and for one previous financial year. The two-year allowance is not based on calendar years. A nominal fee of $26.50 (at the time of writing) is applied per year thereafter, depending on how many years of data you want to bring across.

This data conversion is available for data imported from the following:

>> Reckon Accounts for business, 2016 or earlier (.qbb or .qbw file types)

>> Reckon Accounts Hosted

>> Reckon QuickBooks 2009 or later (.qbb or .qbw file types)

>> MYOB AccountEdge V14 and earlier (.myo file type)

>> MYOB Account Right Enterprise, Premier V19 and earlier (.myo file type)

>> MYOB Account Right V 2012–2016 (.myox file type)

>> Xero (excluding Xero US Version)

To begin a file conversion visit www.odyssey-resources.com/quickbooks_online/Conversion.php. For additional details on importing a file, also see Chapter 14 (or ask your accountant to help you with the import). And don't worry if you don't want to import your entire desktop company; you can import just the list information from that company, as described in Chapter 4. Importing lists will still save you a lot of time and set-up work.

TIP

You can import your lists of customers, suppliers, employees, chart of accounts and products and services via a CSV file or MS Excel spreadsheet at any stage and QBO will recognise any duplicate entries and prompt you for direction.

Understanding the Dashboard

When you first see your QBO company, your Dashboard contains boxes with links to options you can use to set up features in QBO that are important to you (refer back to Figure 3-4). You can use those links and set up those options now, or you can wait until later. To hide the options, slide your mouse over any item, and an X appears in the upper right corner of the box.

When you click the X, QBO offers you the option to permanently dismiss the box or to see it later (see Figure 3-5). Click your choice. If you choose to see the option later, the box will reappear the next time you log in to your QBO company.

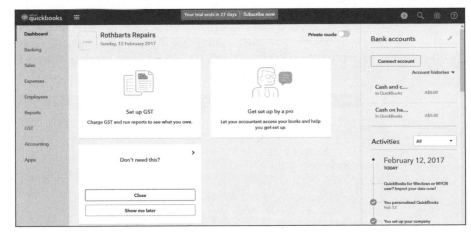

FIGURE 3-5:
You can close or view later the boxes that offer to help you perform some QBO set-up work.

TIP

Don't worry; you can still set up the options associated with any of these boxes. And be aware that each box you dismiss is replaced by another associated with the list of options that matter to you (see 'Setting Up a New Business', earlier in this chapter, for more).

Once you close the boxes, your Home page displays information specific to your company (see Figure 3-6).

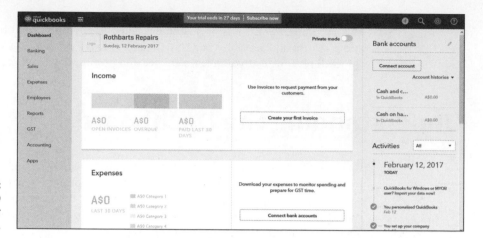

FIGURE 3-6:
The QBO
Dashboard after
closing the boxes.

In the centre of the screen, using most of the Dashboard real estate, you find information that changes depending on what you have clicked while using QBO. For example, when you initially open QBO, the information is overview company information. If you click an entry in the Navigation bar (on the left side of the screen), the information in the centre of the screen changes to information related to the entry you click. Figure 3-7, for example, shows what comes up when you first click on the Banking tab. If you select a setting on the Gear menu (discussed later in this section), the information is related to the setting you select.

FIGURE 3-7:
Moving
through the
Navigation bar.

TIP

You might have noticed the Private Mode button in Figures 3-4 to 3-6 at the top right of the home screen. You can use this button to temporarily hide financial information on your Home page. For example, you might want to turn Private Mode on if you're using QBO in a public place or even in your office when you're not alone. Once you turn Private Mode on, it remains on until you turn it off again.

As we just mentioned, the Navigation bar runs down the left side of the screen. You use the Navigation bar the same way you'd use a menu; click an item in the Navigation bar to, well, navigate to that part of QBO. For example, you can click Sales in the Navigation bar to see invoices.

Back on the Dashboard, on the right side of the screen, you find a list of the bank accounts you've set up as well as the Activities list — a list of things that QBO thinks need your attention. The list is interactive, so you can click items in the list to take various actions.

Above the list of bank accounts, at the top right of the screen, you will see four buttons. When you click the Help button (the question mark button on the far right), you see a menu of common topics related to the area of QBO you are currently viewing, and you can type in the search box to find help on a particular topic (see Figure 3-8).

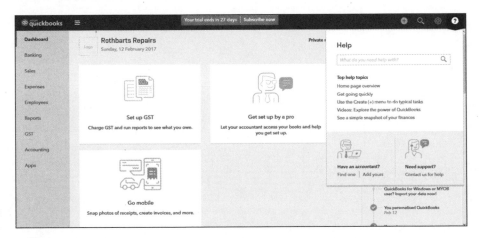

FIGURE 3-8:
The Help menu.

Figure 3-9 shows 'support' in the Help search box and provides a list of frequent topics relating to 'support'.

Next to the Help button is the Gear button. If you click the Gear button, you see the menu shown in Figure 3-10, which you use to look at and change QBO company settings; view lists; work with tools such as import and export, reconciliation and budgeting tools; and view information about your QBO account. Note that the Gear menu is divided into four columns that organise related commands.

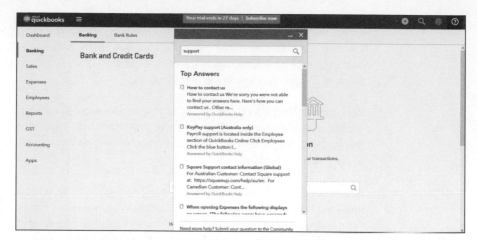

FIGURE 3-9:
A sample
Help topic.

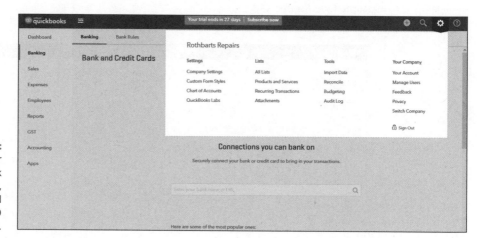

FIGURE 3-10:
Use the Gear
menu to work
with settings,
lists, tools and
your QBO
account.

Located next to the Gear button is the search transactions button (represented as a magnifying glass). Figure 3-11 shows what you see when you click the Search button. You can click any transaction in the list to open that transaction (see Figure 3-12 — here we've used an example from QBOA to give you more transactions).

Lastly, on the left is the Create button. Figure 3-13 shows the Create menu that appears when you click the plus sign menu button.

REMEMBER

The Create button appears as a plus sign (+) when the menu is closed and an X when the menu is open; compare Figures 3-12 and 3-13.

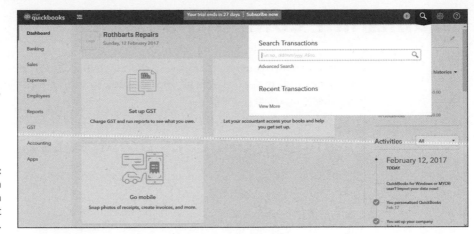

FIGURE 3-11:
Click the Search button to search for past transactions.

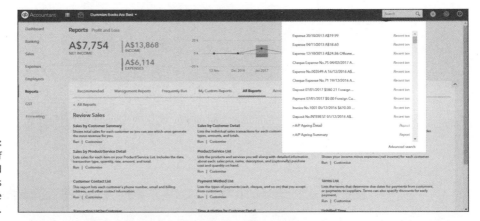

FIGURE 3-12:
Display a list of recently entered transactions through the Search menu.

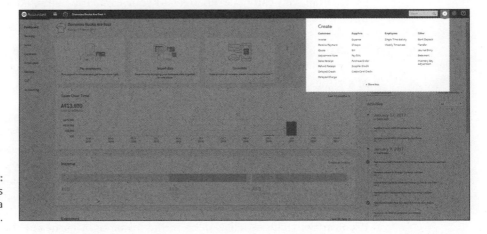

FIGURE 3-13:
Click the plus button to create a new transaction.

Establishing Company Settings

After you set up your company, you should review the default settings Intuit established and make changes as appropriate. To examine and make changes to Payroll settings, see Chapter 9.

Examining company preferences

Choose Gear ⇨ Company Settings to display the Company preferences screen (see Figure 3-14).

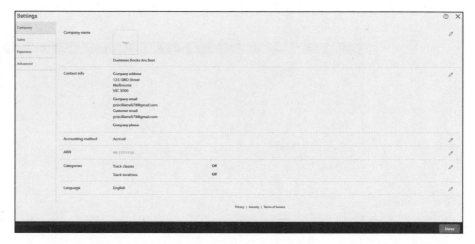

FIGURE 3-14:
Review company settings.

On this tab, you can make changes to your company name, address and contact information.

To change any setting, click anywhere in the group where the setting appears. When you finish making changes, click the Save button that appears in the group of settings. You can then move on to other settings on the page.

TIP

Depending on the version of QBO you use, you can use the Categories section to opt to track information using classes, locations or both. You also can opt to have QBO warn you if you don't assign a class to a transaction. You can opt to assign classes individually to each line of a transaction or assign one class to the entire transaction. For locations, you can choose from seven different labels; one of these choices might better describe your intended use of the Location category.

If you make changes, click Done in the lower right corner of the screen to save them.

Setting sales preferences

Choose Gear ⇨ Company Settings to display the Company preferences screen (refer to Figure 3-14). Then click Sales in the pane on the left.

At the top of the page that appears (see Figure 3-15), you can click the Customise Look and Feel button to customise the appearance of the invoice you send to customers. We return to the customisation process at the end of this section; first, let's examine the settings available to you.

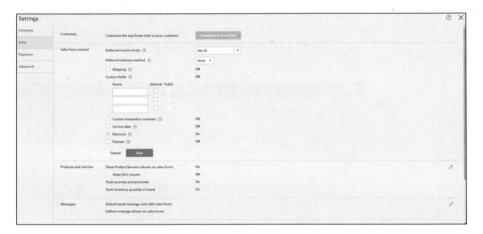

FIGURE 3-15: Review Sales preferences.

Examining sales settings

You can set a variety of options related to sales:

>> In the Sales Form Content section, you can define the fields that appear on the form you complete to prepare invoices, sales receipts and other sales forms.

>> In the Products and Services section, you can make changes to the product- and service-related fields that appear on sales forms. If you're using QBO Plus, this is where you turn on inventory tracking.

>> In the Messages section, you can control the default email message sent to customers with sales forms and the default message that appears on those sales forms.

>> If you scroll down the Sales page, you can, in the Reminder section, create a new message or edit the default email message that gets sent to customers reminding them that their invoice is overdue.

>> In the Online Delivery section, you can set email delivery options for sales forms, such as attaching the sales form as a PDF, showing a summary or details of the sales form in the email, and email formatting options for invoices.

>> In the Statements section, you can specify whether to show the ageing table at the bottom of the statement.

Customising form appearance

To customise forms that your customers receive, click Customise Look and Feel at the top of the Sales preferences page in the Company Settings dialog box (refer to Figure 3-15) to display the Custom Form Styles page shown in Figure 3-16.

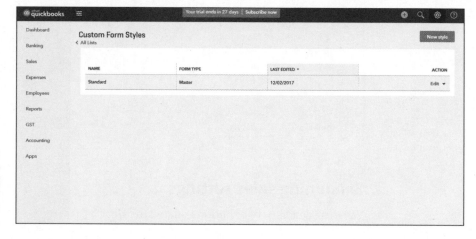

The Custom Form Styles page lists any form styles you have already created. By default, QBO creates one form style for you when you sign up; that form style is named Standard and is used by default for invoices, estimates and sales receipts.

If you are satisfied with the appearance of the majority of the form style, you can edit it instead of creating another form style. Alternatively, you can create separate customised forms for invoices, estimates and sales receipts. To do so, click New Style in the upper-right corner of the Custom Form Styles page. Whether you edit or create a new form style, QBO displays the Customise Form Style dialog box, and its appearance varies only slightly, depending on whether you are editing or creating new form style. In particular, if you opt to create a new form style, the dialog box gives you the option to select the type of form style (see Figure 3-17).

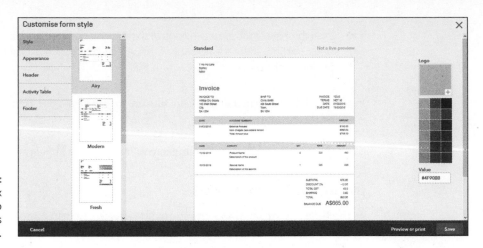

FIGURE 3-17:
The dialog box
you use to
customise sales
forms.

You use the tabs that run down the left side of the dialog box to establish form style settings:

>> From the Style tab, shown in Figure 3-17, you can select a style for the form: Airy, Modern, Fresh, Friendly or Bold.

>> From the Appearance tab, you can modify the appearance and placement of your logo; set the form's font, line height and page margins; and specify whether to print your form to fit in a standard window envelope. You also can opt to show an account summary table, which shows your customers how much past due they are in paying you.

>> From the Header tab, you can define the names used for each form and the fields that appear in the header area of the form — such as your company name, address, contact information, payment terms, due date and form number. You also can opt to show your customer's terms, due date, shipping and payment methods, as well as set up custom fields.

>> From the Activity Table tab, you can control the appearance of the body of the invoice, determining whether to display, in columns, information such as the quantity, rate and description for each item — and the order in which the elements appear. For each row of information, you also can specify whether to display billable time and markup on billable expenses (most people don't display markup on billable expenses), and you can choose whether to show the employee's name and the hours and rate. You also can choose the way you want to group activity (by day, week, month or type) and, if you group activity, you can choose to subtotal by group. You can also combine rows that show the same rate and description and omit the dates for those rows.

TIP

Chapter 6 contains an example of customising the Activity Table so that you can include subtotals on an invoice.

>> From the Footer tab, you can control the information that appears in the footer portion of the form, along with messages to your customer or account details for EFT payments.

You can click the Preview or Print button to preview your invoice in a browser window (in PDF format).

Click the Save button to save changes you make to the appearance of your forms.

Importing form styles

REMEMBER

At the time of writing, importing form styles was a feature 'under construction' in QBO and is therefore not available unless you enable it using QuickBooks Labs. For details on using QuickBooks Labs, see the section 'Taking Advantage of Quick-Books Labs', later in this chapter. For the purposes of this discussion, we have enabled the feature.

If the form templates supplied with QBO don't meet your needs, you can use Microsoft Word 2010 or later to create a form style and then upload it into QBO. As part of the import process, you map fields you've identified on your Word document form style to QBO fields.

The tricky part of this process is getting the form correctly designed in Word. But, luckily, Intuit anticipated the challenge and provides sample forms and instructions to simplify the process. To download the samples and instructions, you need to pretend you've already created your form style in Word. If this feels like we're putting the cart in front of the horse, well . . . we are, sort of.

To get the sample information and instructions, enable the Import Form Styles feature through QuickBooks Labs. Then click Gear ➪ Custom Form Styles. On the Custom Form Styles page, click the down arrow beside New Style, and choose Import Style, as shown in Figure 3-18.

QBO displays the page shown in Figure 3-19.

To download the sample information, click the Download a Sample Invoice link. A Zip file downloads, containing two sample forms you can use as starting points.

REMEMBER

The Zip file also contains detailed instructions that describe what to do and what not to do when creating a form style. For example, the instructions list the fonts QBO will recognise and also describe the best way to use Word tables. Suffice it to say, use these instructions and save yourself some pain.

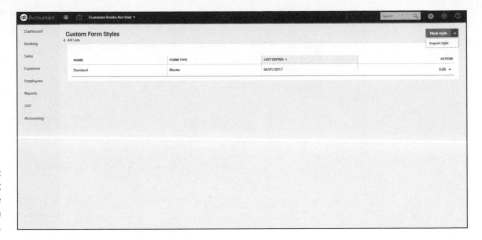

FIGURE 3-18:
Access the Import
Form Style page
from the Custom
Form Styles page.

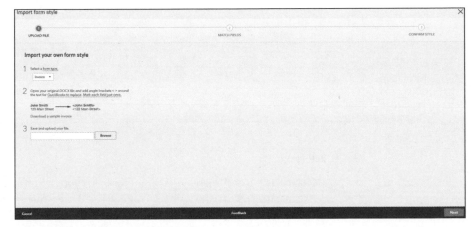

FIGURE 3-19:
Use the Import
Form Style page
to download
sample forms
and instructions
to create your
own form style.

Open either of the sample files to see how a customised form style should look in
Word (see Figure 3-20). Note, for example, that you simply type information that
won't change, but you place less than and greater than brackets around fields you
want to replace with QBO data, such as your customer's billing and shipping
addresses and item information.

When you're ready to upload your form style, follow these steps:

1. **Choose Gear ➪ Custom Form Styles to display the Custom Form Style
page.**

2. **Click the arrow beside the New Style button and choose Import Style to
redisplay the page shown earlier in Figure 3-19.**

3. **Click the Browse button and navigate to the Word document you created
for your form style.**

FIGURE 3-20:
Place information that QBO should replace in brackets.

4. **Click Next.**

   QBO uploads the document and scans it for fields you placed in brackets. If you successfully upload the Word document, you'll see a message telling you that you succeeded in uploading. If this process is not successful you will see errors; review the instruction document included with the sample files for details on errors and how to correct them.

   Assuming your document uploads successfully, a page appears where you can map the fields on your form style to fields in QBO.

5. **Match the fields on your form style to QBO fields; when you finish, click Next.**

   A preview of the new form style appears on the Confirm Style page.

6. **If you're happy with what you see, click Save and supply a name for your form style. It's now ready to use.**

   If you're not happy, click Back and correct any problems.

Taking a look at expense preferences

From the Expenses tab of the Company Settings dialog box, you can control expenses related to purchase orders, bills and payments you make to suppliers (see Figure 3-21). Choose Gear ⇨ Company Settings ⇨ Expenses.

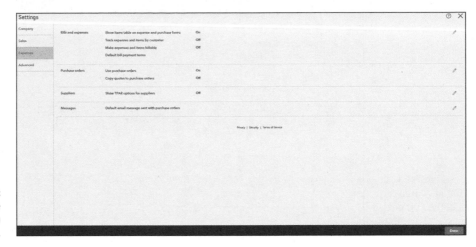

FIGURE 3-21:
Expense preferences you can control.

In the Bills and Expenses group of settings, you can opt to display a table of expense and purchase forms so that you can itemise and categorise the products and services you buy. If you purchase goods and services for your customers, you can

» Add a column to the table so that you can identify the customer for whom you made the purchase.

» Add a column where you identify expenses and items for which you want to bill customers.

You also can set default bill payment terms.

In the Purchase Orders group, you can opt to use purchase orders and you can opt to copy quotes to purchase orders. For more information about converting a quote to a purchase order, see Chapter 6.

Reviewing advanced preferences

The Advanced tab of the Company Settings dialog box enables you to make changes to a variety of QBO settings (see Figure 3-22). Choose Gear ➪ Company Settings ➪ Advanced to view and update these settings:

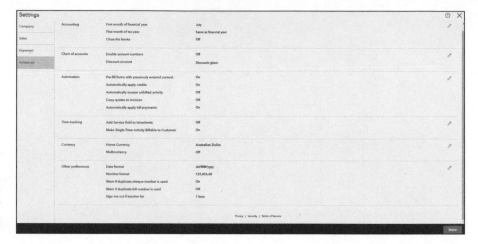

FIGURE 3-22:
The Advanced tab of the Company Settings dialog box.

>> In the Accounting group, you can control fiscal year settings and the accounting method your company uses (cash or accrual).

>> In the Chart of Accounts group, you can turn on account numbers — something most accountants prefer you do.

>> In the Automation group, you can control some of QBO's automated behaviour. For example, if you don't want QBO to prefill new forms with information from forms you entered previously, feel free to turn that setting off.

>> In the Time Tracking section, you can control the appearance of timesheets. For example, you can opt to add a service field to timesheets so that you can select services performed for each time entry. By default, QBO includes a customer field on timesheets so that you can optionally charge work performed to a customer.

>> Use the Currency section to turn on Multicurrency tracking and to set your company's Home Currency. If you change the home currency symbol, QBO changes the symbol for future transactions; existing transactions will still be calculated at the original currency value. For more information about Multicurrency and Home Currency, see the section 'Working with Multiple Currencies', later in this chapter.

WARNING

Turning on Multicurrency eliminates your ability to change your home currency. Further, you can't turn Multicurrency off after you turn it on.

>> In the Other Preferences group, you can make changes to a variety of settings, such as date and number formats, whether QBO warns you if you reuse a cheque number or bill number you used previously, and how long QBO should wait before signing you out because you haven't done any work.

Examining billing and subscription settings

To review the settings related to your QBO billing and subscription, choose Gear ➪ Your Account.

This page, shown in Figure 3-23, shows you the status of your QBO subscriptions. From this page, you can convert your trial version of QBO to a regular subscription — keep in mind that converting cancels your trial.

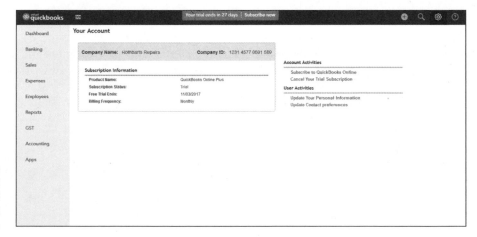

FIGURE 3-23: Review QBO billing and subscription settings.

Working with Multiple Currencies

The Plus version of QBO supports using multiple currencies. Typically, you use the Multicurrency feature when you sell products and services to customers or buy products and services from suppliers whose base currency is different from your home currency. If you don't need to record transactions in multiple currencies, don't turn on this feature because you can't turn it off again. But having said that, the feature simply sits in the background anyway.

CATEGORIES, CLASSES AND LOCATIONS . . . OH, MY!

Don't confuse the options you see in the Categories section of the Company Settings dialog box (QBO classes and locations) with QBO categories. The QBO Category feature is entirely separate from the class and location features shown in the Categories section of the Company Settings dialog box.

If you turn on the Class and Location options shown in the Company Settings dialog box, you can then assign classes and locations to transactions to help you further break down financial data beyond the account level. To create classes and locations, first enable them in the Company Settings dialog box. Then choose Gear⇨All Lists. Then click Classes to create new classes and click Locations to create new locations.

QBO categories, *not* shown in the Company Settings dialog box (and no need to turn them on), replace sub-items and are available to users of QBO Plus to help organise item information for reporting purposes; see Chapter 4 for details.

Because you can assign only one currency to each account, customer or supplier, QBO will add new asset and liability accounts, customers and suppliers for each different currency that you will use in transactions. Be aware that, once you've set up a customer or supplier in a certain currency, you can't change it. To correct the problem, you will need to create another customer or supplier with the correct currency and make the original entry inactive.

REMEMBER

Income and expense accounts continue to use your home currency — the currency of the country where your business is physically located.

So, if you've decided to use the Multicurrency feature, do these things in the order listed:

1. **Turn on the Multicurrency feature.**

2. **Set up the currencies you intend to use.**

3. **Add customers, suppliers and necessary asset and liability accounts for each currency you expect to use.**

   Note: QBO automatically creates Accounts Receivable and Accounts Payable accounts in the foreign currency after you create one foreign sales and one foreign purchasing transaction, so you don't need to set up those accounts.

4. **Enter transactions.**

How the Multicurrency feature changes QBO

After you turn on the Multicurrency feature, you will see new fields in QBO. Specifically, you'll see changes on these screens:

» When you open the Gear menu, you'll see the Currencies option at the bottom of the Lists column. You use the Currencies list to establish the foreign currency you want to use, along with the exchange rate. We describe using this option after we show you how to turn on the Multicurrency feature (see the following section).

» When you view the Chart of Accounts, you'll find a Currency column that shows the currency assigned to each account. You'll also find a new account — an Other Expense account called Exchange Gain or Loss.

» When you view Bank and Credit Card ledgers, the currency of each transaction appears in brackets in the Payment, Deposit, Sales Tax and Balance Due columns.

» Sales and purchase forms use both your home currency and the foreign currency; QBO does all the conversions for you on the screen.

» On QuickBooks reports, you find that QBO converts all foreign currency amounts to home currency amounts, automatically reflecting exchange rate changes.

Turning on the Currency feature

You can change your home currency from the same place that you enable the Currency feature.

WARNING

Once you turn on the Currency feature, you cannot change your home currency.

Follow these steps to enable the currency feature:

1. Click Gear ➪ Company Settings.

QBO displays the Company Settings page.

2. Click Advanced.

3. Scroll down to the Currency section.

4. Set your home currency by clicking the Home Currency list box.

Choose the currency of your country. If you're not in Australia, don't set Australia as your home currency.

5. Select Multicurrency (see Figure 3-24).

QBO warns you that, once you turn on the Multicurrency feature:

(a) You can't turn it off.

(b) You can't change your home currency.

6. Select I Understand I Can't Undo Multicurrency.

7. Click Save.

8. Click Done.

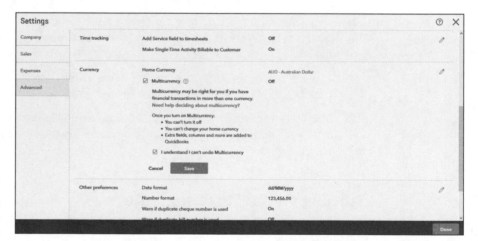

FIGURE 3-24:
Turning on
Multicurrency.

REMEMBER

You can't turn off the Multicurrency feature because it affects many accounts and balances in QBO.

Setting up currencies

After enabling the Currency option, you find an option to display the Currencies list if you click the Gear button; the Currencies option appears at the bottom of the Lists section on the Gear menu (see Figure 3-25).

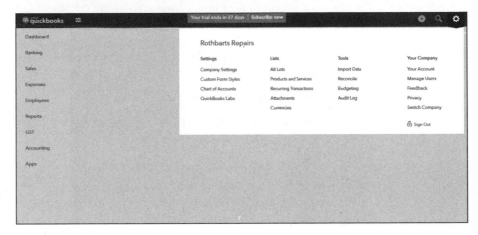

FIGURE 3-25:
The link to the Currencies page.

Follow these steps to set up the currencies you need to use:

1. **Click Gear ⇨ Currencies.**

   QBO displays the Currencies page (see Figure 3-26).

2. **In the upper right corner of the page, click Add Currency.**

   QBO displays a drop-down list.

3. **Select a currency you want to use.**

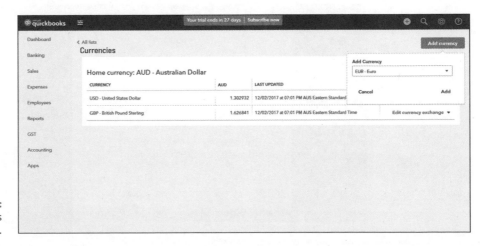

FIGURE 3-26:
The Currencies page.

4. Click Add.

QBO redisplays the Currencies page with the new currency added.

QBO always records exchange rates, shown on the Currencies page, as the number of home currency units needed to equal one foreign currency unit. QBO downloads exchange rates every four hours from Wall Street On Demand, but you can, if you want, provide your own exchange rate. Click the Edit Currency Exchange link beside the rate you want to edit and supply the rate you want to use. You can also alter exchange rates from within individual transactions.

Using multiple currencies

Let's examine, briefly, the effects of creating an invoice that uses multiple currencies; creating a purchase transaction for an overseas supplier also works in a similar way.

Suppose that you have a customer whose base currency is the Canadian dollar and your home currency is the Australian dollar (that is, AUD). So, in this example, when we refer to the 'foreign currency', we mean the Canadian dollar.

REMEMBER

At this time, QBO doesn't support letting either your employees or contractors record time entries (using either the Weekly Timesheet or the Single Time Activity) associated with a foreign currency customer.

First, create the customer: Click Sales⇨Customers⇨New Customer. Fill in the window as you usually would with the following addition: Click the Payment and Billing tab. Then open the This Customer Pays Me With list and select the customer's currency. In Figure 3-27, our customer, uninspiringly named Foreign Currency, uses the Canadian Dollar.

FIGURE 3-27: Assigning a foreign currency to a new customer.

REMEMBER

You find a similar setting available when you create a new supplier.

Once you save the customer, if you look at the Customer list page, you see the customer listed and, in the Currency column, you see the foreign currency. Your home currency customers display your home currency.

Next, in the Invoice window, select your 'foreign transaction' customer. QBO automatically displays, below the customer's name, the two currencies (first the foreign currency and then your home currency) associated with the transaction (see Figure 3-28).

FIGURE 3-28:
Creating an invoice for a customer who uses a foreign currency.

Once you add products or services to the invoice, as shown in Figure 3-29, the amounts for each line appear in the foreign currency, and totals appear in both currencies. The Balance Due on the transaction appears in the foreign (customer's) currency so that your customer knows how much to pay.

REMEMBER

Saving your first sales or purchase document for a customer or supplier using a foreign currency makes QBO automatically establish a foreign currency-related Accounts Receivable and Accounts Payable account.

Reports in QBO show values in your home currency. Figure 3-30 shows the A/R Ageing Summary.

Figure 3-31, the Balance Sheet, shows the multiple Accounts Receivable accounts QBO uses when you've enabled the Multicurrency feature and created a sales transaction using a foreign currency; the values on the report appear in the home currency.

FIGURE 3-29:
An invoice for a foreign currency customer shows values in both the home and foreign currency.

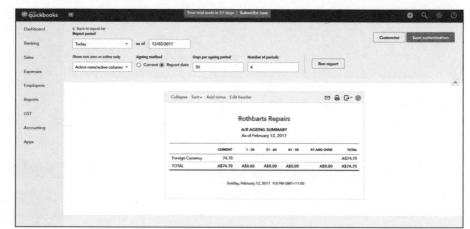

FIGURE 3-30:
Values on reports appear in your home currency.

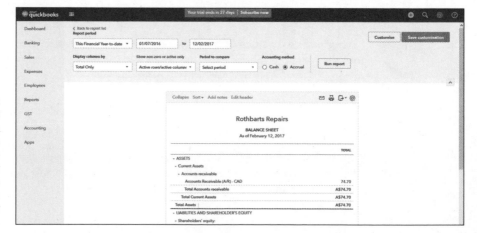

FIGURE 3-31:
QBO establishes separate Accounts Receivable accounts for transactions involving foreign currency customers.

Updating the Chart of Accounts

On the Advanced tab of the Company Settings screen, you see that you can turn on account numbers for the accounts in your Chart of Accounts. To make changes to those accounts, choose Gear⇨Settings⇨Chart of Accounts. On the page that appears (see Figure 3-32), you can perform a variety of functions. For example, you can print a list of your accounts if you click the Run Report button, which is at the top of the page, and then select the printer icon.

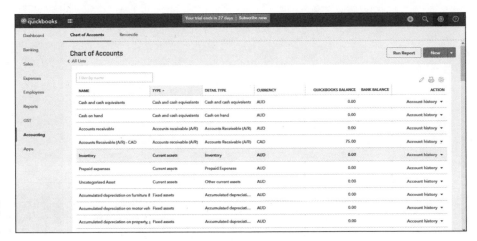

FIGURE 3-32:
The Chart of
Accounts page.

REMEMBER

If you've enabled the Currency feature, you see a Currency column on the Chart of Accounts page.

For individual accounts, you can perform a few actions. Balance Sheet accounts have ledgers known in QBO as Account Histories; you can view the transactions in the account by clicking Account History in the Action column to the right of the account name. You can identify Balance Sheet accounts by looking in the Type column. Balance Sheet accounts display one of the following account types:

>> Bank (Cash & Cash Equivalent)

>> Accounts Receivable

>> Other Current Assets

>> Fixed Assets

>> Other Assets

>> Credit Card

>> Other Current Liabilities

>> Long Term Liabilities

>> Accounts Payable

>> Equity

A FEW NOTES ON PAYING OWNERS

Many small business owners wonder about the accounts they should use to pay themselves. Owners and partners typically are not considered employees and therefore are not paid through payroll. To pay an owner or partner, use the Chart of Accounts page to set up a Drawings account (Owner's Drawings, Partner's Drawings, whatever is appropriate; if you have multiple partners, set up drawings accounts for each partner) and use it to pay owners. The Drawings account is an equity account.

Similarly, owners and partners sometimes put their own money into the business; to account for these contributions, set up equity accounts (again, one for each owner or partner) called Owner's Contribution, Partner's Contribution — again, whatever is appropriate.

Typically, Australian accounting practice would allow for a header account and two sub-accounts to calculate moneys put into and moneys taken out of the business by the owners, and also to give a current balance as follows:

- **Header Account–Owners Equity: A J Smith**

  This is the account used to calculate the balance of equity, including money put into the business and money taken out of the business by A J Smith. It will automatically calculate the value of equity, taking into account the balance of the following sub-accounts.

- **Sub-Account 1: A J Smith Current**

  This is the account used for the money A J Smith puts into the business.

- **Sub-Account 2: A J Smith Drawings**

  This is the account used for the money A J Smith takes out of the business.

You use the Drawings account not only to pay the owner but also to account for personal items an owner might buy using the business's money, or purchases for the business that the owner makes using their own money. You record the withdrawals using the appropriate Bank account and the appropriate Drawings account. These Drawings transactions don't show up on your Profit and Loss report because they are *not* business expenses. However, purchases made by an owner from their own funds that are posted to the owner's Current account will. To find out the total amount paid to an owner, run a report for the Drawings account. To run a report on how much money the owner has put into the business, run a report on the owner's Current account.

And, finally, a note on housekeeping for the Drawing and Contribution/Current accounts: At the end of your financial year, you need to enter a journal entry, dated on the last day of your financial year, that moves the dollar amounts from the appropriate Drawing or Contribution account to Retained Earnings — another equity account. If you're at all unclear on any of this, talk to your accountant.

For other accounts — the ones without ledgers or Account Histories — you can run reports for the account by clicking Run Report in the Action column.

You also can edit any account and you can delete an account you have not yet used. Click the down arrow in the Action column (at the right edge of the account's row) to display a short menu of the actions you can take for the account.

WARNING

If you edit an account, don't change its type unless you're sure you know what you're doing. Consider consulting your accountant or bookkeeper before you make a change to an account's category or detail type. You also can identify if the account is actually a sub-account of another account.

If you decide to turn on account numbers, you can click the Batch Edit icon (it looks like a pencil and appears just above the Action column). The appearance of the Chart of Accounts page changes to enable you to quickly assign account numbers (see Figure 3-33).

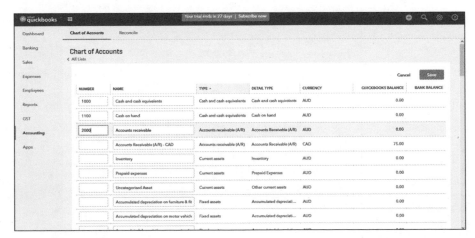

FIGURE 3-33:
The Chart of Accounts page in Batch Edit mode.

If you've enabled the Multicurrency feature, the Chart of Accounts page in Batch Edit mode also contains a Currency column.

Type a number for each account; when you finish entering all the numbers, click the Save button at the top of the page. QBO displays the account number as part of the account name on the Chart of Accounts screen.

You also can establish budgets for accounts; see Chapter 12 for details.

The screens you use to add or edit an account look almost exactly alike. Because you need a bank account for your company, we examine the screens as you create your bank account. If you plan to connect your QBO Bank Account to its corresponding account at a financial institution, don't follow these steps; instead, see Chapter 8 for details on creating the account. And, if you decide now that you don't want to connect and later you decide that you *do* want to connect, all isn't lost. Once again, see Chapter 8 for details on merging the bank account you create here with an online version.

To ensure an accurate bank balance in QBO, reconcile your bank account before you set up the account in QBO. Follow these steps to create an account in QBO:

1. **Click the New button on the Chart of Accounts page to open the Account dialog box (see Figure 3-34)**

FIGURE 3-34:
The dialog box you use to create an account.

2. **Open the Category Type list and choose Cash & Cash Equivalent.**

3. **Click the entry in the Detail Type list that most closely matches the type of account you want to add.**

   QBO uses the choice you make in the Detail Type list as the account's name, but you can change the name to something else. For example, you can choose Cash and Cash Equivalent, change the account name to NAB Cheque Account, and supply the account number as the description.

4. **If you're using account numbers, supply a number for the new account.**

   You can, optionally, supply a description for the account.

REMEMBER

   If you've enabled the Currency feature, the dialog box you use to create a bank account — or any type of asset or liability account except an Accounts Receivable (A/R) or Accounts Payable (A/P) account — also contains a list box from which you select the currency for the account. QBO automatically creates currency-related A/R and A/P accounts when you create transactions for foreign customers and suppliers.

5. **You can enter your account's balance as it appears on the last statement you received from your bank.**

   If you're entering an opening journal to set up your balances, don't enter the balance again here; ask your accountant or bookkeeper if you are not sure.

6. **Click Save and Close.**

   QBO redisplays the Chart of Accounts page and your new account appears in the list.

ENSURING ACCURATE ACCOUNT BALANCES

If you've been in business for a while, transactions have occurred. To ensure your account balances are accurate, you need to account for these transactions in QBO.

To make sure that you start your work in QBO with correct account balances, begin by deciding on the first date you intend to use QBO. This date determines the 'as of' date of historical information you need to collect. Try to start using QBO on the first day of an accounting period — either on the first day of your company's financial year or on the first day of a month.

Although it might seem like more work, we suggest that the easiest way for you to ensure proper account balances is to enter $0 as your bank account's opening balance

(continued)

(continued)

in Step 5 in the preceding steps for creating a bank account. Then enter all transactions that have occurred so far this year.

If you've been in business since before the beginning of the year, enter $0 for your bank account's balance and ask your accountant for opening amounts for your Balance Sheet and Profit and Loss Statement. Enter these amounts by entering a journal entry: Click the plus sign (+) icon at the top right of QBO and choose Journal Entry from the Other column in the list.

The transactions you enter for the current year will ultimately affect your bank balance (for example, when a customer eventually pays an invoice), and, when you finish entering the transactions, your QBO Bank Account balance should agree with the one your financial institution has. So we suggest that you enter transactions for *all* customer invoices (and corresponding payments customers made) and *all* supplier bills (and corresponding payments you made) during the current year.

If you choose to ignore our suggestion and enter an opening amount for your bank balance in Step 5, you need to then enter all transactions that have affected your bank account *since the last statement*.

QBO posts balances you enter while creating an account to the Opening Balance Equity (Equity) account, an account created by QuickBooks. Most accountants don't like this account and will want to create journal entries to move the balances to proper accounts.

That second approach sounds like a lot less work and, if you don't use payroll or you make payroll payments from a separate bank account, you can safely ignore our suggestion and enter an opening amount for your bank balance in Step 5 and then enter outstanding customer invoices and unpaid supplier bills.

However, if your company does prepare payroll, has prepared one or more payrolls so far this year and you use only one bank account, we strongly urge you to take our suggestion because you need accurate *annual* information to successfully manage payroll. The easiest way to ensure that you have accurate annual payroll information is to enter all payrolls you've completed this year so far — and these payrolls will affect your bank account, so, entering a bank account balance in Step 5 will lead you into trouble. Yes, you can try to do a mix of both approaches and subtract payroll amounts from the bank balance you previously entered in Step 5, but that approach is seriously error-prone.

If you use one bank account for everything and you feel that entering all transactions that have occurred so far this year is just too much work, we suggest that you enter your bank account's balance as of your last bank statement, enter outstanding invoices and unpaid supplier bills, and then contact Intuit technical support for help entering historical payroll information.

Activating the GST Centre

If you're earning over $75,000 per year or operate certain types of business, you have probably registered for GST. Even businesses that earn under the threshold often register because doing so makes life easier when dealing with customers and suppliers. If you are registered for GST or other taxes such as WET or FTC, you will need to activate the GST Centre.

To activate the GST Centre, go to the Navigation menu and select the GST tab. You see a Set up GST button to the right (see Figure 3-35). Enter in your businesses tax settings (if unsure, ask your accountant or bookkeeper for help). For information on using the GST Centre and lodging IAS, BAS and other taxes, see Chapter 10.

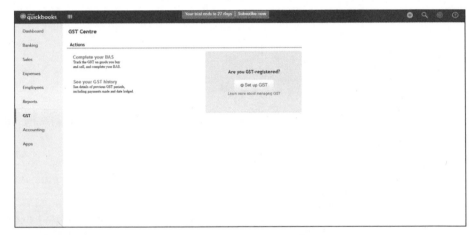

FIGURE 3-35:
Activating the
GST Centre.

Taking Advantage of QuickBooks Labs

You might be wondering about the QuickBooks Labs option on the Gear menu (you can see it if you refer back to Figure 3-10). Intuit calls QuickBooks Labs its 'high-tech playground'. If you're adventurous, check out the lab and turn on experimental features to see how they work.

REMEMBER

In most cases, features you find in QuickBooks Labs eventually become part of QBO. For example, at the time of writing, the Import Style feature discussed earlier in this chapter was a QuickBooks Labs feature and therefore didn't appear by default.

Here's how you turn on a QuickBooks Lab feature:

1. **Log in to your company.**

2. **Click Gear ⇨ QuickBooks Labs.**

   The QuickBooks Labs window appears (see Figure 3-36).

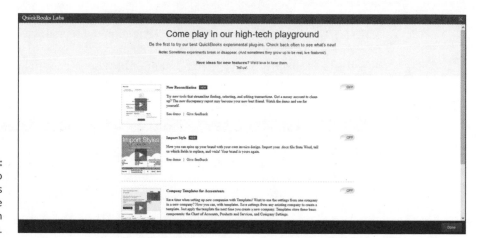

FIGURE 3-36:
Use this page to turn on features not yet available by default in QuickBooks.

TIP

Note: You can provide feedback on QuickBooks Labs features. The more positive feedback a feature receives, the more likely it is that feature will become a standard part of QBO.

3. **Check out the features available and, for any you want to try, click the Off button.**

   The Off button changes to the On button.

4. **When you finish turning on features, click Done.**

   Your QBO company reappears, with the features you selected enabled.

REMEMBER

You might need to refresh the browser page to see the new features you choose to make available. Click your browser's Refresh button or press F5 on your keyboard.

Signing In to and Out of QBO

If you followed the process in this chapter to sign up for QBO, you're currently signed in to QBO. But, obviously, you don't sign up for QBO every time you want to use it. And then, of course, there's the question of how you sign out of QBO each time you finish using it.

To sign out of QBO, click the Gear button and, from the menu shown earlier in Figure 3-10, click Sign Out (at the bottom of the list of commands under Your Company).

To sign in to QBO in the future, visit intuit.com.au (you get redirected to a long web address you don't need to type) and click the Sign In button on the top right (see Figure 3-37). You then need to supply your username and password. We suggest you bookmark this page to make signing in easy.

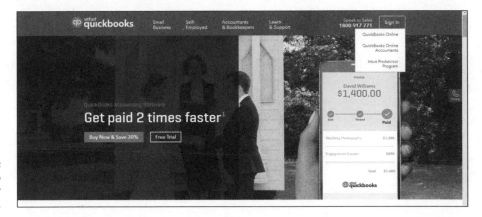

FIGURE 3-37: Use this page to sign in to your QBO account.

IN THIS CHAPTER

» **Adding new list entries by typing or importing**

» **Searching lists for people**

» **Changing settings for lists**

» **Understanding Products and Services items**

» **Displaying other lists**

Chapter **4**

Managing List Information

L ike its cousin, the QuickBooks desktop product, QBO relies on lists to help you store background information that you use again and again. For the most part, you enter information about the people with whom you do business — customers, suppliers and employees — and the stuff you sell or buy. But you also store other background information in lists, such as the accounts your company uses and the payment methods your company accepts.

In this chapter, you find information that all QBO users need about setting up customers and suppliers. And some QBO users will be interested in the portions of this chapter that focus on setting up items you sell or buy. Finally, at the end of the chapter, you learn where to find other lists you might need.

Importing People into a List

If you've been running your business for a while, you probably have lists of customers and suppliers. If they're stored electronically, you might be able to save yourself some set-up time in QBO if you import them. And, because most people tend to worry about accounting 'later', after they've been running the business for a bit, we start this chapter by assuming you do have lists stored in some electronic form. In the 'Adding New People to a List' section of this chapter, we show you how to manually set up a customer or supplier. That will be important if you don't have anything already in electronic form, and also as your business grows and you add new customers and suppliers.

If you've been using other accounting software or Excel to do your bookkeeping, you can import list information as an Excel file or a CSV file. CSV stands for *comma-separated values*; most programs, including QuickBooks desktop, enable you to export information to a CSV format. Coincidentally, Excel can open and save CSV files. So you can open a CSV file, edit it in Excel as needed, and then resave it as a CSV file. Or, after editing, you can save the file as an Excel 97-2003 workbook.

TIP

You can create a CSV file by saving an Excel file in CSV format. With the Excel file open, choose File ⇨ Save As. In the Save As dialog box, change the Save As Type list below the filename from Excel Workbook to CSV (Comma Delimited).

You use the same process to import customers or suppliers from a QuickBooks desktop or Xero/MYOB accounting product. Because the screens for importing customers or suppliers are the same, we'll go through the process of importing customers and let you take it from there.

The steps that follow assume you have installed Excel on your computer. If you don't own a copy of Excel, you can use Excel Mobile, the free app from Microsoft. To make editing changes to your files in Excel Mobile, you need to sign in to Excel Mobile with your Microsoft account email and password.

Follow these steps to import customers:

1. **Click the Gear button on the top right of your screen and select Import Data from the Tools menu.**

2. **From the Import Data screen, select Customers (see Figure 4-1).**

   The import wizard has three steps: Upload the file, map data and confirm import.

3. **Click the Download a Sample File link (see Figure 4-2).**

   To successfully import information into QBO from a CSV file or an Excel workbook, the information must conform to a specific format. And, luckily, QBO gives you the option to download a sample file in Excel format so that you can view the required format for importing list information; you can use this sample as a guideline for setting up the data in your own file. A sample file is available for customer, supplier, chart of accounts and product and services data importing. If you *don't* want to download a sample file, skip ahead to the next set of steps.

   Once you click the Download a Sample File link, QBO downloads the sample file and displays a button in the Windows taskbar for it.

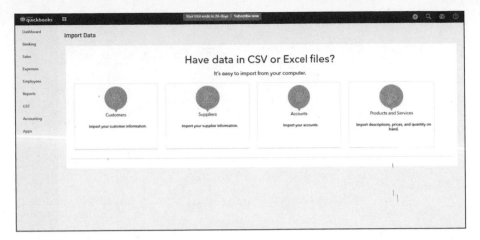

FIGURE 4-1:
The Import Data
screen.

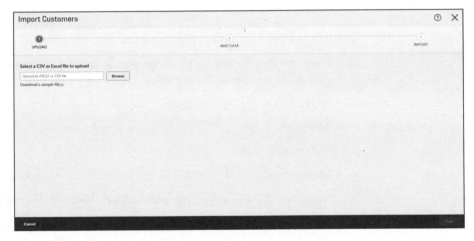

FIGURE 4-2:
The Import
Customer wizard.

4. **Click the sample file's button in the Windows taskbar.**

   The sample file opens in Excel (see Figure 4-3).

5. **Examine the file's content by scrolling to the right to see the information stored in each column.**

6. **Create your own file, modelling it on the sample file.**

TIP

   Importing your data works best if you can match the headings in your data file to the ones found in the sample data file. Also, your data file cannot contain more than 1,000 rows or exceed 2MB in size. Don't forget to save your data file as either an Excel 97–2003 workbook or as a CSV (comma-delimited) file.

REMEMBER

   If you're working on importing suppliers, the process outlined in the preceding and following steps is identical; however, you must make the appropriate selection at the Import Data screen.

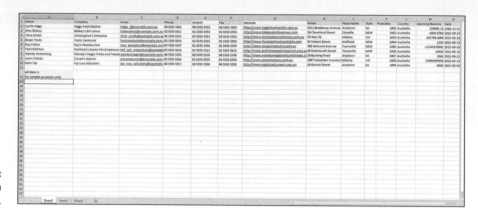

FIGURE 4-3:
A sample file in
Excel.

Once you're happy with your Excel or CSV file, you can import it into QBO. Follow these steps:

1. **Follow Steps 1 to 2 in the preceding list.**

2. **Select the Browse button to navigate to where the CSV file is located on your computer (refer to Figure 4-2).**

3. **Select the file and choose Open.**

   QBO updates the Import Customers page with the name of the file you selected.

4. **Click Next.**

   QBO uploads your file and displays the Map Data screen shown in Figure 4-4.

5. **Make sure that the fields in your data file correctly match the fields in QBO.**

   As needed, open the list box beside each QBO field name and match it to the labels in your data file.

THE DATA FILE'S LAYOUT IN EXCEL

Excel stores the information in the sample file (and you need to store the information in your data file) in a table format, where each row in the Excel file contains all the information about a single supplier or customer (each row is referred to as a *record*), and each column contains the same piece of information for all customers and suppliers (each column is referred to as one *field* in a record). For example, in Figure 4-3, all the information about Alex Blakey appears in Row 3, and all email addresses appear in Column C. Also note that Row 1 contains a label that identifies the type of information found in each column; don't forget to include identifying labels in your data file.

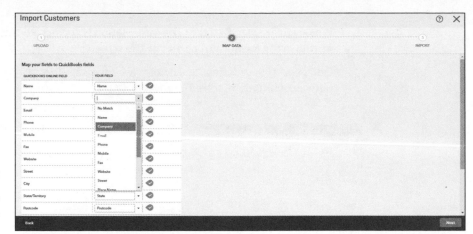

FIGURE 4-4:
Mapping the data from your spreadsheet to QBO.

6. **Click Next.**

   QBO displays the records it has identified (see Figure 4-5).

7. **Review the records QBO proposes to import to make sure the information is correct.**

   You can make changes to the information in any field by clicking that field and typing. You also can uncheck any row to avoid importing the information in that row to QBO.

TIP

   If you notice any errors with your records on the confirmation page — for example, if your customer's name is Edwin but it is recorded as Adwin, or if an email address is missing — you can simply update the records from the confirmation page rather than needing to edit and reimport your spreadsheet file.

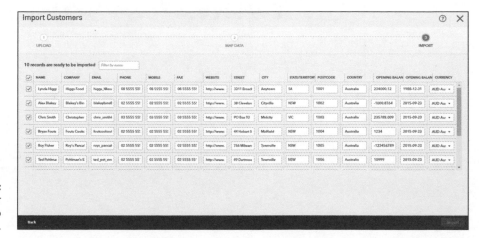

FIGURE 4-5:
Previewing your records to import.

8. **When you are satisfied that the information is correct, click the Import button in the lower right corner of the screen.**

QBO imports the information and displays a message that identifies the number of records imported (see Figure 4-6).

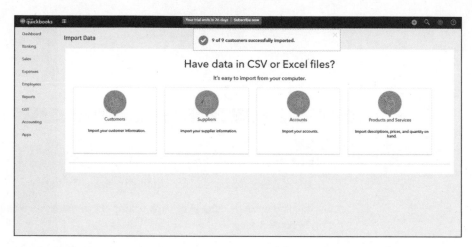

FIGURE 4-6: Confirmation of imported records.

Once you have imported your list of customers, you can view them in the Customers section of QBO by going to Sales in the Navigation menu on the left and then selecting the Customers tab (see Figure 4-7).

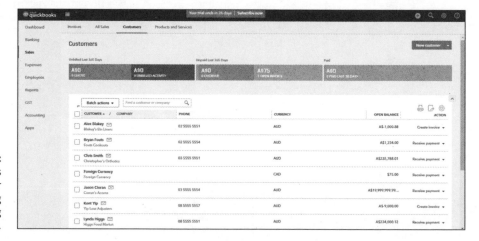

FIGURE 4-7: The Customers page after importing customers using an Excel file.

REMEMBER

You're not limited to only importing lists when you first set up a file. You can import lists at any time, and you don't have to worry about duplicates because QBO will detect a duplicate and will prompt you to remove it from the import process — very smart!

Merging Accounts

WARNING

Sometimes QBO won't detect what are actually duplicate entries if they're not identical. For instance, if you have a listing for Edwin Ko and one for Adwin Ko, QBO sees these as two separate entities — while your human brain can work out that they are one and the same. If this occurs, you can easily merge the two entries into one, keeping both sets of data already attached to each individual's name. This works for all accounts — Customers, Suppliers, Bank accounts, Expenses and Income.

To merge accounts or people, select the correct entry and copy that name exactly (you can use your mouse to highlight and copy), and then go to the incorrect entry and rename that entry to the exact match of the entry you want to keep (again, use your mouse for pasting). QBO will then advise you that you have two duplicate entries and will offer to merge them (see Figure 4-8), which you will accept by clicking Yes and voila! Two become one and no data is lost!

FIGURE 4-8:
QBO will offer to merge identical entries.

Adding New People to a List

You use the Sales and Expenses links in the Navigation bar to work with your customers and suppliers. In this section, we show you how to set up a new customer. The steps are the same to set up a new supplier; you just start by clicking the appropriate link in the Navigation bar.

REMEMBER

If you have determined that your company needs to use the Multicurrency feature, turn it on before you start creating people so that you have available the fields you need to establish each person's currency. See Chapter 3 for details on the Multi-currency feature.

Follow these steps to set up a new customer in QBO:

1. **Click Sales in the Navigation bar and then navigate to the Customers tab to display the Customers page shown in Figure 4-7.**

Figure 4-9 shows the Customers tab to click.

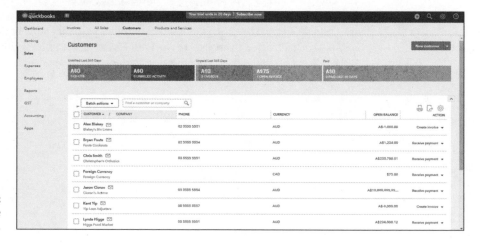

FIGURE 4-9:
Navigating to the Customer page.

2. **Click the New Customer button in the upper right corner of the page.**

QBO displays the Customer Information dialog box shown in Figure 4-10.

3. **Type the requested information.**

4. **Click Save.**

QBO saves the customer and displays a page showing information specific to that customer, such as the customer's transactions. If you click Sales in the Navigation bar and then head to the Customers tab, the Customers list page reappears and the new customer now appears in the list.

FIGURE 4-10:
Use this dialog box to enter information for a new customer.

TIP

You can make any list entry inactive. Click that entry in the appropriate list, and then click the Action down arrow at the right edge of the list. In the list that opens, click Make Inactive. This also applies to Suppliers or accounts in your Chart of Accounts.

WHAT'S A SUB-CUSTOMER?

Sub-customers are a way for you to create a hierarchy for customers, and you can use sub-customers pretty much any way you want. For example, if you're an architect, sub-customers might represent jobs or projects. If you're an attorney, sub-customers could represent cases.

If you set up sub-customers, you can choose to bill either the parent or the sub-customer. Sub-customers' balances are included in the parent customer's balance. Transactions for sub-customers appear in the sub-customer's register as well as the parent customer's register.

You can create as many sub-customers as you want and, for any given customer, you can assign sub-customers up to five levels deep, including the parent customer.

Searching Lists for People

You can use the Customers and Suppliers pages in a variety of ways. From the Customers or Suppliers pages that list all the people in those categories, you can sort the people in the list, export the list to Excel, and perform actions on a selected group of people on the list.

Working with a particular person

You can select a particular customer or supplier and view the transactions associated with that person as well as the person's details, and you can attach files to the person. For this section, we work with customers.

To search for a particular person, type some characters that match the person or company name in the search box that appears above the list of people (see Figure 4-11).

FIGURE 4-11: To find a particular person on a list, use the search box that appears above the names on the list.

When you select any person from the list, QBO displays the page specifically associated with that person. The page has two tabs; in Figure 4-12, you see the Transaction List tab, and in Figure 4-13, you see the Customer Details tab.

From either tab, you click the Edit button to edit information on the page; you can also click the New Transaction button to add a transaction associated with that person.

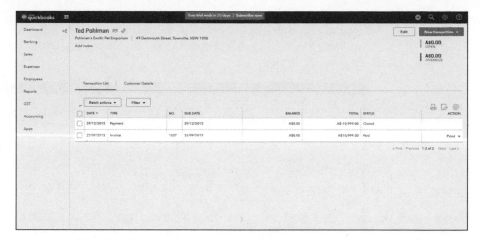

FIGURE 4-12:
The Transaction List tab shows transactions in QBO associated with the selected person.

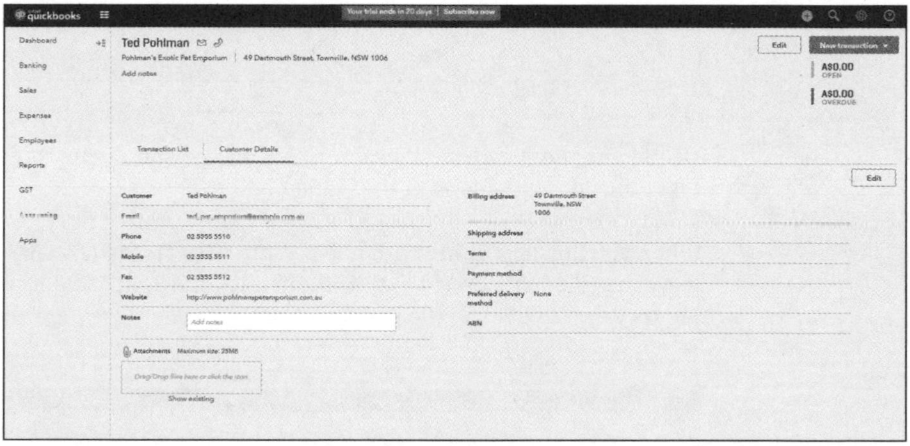

FIGURE 4-13:
The Customer Details tab; all detail tabs show, well, details for that person.

From the details page of a person, you can attach files to keep track of important financial information. For example, you can attach a supplier's price list or a customer's contract. You're not limited to text documents; you also can attach photos. Simply drag and drop the item into the Attachments box at the bottom left side of the appropriate details page; if you prefer, you can click the box and a standard Windows Open dialog box appears so that you can navigate to and select the document you want to attach.

The attachment size is limited to 25MB. To view documents you've already attached, click the Show Existing link below the Attachments box.

While viewing the Transaction list of a particular person, you can add the Attachments column to the table. Display the person's Transaction List page and then click the small Gear button just above the Action column. From the list that appears, click Show More. Show More changes to Show Less and a check box for Attachments appears (see Figure 4-14); click it and the Attachments column appears as part of the table grid. You can identify it as the column heading with a paper clip.

TIP

Displaying the Attachments column for one person displays it in the Transaction List table for all persons in that category.

When you finish working with one person, you can easily switch to another in that list using the list's Split View. You can click the Split View icon, shown earlier in Figure 4-14, to display the people stored in the list (see Figure 4-15).

FIGURE 4-15:
Displaying a list's Split View.

From the Split View, you can scroll down to find a person, or you can type a few letters of the person's name or company name in the search box at the top of the list to find that person in the list. Or you can sort the list by name or by open balance. Click a person to switch to that person's page.

To add a new person to the list, click New Customer on the top right of the page to see the dialog box shown earlier in Figure 4-10.

Sorting a list

In addition to sorting in Split View, you can sort the lists on the Customers and Suppliers pages by name or open balance. By default, QBO sorts the entries on these pages alphabetically by name in ascending order.

To change the sort order for either of these lists, click the Sales or Expenses link in the Navigation bar to display the appropriate Customers or Suppliers page; for this example, we use the Customers page.

Next, click the heading for the column by which you want to sort. If you click the Customer/Company column heading, QBO displays the customers in descending alphabetical order. If you click the Open Balance column heading, QBO sorts the list in Open Balance order, from lowest to highest.

Exporting a list to Excel

You can export a list of your customers or suppliers to Excel.

In this section, we assume you have a copy of Excel on your computer; otherwise, downloading your list to an Excel file wouldn't make much sense. If you don't have a copy of Excel on your computer, you can download and use the free mobile version of Excel.

Click the appropriate link in the Navigation bar to display either the Customers page or the Suppliers page; we use the Customers page in this example. At the right edge of the page, just above the list, three buttons appear: The first with a symbol of a printer; the second, a tablet with an arrow; and the last icon is another gear wheel. Click the middle button, and QBO exports the list to an Excel file; a button for the file appears at the bottom of the screen (see Figure 4-16).

Click the button at the bottom of the screen, and Excel opens the file. You can edit the file if you click the Enable Editing button in the yellow bar at the top of the window.

REMEMBER

If you're using Excel mobile, you need to sign in using your Microsoft account to edit the file.

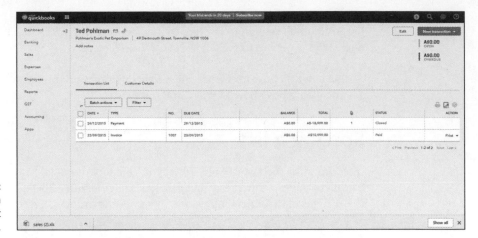

FIGURE 4-16:
Exporting a
customer list
to Excel.

Working with a batch of people

When you work with customers or suppliers, you can take certain actions simultaneously for a group of people. For example, you can select specific suppliers by clicking the check box beside each name and then send the same email to those suppliers. For customers, in addition to sending email, you can send statements.

To use one of these actions for a group of people, click the appropriate link in the Navigation bar to display the associated page. For this example, we used the Customers page.

Next, click the check box beside the names you want to include in your action and then click the Batch Actions button (see Figure 4-17). Select the action you want to take, and then follow the prompts onscreen to complete the action.

FIGURE 4-17:
Performing an
action for several
customers.

Changing Settings for People Lists

You can, to some extent, control the appearance of the lists on the Customers page and the Suppliers page. For example, you can opt to show or hide street address, email and phone number information, and you can opt to include or exclude inactive entries in the list. You can also control the number of entries displayed on each page, and adjust those entries' column widths.

Click the appropriate link in the Navigation bar to display the associated page; for this section, we worked on the Customers page.

To control the information displayed in the list, click the Gear button at the right edge of the page just above the list's labels (see Figure 4-18). Then select or deselect check boxes to display or hide information. Click outside the list when you finish.

FIGURE 4-18:
Controlling the information that appears in the list.

TIP

When you click outside the list, click in the empty area at the bottom of the Navigation bar (below the Apps link) so that you don't accidentally navigate away from the current page.

To adjust the width of any column, slide the mouse pointer into the row of column heading labels above the list and place it over the right edge of the column you want to adjust. Drag the mouse when the mouse pointer changes to a pair of vertical lines and a pair of horizontal arrows pointing outward. A vertical bar appears to guide you in resizing the column. Release the mouse button when you're satisfied with the column width (see Figure 4-19).

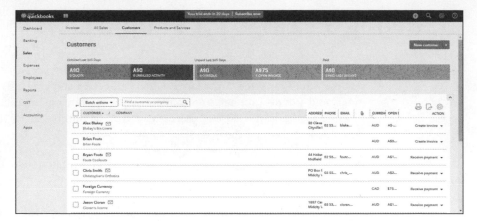

FIGURE 4-19:
Adjusting the width allotted to the customer's name on the Customers page.

TIP

QBO remembers column width adjustments you make in ledgers (Account Histories) and on pages like the Customers and Suppliers pages, even after you sign out of QBO and then sign back in again.

Working with Products and Services Items

Inventory tracking is available in the QBO Plus edition, and you need to turn on the feature. Click Gear ⇨ Company Settings and click the Sales tab. Then, in the Products and Services section, click Track Inventory Quantity On Hand (see Figure 4-20).

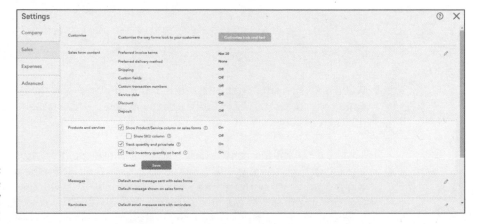

FIGURE 4-20:
Turning on the Inventory Tracking feature.

The Products and Services list, shown in Figure 4-21, is the QBO equivalent to the QuickBooks desktop product's Items list.

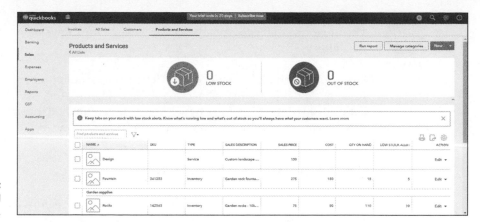

FIGURE 4-21:
The Products and
Services list.

You use the Products and Services list pretty much the same way you use the Customers and Suppliers lists; for example, you can search for an item by its name, SKU (stock keeping unit) or sales description. You can identify the columns you can use to sort the list if you slide your mouse over the column heading; if the mouse pointer changes to a hand, you can click that column to sort the list using the information in that column.

REMEMBER

Enabling the Multicurrency feature, described in Chapter 3, has no effect on inventory item valuations; QBO assesses and reports inventory item values in home currency units, regardless of the currency used by the supplier who sold you the items. For that reason, the Products and Services list shows no distinctions related to currency.

You can import and export items using an Excel or CSV file, the same way you import and export people information. See the sections 'Importing People into a List' and 'Exporting a list to Excel', earlier in this chapter.

TAKING ADVANTAGE OF SKUs

You can control whether SKU information appears on the Products and Services list and on transaction forms from the Company Settings dialog box. Click Gear ⇨ Company Settings ⇨ Sales. Click in the Products and Services section and check or uncheck the Show SKU column. Click Save and then click Done. Using a custom form style (refer to Chapter 3 for information on creating custom forms), you can add the SKU to your invoice form. Or it can be added from the Custom Form Style screen, to the standard Airy invoice template by selecting the SKU check box in the Activity Table tab under the column heading.

REMEMBER

The importing and exporting processes include the information about the item's taxability.

You also can print a basic report by clicking the Print button on any list page; the Print button appears just above the Action column. And you can print a more detailed report for a list entry by selecting the account and then clicking the drop-down menu and the Run Report button under the Actions heading.

Establishing categories

Categories replace sub-items for QBO Plus users in all regions except France. You can use categories to organise what you sell and, using various Products and Services reports, hopefully help you better understand what people are buying from you. Categories do not affect your accounting or your financial reports and you cannot assign categories to transactions.

TIP

Use classes and/or locations to help further catalogue transactions and financial information. Refer to Chapter 3 for more information.

You can create new categories as you create items or, if you prefer, you can click the Manage Categories button and create categories so that they are available as you create items. Yes, you can do both.

From the Product Categories page shown in Figure 4-22, you can click the New Category button to add a category; the Category Information panel appears on the right side of your screen and you simply supply the category name. If the category is a sub-category of an existing category, check the Is a Sub-Category box and select the name of the existing category. Click Save at the bottom of the panel to set up your category.

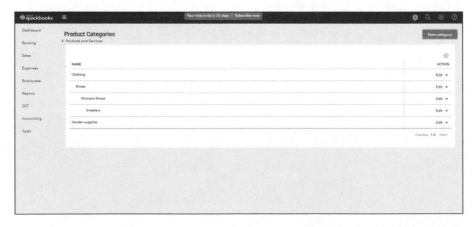

FIGURE 4-22:
The Product
Categories page.

TIP

You can create sub-categories up to four levels deep. That is, you can create a category called Clothing and then create a sub-category of Clothing called Shoes. For the Shoes sub-category, you can create a sub-category called Women's Shoes and, for the Women's Shoes sub-category, you can create one last sub-category called Sneakers. You can't create a sub-category for Sneakers, but you can create another sub-category for Women's Shoes called Dress Shoes.

If necessary, you can edit an existing category; click the Edit link beside the category you want to modify in the table on the Product Categories page. Once again, the Category Information panel appears, displaying the category's current information. Make changes and click Save; alternatively, you can click Remove to remove a category.

REMEMBER

The effect on items of removing a category depends on whether you remove a sub-category or a category. If you remove a sub-category, QBO moves the items assigned to it up one level. If you remove a category (with no sub-categories) QBO reclassifies the items as uncategorised.

Adding service and non-inventory items

You can create inventory, non-inventory and service items, and you can edit batches of items to change their type; we show you how to change an item's type after we show you how to add an item to the list.

Here's how to add an item to the list:

1. **To display the Products and Services list, click Gear ⇨ Products and Services.**

The list can also be accessed by selecting Sales in the Navigation menu and then clicking on the Products and Services tab.

2. **Click the New button.**

QBO displays the Product/Service Information panel on the right side of your screen (see Figure 4-23), where you can select whether you're creating an inventory item, a non-inventory item, a service or a bundle.

3. **Click a type to select it.**

For this example, we chose Non-inventory item. You create a service item the same way you create a non-inventory item, supplying the same kind of information shown in these steps. See the next section, 'Creating an Inventory Item,' for details on the additional information you supply when creating an inventory item.

QBO then displays the panel for the type of item you chose; Figure 4-24 shows the Non-inventory panel.

FIGURE 4-23:
Select a type of
item to create.

4. **Supply a name for the item and, if appropriate, a stock keeping unit (SKU).**

   You also can select the item's category.

   TIP

   You can upload a picture of the item by clicking the Upload button and navigating to the location where you store the picture.

5. **In the Sales Information section, you can:**

   a. **Select the I Sell This Product/Service to My Customers check box and supply a default description**

   b. **Supply the price you charge when you sell this item**

   c. **Select the income account associated with the item**

   QBO uses this information when you select this item on sales transactions; however, these are the item's default values only and can be overridden from within the individual sale or purchase transactions.

6. **Select the I Purchase This Product/Service from a Supplier check box at the bottom of the window to display the Purchasing Information section (see Figure 4-25).**

7. **Supply a default description, the cost you pay when you purchase the item and the expense account associated with the item.**

   QBO uses this information when you select this item on expense transactions.

FIGURE 4-24:
Use this window
to create a
non-inventory
item.

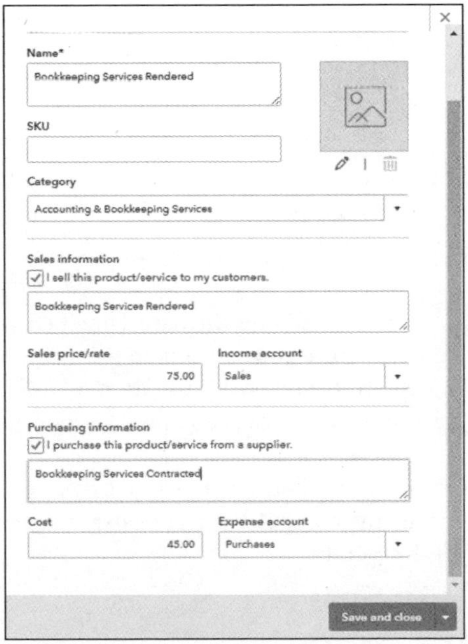

FIGURE 4-25:
Add purchasing
information for
the item.

8. **Click Save and Close.**

QBO saves the item and redisplays the Products and Services list; the new item
appears in the list.

Creating an inventory item

Creating an inventory item has a few additional types of information you need to supply. As you can see in Figure 4-26, in addition to the other information you supply when you create a service or non-inventory item, for an inventory item you supply quantity on hand information as well as the inventory asset account that tracks your inventory items.

FIGURE 4-26: Supply quantity on hand and inventory asset account information for inventory items.

Supply the quantity you have on hand and the date on which you determined the quantity on hand. Remember, before you can sell an item, you must own some of it. If you don't own any at the time you create the item, you'll probably buy some of it using an expense transaction, and that will update your quantities for you.

REMEMBER

If you put in a date for quantity on hand, you are not able to record expenses or bills from suppliers for that inventory if the bill or expense is dated prior to the date you are recording in this screen.

Changing item types

You can change a service or non-inventory item's type individually or you can select several items and change their item types simultaneously.

TYPES OF CHANGES YOU CAN MAKE

Be aware that you can change item types with some limitations. Specifically, you can't change Inventory items to any other item types. You can make the following types of changes:

- Non-inventory and Service items to Inventory items
- Service items to Non-inventory items or Inventory items
- Non-inventory items to Service items

When changing item types, you change several items at one time only if you are changing Non-inventory items to Service items or Service items to Non-inventory items. If you need to change either a Service item or a Non-inventory item to an Inventory item, you can make the change only one item at a time.

To change any single item's type, edit that item by clicking Edit in the Action column of the Products and Services list; QBO displays the item in the Product/Service information panel (refer to Figure 4-24). Click the Change Type link at the top of the panel above the item's name.

QBO displays a panel very similar to the one shown in Figure 4-23; the only difference you'll notice is that current item type contains a check. Click the new item type, and QBO redisplays the Product/Service Information panel using the new item type. Make any other necessary changes and click Save and Close.

Changing the type of a single item using the method just described works well when you only need to change one or two items. But when you need to change multiple items, use a different approach to save time when changing items of the same type to a different type; follow these two steps:

1. **On the Products and Services page, select the check box that appears to the left of each item you want to change.**

   Make sure that you select either service items or non-inventory items, but not both.

   QBO displays two buttons above the table of items (see Figure 4-27).

2. **Click the Batch Actions button and select the new type for the selected items.**

   QBO redisplays the Products and Services list, showing the new item types for the items you selected in Step 1.

FIGURE 4-27: Changing the type of multiple items simultaneously.

TIP

The Assign Category button at the top of the Products and Services list appears when you select multiple items, and you can use it to simultaneously assign the same category to multiple items.

Adjusting inventory item information

On occasion, you might need to make adjustments to inventory item information. Specifically, you might need to adjust inventory item quantities on hand or starting values.

TIP

You can edit any item to change descriptive information, such as its name or description; just click the Edit link in the Action column beside its name on the Products and Services page to view the item's information in the panel shown previously. In this section, we're talking about adjusting inventory item information, which encompasses more than editing descriptive information.

Adjusting inventory quantities

You might discover, particularly after physically counting inventory, that you have a different number of an inventory item than reported in QBO. In this case, you need to adjust the quantity in QBO to match what you actually have in stock.

To create an adjustment for just a few inventory items, follow these steps:

REMEMBER

1. **Click the Create menu (+ at the top right of the QBO window) and choose Inventory Qty Adjustment (see Figure 4-28).**

   The Create menu plus sign changes to an X when the menu is open.

   QBO displays the Inventory Quantity Adjustment window (see Figure 4-29).

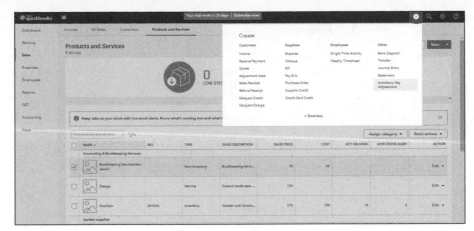

FIGURE 4-28:
Starting an inventory item adjustment for a single inventory item.

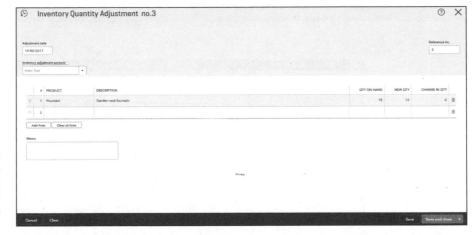

FIGURE 4-29:
You can use this window when you have just a few adjustments to make.

2. **If necessary, change the adjustment date and the Inventory Adjustment Account.**

3. **In the table, click the Product field, click the drop-down arrow that appears and select an inventory item.**

   QBO fills the inventory item's SKU, description and quantity on hand. QBO also suggests the Qty On Hand value for the New Qty value.

   If you've enabled class and location tracking, you can supply information for those fields as you complete the Inventory Quantity Adjustment window.

REMEMBER

4. **Enter either a new quantity or a change in quantity.**

Suppose that the Qty On Hand field indicates you own 25 of your item and you need to reduce the quantity you own by 5. You do either of the following:

a. Enter 20 in the New Qty field

b. Enter -5 in the Change in Qty field

5. **Repeat Steps 3 and 4 for each inventory item you need to adjust.**

6. **In the Memo field, enter a description that explains why you made this adjustment.**

7. **Click Save and Close.**

If you have a lot of inventory items to adjust, you can save some time by preselecting them and adjusting them as a batch. Choose Gear⇨ Products and Services to display the Products and Services page (see Figure 4-30).

FIGURE 4-30:
Selecting multiple
inventory items
to adjust.

Then select the inventory items you want to adjust by placing a check in the column to the left of the item name. Click the Batch Actions button and choose Adjust Quantity. QBO displays the Inventory Quantity Adjustment window shown previously in Figure 4-29, but prefills the window with the information about the inventory items you selected. Complete Steps 4, 6, and 7 from the preceding list for each item in the window.

Editing an inventory quantity adjustment

If you need to edit an inventory quantity adjustment you previously saved (hey . . . it happens), follow these steps:

1. **In the upper right corner of your screen, click the Search button to display Recent Transactions (see Figure 4-31).**

   QBO displays recent inventory adjustment transactions.

FIGURE 4-31:
Searching for a recent inventory adjustment transaction to edit.

2. **If the adjustment appears in the list, click it.**

   If the adjustment doesn't appear, click View More to display the Search page, where you can expand your search for the transaction. In most cases, changing the date range will do the trick.

3. **Make the necessary changes.**

   You can remove a line from an adjustment by clicking its Delete button at the right edge of the row.

TIP

4. **Click Save and Close.**

Adjusting an inventory item's starting value

Suppose that you made a mistake when you set up the starting value for an inventory item; you can edit the item's starting value as long as you created the inventory item after the November 2015 QBO release.

WARNING

Changing an item's starting value can have wide-ranging effects, and QBO will display a warning to this effect when you start your inventory item starting value adjustment. If you're not sure about what you're doing, ask your accountant or bookkeeper. Please.

To adjust an inventory item's starting value, follow these steps:

1. **Choose Gear ⇨ Products and Services.**

2. **In the Action column beside the inventory item you want to adjust, click the drop-down arrow and select Adjust Starting Value (see Figure 4-32).**

QBO displays a warning explaining that changing an inventory item's starting value may affect the initial value of your inventory.

FIGURE 4-32:
Getting ready to adjust the starting value of an inventory item.

3. **Assuming you've heeded the preceding warning and know what you're doing, click Got It!**

QBO displays the Inventory Starting Value window (see Figure 4-33).

TIP

If you've enabled class and location tracking, you can supply information for those fields along with other fields that affect the inventory item's starting value.

4. **Make the necessary changes.**

REMEMBER

You can't change an item's inventory asset account from the Inventory Starting Value window. To change the item's inventory asset account, display the Products and Services page and click the Edit link to display the item's information in the Inventory Item Product/Service Information panel shown previously in Figure 4-26.

5. **Click Save and Close.**

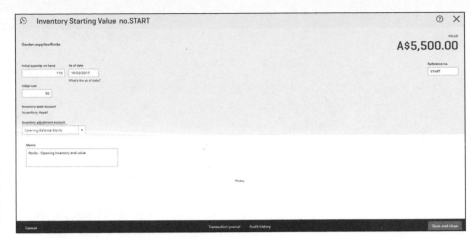

Looking at Other Lists

Just as QuickBooks desktop has other lists besides lists of people and items, QBO also has other lists. To find them, click the Gear icon in the upper right corner and, from the menu that appears, click All Lists in the second column from the left. QBO displays the Lists page shown in Figure 4-34.

Click any list name to open that list and work with it. You can add new entries, select and edit existing entries, and select and delete entries that have never been used. The steps to create any new list element are pretty much the same as the steps you've seen in this chapter to create people, items and product categories.

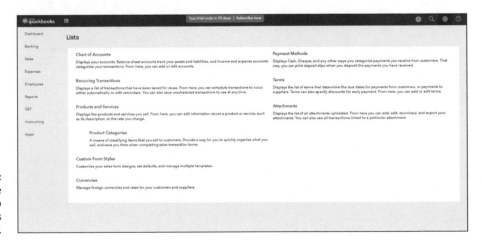

IN THIS CHAPTER

» **Issuing cheques**

» **Entering expenses**

» **Creating Transaction Templates**

» **Using purchase orders**

» **Entering and paying bills**

Chapter **5**

Dealing with the Outflow of Money

I t's always more fun to make money than to spend it, but paying bills is part of life — unless you're living in *Star Trek: The Next Generation,* where they have no bills . . . but, we digress. This chapter explores the transactions you use in QBO to meet your financial obligations.

To record most expense-related transactions, you can choose the Expenses tab in the Navigation menu to display the Expense Transactions page shown in Figure 5-1. Click the New Transaction button to select a transaction type.

If the transaction type you want to record isn't available, click the Create plus sign (+) icon at the top right of QBO and choose the type of transaction you want to record from the Create menu that appears; expense-related transactions show up in the Suppliers column (see Figure 5-2).

REMEMBER

The Create icon changes to an X when you open the menu.

FIGURE 5-1:
The Expense
Transactions
page.

FIGURE 5-2:
Expense
transactions
appear in the
Suppliers column
of the Create
menu.

Writing a Cheque

Typically, you enter a cheque transaction when you intend to print a cheque to pay for an expense. Suppose that the courier guy has just made a delivery for which you owe money and you want to give him a cheque: Use the Cheque transaction.

Assigning a cheque to accounts or items

When you write a cheque, you need to assign the expense for which you're writing the cheque to either an account or an item, and you can assign one cheque to both accounts and items. Follow these steps to enter and print a cheque:

1. **From the Navigation menu on the left side of your screen, select the Expenses tab. From the Expenses screen, click the New Transaction button at the top right of the screen.**

2. **From the list that appears, click Cheque.**

   QBO displays the Cheque window, which is divided into four sections:

   - **The Header section:** Shown in Figure 5-3, this section displays the balance in the selected cheque account, the selected payee and the payee's mailing address, the payment date, the cheque amount and number.

FIGURE 5-3:
The Header section of the Cheque window.

   - **The Account Details section:** You use this table when the expense is not related to an item you've defined as one of your products or services; for example, an office expense.

   - **The Item Details section:** You use this table when you're writing a cheque to pay for a product or service you purchased that relates to your inventory. If you don't see this table, its preference isn't enabled. To display the table, choose the Gear icon and then go to Company Settings ⇨ Expenses ⇨ Bills and Expenses and edit the Show Items Table on Expense and Purchase Forms option.

If this is already activated, the reason that it's not showing up on your screen may be because it is minimised. Select the drop-down arrow near Item Details and the section will expand.

REMEMBER

You typically write a cheque using *either* the Account Details section or the Item Details section, but not both. However, you can use both sections. As an example, you would use both sections if you were paying for a box of shampoo (which gets added to your inventory) plus a packet of stickers to go on the shampoo (which you don't calculate as inventory but post to an advertising expense account), and you could also use the account section for posting delivery or freight charges. If you won't be using a section, you can hide it by clicking the downward-pointing arrow beside the section name.

- **The Footer section:** This contains the cheque total, the Memo box, and the box you use to attach an electronic document to the cheque, such as a copy of any delivery documentation or warranties.

3. **Choose a payee and an account from which to make the payment.**

   Along with the payee's address information, QBO displays information from previously entered transactions — unless you haven't entered any transactions for that payee yet, or you have disabled the setting to display previously entered transaction information in Company Settings. This is known as a *sticky preference*, which can make the task of entering data much easier. For example, if you enable this preference and each time you pay Caltex you use the Fuel account to post the transaction to, QBO (being super intelligent) will know when you choose Caltex that you want to post to the fuel account, so it will pre-populate that information for you along with the last value that you entered. So all you need to do is change the value of the transaction to reflect your current expense.

TIP

If a pane appears on the right side, it displays transactions you might want to link to the cheque you're writing — and, if that's the case, see the next section, 'Writing a cheque for an outstanding bill'. On the other hand, if the cheque you're writing has nothing to do with any transaction that appears in the pane, just ignore the pane; you can hide it as described in the next section.

4. **Double-check the payment Date and Cheque Number.**

5. **Assign part or all of the cheque to an expense account or an item using the Account Details section or the Item Details section (see Figure 5-4).**

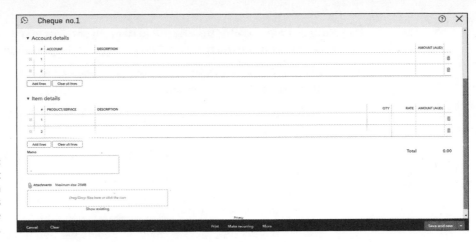

FIGURE 5-4:
The Account Details and Item Details sections of the Cheque window.

To assign a portion to an expense account:

a. Click in the Account column and select an appropriate expense account for the cheque you are recording.

TIP

You can type characters that appear in the account name and QBO will help you find the account, or account numbers if you have enabled them in your chart of accounts.

b. In the Description column, describe the expense you're paying.

c. In the Amount column, supply the amount of the cheque that you want to apply to the selected account.

d. If you incurred the expense on behalf of a customer and you want to bill the customer for the expense, check the Billable box and select the customer's name in the Customer column.

TIP

Billable and customer columns are available in the Cheque window only if these features are turned on. To turn on these features, return to the Home page and select the Gear icon ⇨ Company Settings. Go to the Expense tab and under Bills and Expenses, select the check boxes for Track Expenses and Items by Customer and Make Expenses and Items Billable. Click Done to save.

e. Make sure to select the appropriate tax code that applies to the transaction or each line of the transaction (for example, GST or GST Free), and choose the correct preference in the header section that advises if the values that you are entering are inclusive or exclusive of tax. Always make sure the total of the cheque as shown in the top right of your screen equals the exact amount that you are paying.

TIP

The tax rate option is only available on a cheque transaction if you have turned on the GST Centre by choosing the left Navigation menu ⇨ GST ⇨ Set up GST.

f. Repeat Steps a to e to add more lines to the cheque.

6. **To assign part or all of the cheque to items or services you have defined as your inventory, use the Item Details section (also shown in Figure 5-4):**

   a. **Click in the Product/Service column and select an appropriate item for the cheque you are recording.**

   You can type characters in the Product/Service column and QBO will help you find the item.

   b. **Optionally, edit the Description column for the selected item.**

   c. **Use the Qty, Rate and Amount columns to supply the quantity of the selected item you are purchasing, the rate you're paying for each item and the amount you're paying.**

   If you entered purchase prices in for the items when you set up your inventory, these prices will appear on your screen (which you can easily override if necessary).

   When you supply any two of the Qty, Rate and Amount values, QuickBooks calculates the third value.

   d. **Repeat Steps a to c to add more items to the cheque.**

7. **You can scroll down in the cheque window to the Footer section, type a message to the payee, and attach an electronic document (such as the payee's invoice) to the cheque.**

   To attach an electronic document to the cheque, click in the Attachments box; a standard Open dialog box appears that you can use to navigate to the document. Alternatively, you can drag and drop the electronic copy into the Attachments box.

8. **At the bottom of the window, you can**

   • **Cancel your action or clear the window and start again.**

   • **Click Print to print an expense receipt with provision for you to load preprinted cheques into your printer.**

   You must fill in the actual cheque component by hand as QBO only prints details into the top remittance section of the cheque.

The Save and New button is a sticky preference. That means, if you click the drop-down arrow to the right of the button and select Save and Close, the next time you open the window to write a cheque, the default button will be the Save and Close button.

Writing a cheque for an outstanding bill

You can use the cheque window to write a cheque to pay a bill you previously entered — something that you cannot do in the QuickBooks desktop product.

TIP

Don't use the cheque transaction if you're planning on paying several bills. Instead, see the section 'Paying bills' at the end of this chapter.

If you select a payee for whom an outstanding bill exists, QBO displays a pane at the right side of the Cheque window (see Figure 5-5) that shows all transactions linked to the selected payee; each transaction appears as a separate entry. If nothing in the pane applies to your transaction, you can hide the pane by clicking the button shown in Figure 5-5.

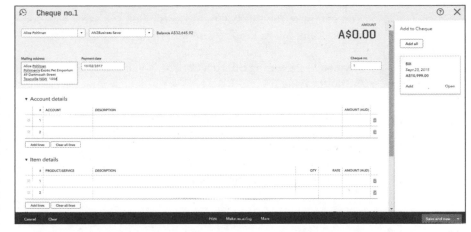

FIGURE 5-5:
If you select a payee for whom you previously entered a bill, the outstanding bill appears in the pane on the right side of the Cheque window.

If you're writing the cheque to pay a bill that appears in the pane, click Add in the bill transaction you want to pay. That way, QBO appropriately applies the cheque you're writing to the outstanding bill and correctly reduces your outstanding obligations.

WARNING

If you write a cheque to pay a bill and you *don't* apply the cheque to the bill, your reports show that you continue to owe the bill amount to the payee, which really messes things up.

When you click Add, QBO adds that bill to the cheque and switches to the Bill Payment window, essentially converting the cheque to a Bill Payment transaction. In Figure 5-6, you see the Bill Payment window after we added an outstanding bill to a cheque in the Cheque window.

FIGURE 5-6:
The Bill Payment window.

You complete the Bill Payment transaction the same way you complete a Cheque transaction; follow Steps 7 and 8 in the preceding section.

TIP

If you add the wrong bill to a cheque, you can cancel the Bill Payment transaction without saving it.

Each time you open the Cheque screen, the next cheque number as per your cheque book or pre-printed cheques will appear. Although essentially the same journal entry is used in the back end for creating cheques and entering in expenses, if you are not using a cheque to pay for something, enter the expense in the Expenses screen as outlined in the following section.

Creating an Expense Transaction

You use an Expense transaction when you're trying to record an expense without printing a cheque. For example, you record Expense transactions in QBO to account for a payment you make using cash or a credit or debit card.

The Expense transaction window contains a Payment Method list box that you don't find in the cheque transaction window. Other than that one difference, the windows appear and function the same way.

Setting Up Transaction Templates

When you're entering transactions into QBO, an option shows on the bottom of your screen to make the transaction recurring. You can select this option to save a transaction template, which you can allocate a schedule to. For example, you may have a monthly payment for account fees that is the same amount every month, and comes out on the same day each month. This transaction can be made recurring and you can set a schedule so the transaction will post automatically until you want it to stop.

TIP

If you don't want the transaction to automatically post, you can still make it recurring — just don't set a schedule for it.

You can make all kinds of transactions recurring, including expenses, cheques, bills, purchase orders, supplier credits, credit card credits, bank deposits, transfers, journal entries, invoices, quotes, adjustment notes, sales receipts, refund receipts, delayed credits and delayed charges.

QBO AND CREDIT CARD TRANSACTIONS

By default, QBO treats Credit Card account transactions as cash transactions, a conservative approach that recognises expenses as they occur. To account for credit card transactions, set up both your credit card company as a supplier and a Credit Card account for the credit card in your Chart of Accounts, and use Expense transactions to record credit card purchases to the account as you make each purchase. If you need to record a credit card return, use the Credit Card Credit transaction found in the Create menu.

When the credit card bill arrives, you can pay it in a number of ways:

- To pay by cheque, use the cheque transaction, select your credit card company as the supplier and, in the Account Details section, select your Credit Card account.

- To pay by EFT or BPAY, use the expense transaction, select your credit card company as the supplier and, in the Account Details section, select your Credit Card account.

- To pay by transfer (where you transfer money electronically or manually from a bank account to your Credit Card account, which reduces both accounts), use the Transfer transaction, selecting the bank account you'll use to pay the bill as the Transfer Funds From account and the Credit Card account you're paying as the Transfer Funds To account.

- To pay the bill while reconciling the Credit Card account, follow the steps in Chapter 8 to reconcile the account. When you click Finish, you'll be given the option to write a cheque to pay the amount due.

If you want to download credit card transaction information into QBO, see Chapter 8.

Entering a Purchase Order

Businesses that order lots of stuff from suppliers often use purchase orders to keep track of the items on order. Purchase orders in QBO do not affect any of your accounts; instead, they simply help you keep track of what you order. And, when the order arrives, you can compare the goods that come in the door with the ones listed on the purchase order to make sure they match.

If you plan to use purchase orders, your ordering process typically happens in the following way:

» You place an order with a supplier and you enter a purchase order in QBO that matches the order you placed.

» You receive the items you ordered, typically along with a bill for the items; you then match the items you receive to the purchase order and enter a bill for the items. Note that sometimes you receive the bill without the items or the items without the bill.

» You pay the supplier's bill.

You can send a copy of the purchase order via email direct to the supplier and, when creating a bill for that supplier, QBO will prompt you to add the purchase order via the pane on the right of the screen.

You enter a purchase order transaction using the Purchase Order window; you can open this window either from the Expense Transactions page or from the Create menu (the plus sign). A typical purchase order looks like the one shown in Figure 5-7, and you'll notice the window closely resembles the Cheque window shown earlier in Figure 5-4.

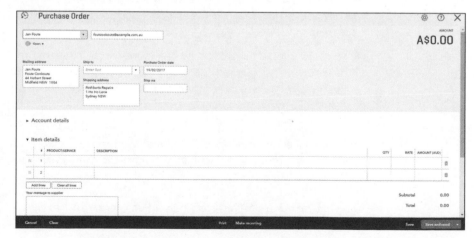

FIGURE 5-7:
The Purchase Order window.

As you fill in the Purchase Order transaction window, QBO assigns a status of Open to the purchase order; the status appears just below the supplier's name in the upper left corner of the transaction window.

When you receive the goods, the supplier's bill or both, you record a bill as described in the next section, or a cheque, an expense transaction, or a credit card charge as described earlier in this chapter, showing what you paid (or what you owe) the supplier.

When you select a supplier who has open purchase orders on any of these types of transactions, a pane appears on the right side of the window, showing available purchase orders. You add a purchase order to the transaction the same way you add a bill to a Cheque transaction: By clicking the Add button. In Figure 5-8, we open a Cheque transaction and select a supplier who has open purchase orders.

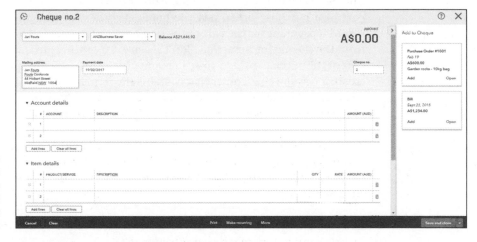

FIGURE 5-8:
The Cheque window, with a supplier selected who has open purchase orders.

When we click Add to add the purchase order to our transaction, QBO adds the purchase order lines to the first available line in the Item Details section of our Cheque transaction. QBO also indicates, immediately below the supplier's name, that the Cheque transaction has one linked transaction (see Figure 5-9).

If you save the Cheque transaction and then reopen the purchase order, QBO has changed the purchase order's status from open to closed so that you don't accidentally add the purchase order to another transaction.

TIP

If you add the wrong purchase order to a transaction, you can remove the purchase order line in the Item Details section by clicking the Trash Can icon at the right edge of the line.

FIGURE 5-9:
A Cheque
transaction
after adding
a purchase
order to it.

QBO can't add only part of a purchase order to a transaction. So, if you receive only part of a purchase order, add the purchase order to your transaction and then record a payment for the part of the purchase order you received by deleting lines from the cheque for items you didn't receive. To continue to track the outstanding part of the purchase order, you can manually close the original purchase order and create a new purchase order that contains the remaining outstanding items; when you create the second purchase order — essentially a back order — try to assign a number to it that helps you track it in relation to the original purchase order.

TIP

You can use your own custom purchase order numbers if you choose Gear⇨ Company Settings⇨Expenses. Then click in the Purchase Orders section to edit purchase order settings, select the Custom Transaction Numbers check box, and click Save.

When you need to identify open purchase orders, use the Open Purchase Order List report. For more on reports, see Chapter 11.

Entering and Paying Bills

You use QBO's Bill transaction to enter a bill from a supplier that you don't want to pay immediately. QBO tracks the bill as a *payable*, which is a liability of your business — money you owe but have not yet paid. Most companies that enter Bill transactions do so because they receive a fair number of bills and want to sit down and pay them at one time, but they don't want to lose track of the bills they receive. They also want to be able to easily determine how much they owe; if you enter Bill transactions, you can print the A/P Ageing Summary and Details reports to find that information.

Depending on the version of QBO that you use, the Bill transaction might not be available to you; if that's the case, pay your bills using the Cheque or the Expense transaction.

Entering a bill

To enter a bill you receive from a supplier, use QBO's Bill transaction. Follow these steps:

1. **Choose Expenses from the Navigation menu.**

2. **Click the New Transaction button in the upper right corner of the Expenses page and select Bill.**

   QBO displays the Bill transaction window shown in Figure 5-10.

3. **Select the supplier from whom you received the bill.**

   QBO fills in the supplier's mailing address information.

4. **Check and, if necessary, change the bill date and the due date.**

5. **Use the Account Details section, the Item Details section or both to record information about the bill.**

   Refer to the section 'Writing a Cheque', earlier in this chapter, for details on filling out the Account Details section and the Item Details section.

6. **Optionally, scroll down to the Footer section and enter information in the Memo field and attach electronic documents to the bill.**

7. **Click Save.**

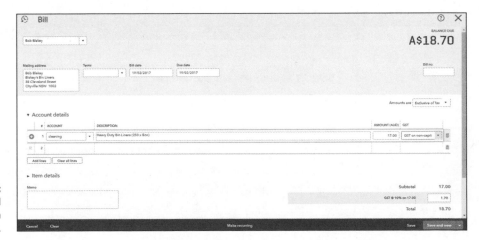

FIGURE 5-10:
The Bill transaction window.

Recording a supplier's credit

You enter a supplier credit to record returns to suppliers or refunds from suppliers. A supplier might provide you with a credit document that indicates you no longer owe the amount stated on the document, or the supplier might issue a refund payment to you. If this is the case and you have received a monetary refund from a supplier into your account, use the Bank Deposit screen available from the Create menu (plus sign).

If a supplier issues a credit document adjustment note, you enter a supplier credit and then apply it when you pay the supplier's bill.

Follow these steps to enter the supplier credit:

1. **On the Expense Transaction page, click New Transaction ⇨ Supplier Credit.**

QBO displays the Supplier Credit window shown in Figure 5-11.

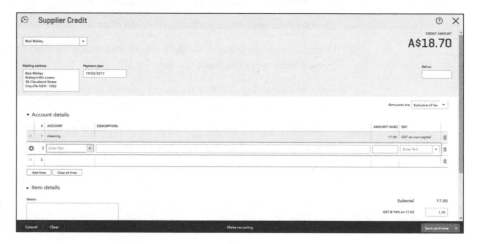

FIGURE 5-11:
A Supplier Credit
transaction.

2. **Select the supplier who issued the credit.**

3. **Enter the date of the credit.**

4. **Enter the credit amount.**

5. **In the Account Details section, select the account used on the original bill.**

If you received the credit because you returned items to the supplier, select the items you returned in the Item Details section because this will also affect your inventory.

6. **You can optionally scroll down and attach an electronic copy of the credit to the Supplier Credit transaction.**

7. **Click the arrow beside Save and New and choose Save and Close.**

REMEMBER

The Save option referenced in Step 7 is called a *sticky preference*, which means that after you select Save and Close, it will appear as the default Save option the next time you display this screen.

If the supplier issued a credit document, read the section 'Paying bills', later in this chapter, to learn how to use the supplier credit you just entered to reduce the amount you owe the supplier when you pay the supplier's bill.

Recording a supplier's refund cheque

If the supplier issued a refund cheque to you, you need to complete the steps in the preceding section to enter a supplier credit. You next need to enter a deposit to record the refund cheque in your bank account and then create an expense to link the deposit to the supplier credit. Here's how:

1. **Click the Create plus (+) sign and, from the Other section of the Create menu that appears, choose Bank Deposits.**

   QBO displays the Deposit transaction window shown in Figure 5-12.

2. **In the Add New Deposits section, enter the following information:**

   - **In the Received From column, select the supplier who issued the cheque.**

   - **In the Account column, select the Accounts Payable account.**

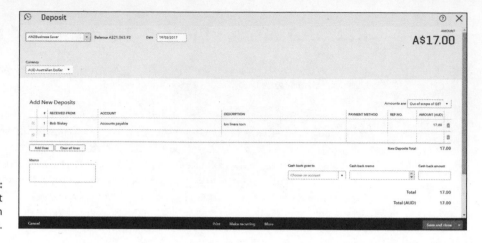

FIGURE 5-12:
The Deposit
transaction
window.

WARNING

You may be tempted to enter the account for which you post that supplier's expenses to — for example, fuel or office expense. However, the deposit won't show up in the supplier's transaction list unless Accounts Payable is entered into the account field.

- **In the Amount column, enter the amount of the cheque.**

3. **Click the arrow beside Save and New and choose Save and Close.**

REMEMBER

The Save option functions as a sticky preference, and you might not see Save and New because you previously made a different choice.

4. **Click the Create plus (+) sign and, from the Create menu that appears, choose Expense.**

5. **Select the supplier whose refund cheque you deposited.**

QBO displays available deposits, credits and bills.

6. **Click Add in the Deposit transaction.**

7. **Click Add in the outstanding Supplier Credit transaction.**

When you add these two transactions, in this order, to the Expense, QBO creates a Bill Payment transaction with a net value of $0 because QBO applies the deposit to the supplier credit.

8. **Click the arrow beside Save and New and choose Save and Close.**

Paying bills

If you've been entering bills from suppliers, at some point you need to pay those bills. Most people sit down once or twice a month and pay outstanding bills. To pay bills in QBO, follow these steps:

1. **Click the Create plus (+) sign and, from the Create menu that appears, choose Pay Bills in the Supplier column.**

   QBO displays the Pay Bills page shown in Figure 5-13.

   Overdue bills display a red flag.

TIP

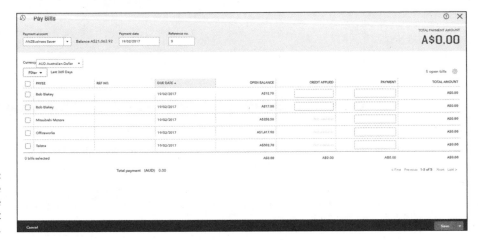

FIGURE 5-13:
The Pay Bills page lists bills you owe but have not yet paid.

2. **In the Payment Account list, select an account to use to pay the bills.**

3. **Provide a payment date at the top of the screen.**

4. **Enter the number of the first cheque you'll use to pay bills.**

5. **In the Filter list, select an option to specify the outstanding bills you want to consider paying.**

   By default, QBO displays unpaid bills for the last year, but you can limit what appears onscreen for your consideration by a variety of dates and even for selected payees.

6. **By clicking the appropriate column heading, you can opt to sort the listed bills by Payee, Reference Number, Due Date or Open Balance.**

7. **Select the check box in the column at the left side of each bill you want to pay.**

   As you select bills to pay, QBO updates the Payment column using the bill amount as the default payment amount (see Figure 5-14). You can change the payment amount of any bill by typing in the Payment column.

REMEMBER

   If a supplier credit exists, QBO will display a field to which you can enter the credit amount you wish to include with the bill payment.

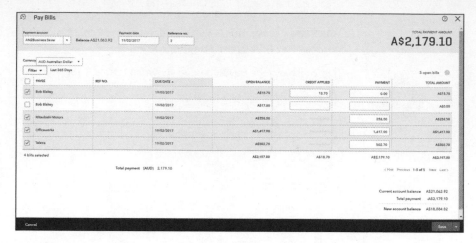

FIGURE 5-14:
QBO uses the bill
amount less any
supplier credits to
calculate a
payment amount.

8. **Click Save and Print, or click the arrow beside Save and Print to choose either Save or Save and Close.**

   Click Save or Save and Close to mark the bills paid without printing any cheques. Click Save and Print to print cheques and mark the bills paid.

TIP

If you choose to pay your bills using a credit card instead of a bank account, the window and process are the same as those outlined in the preceding steps.

Chapter **6**

Managing the Inflow of Money

This is where the fun starts. 'Why?' you ask. Because this chapter covers stuff related to bringing money into the business, which, from any business-person's perspective, is the reason you started your business — and therefore the most fun part!

To record most sales-related transactions, you can choose Sales from the Navigation menu on the left side of your screen and choose the All Sales tab to display the Sales Transactions page shown in Figure 6-1; then click the New Transaction button. If the transaction type you want to record isn't available on the Sales Transactions page, open the Create menu by clicking the Create button — the plus sign (+) icon at the top of QBO, which changes to an X after you click it. Then, choose the type of transaction you want to record; sales-related transactions appear in the Customers column (see Figure 6-2).

GETTING UP-AND-RUNNING

If you've already been in business when you start using QBO, and you have some invoices you've issued but customers haven't yet paid, you can use those invoices as a learning tool and enter them as described in this chapter. If you recorded an opening bank account balance back in Chapter 3, be sure to enter into QBO the deposits you've made since your last bank statement. If you didn't record an opening bank account balance back in Chapter 3, or you recorded a bank account balance as of the end of the financial year, be sure to enter into QBO all the deposits you've made this year, even if they have cleared the bank.

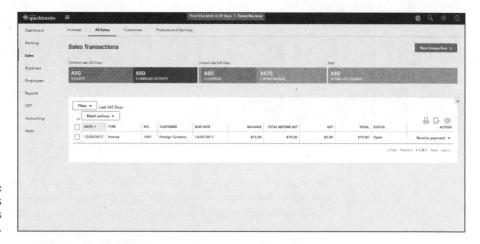

FIGURE 6-1:
The Sales Transactions page.

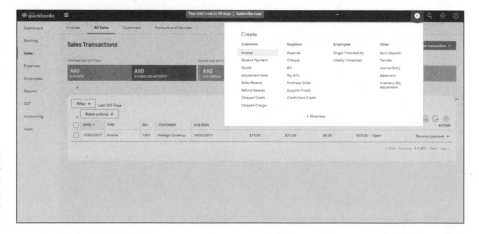

FIGURE 6-2:
Sales transactions appear in the Customers column of the Create menu.

Customising Forms to Handle Subtotals

Before we dive into preparing various types of forms, you should address a house-keeping task: setting up sales forms so that you can include subtotals on them. If you have no need to subtotal information on your sales forms, you can skip this section and move on to the next one.

You can subtotal lines on an invoice, a quote or a sales receipt. First, turn on the feature; for this example, we turn on the feature for the Invoice form. Follow these steps:

1. **Choose Gear ⇨ Custom Form Styles.**

   The Custom Form Styles page appears, which displays the form styles you have set up.

   REMEMBER

   In Chapter 3, you saw how to customise forms. If you opted not to set up any custom forms, you might not see anything listed on the Custom Form Styles page. In that case, click the New Style button and continue with these steps.

2. **Select a form to customise, and then click Edit in the Action column.**

   The Customise Form Style dialog box appears.

3. **On the left side of the dialog box, click the Activity Table section.**

4. **In the More group, select the Group Activity By check box and make a selection from the list.**

   For our example, shown in Figure 6-3, we choose Type.

FIGURE 6-3: Turn on the setting to enable grouping on the selected sales form.

TIP

You can select Subtotal Groups if you want QBO to group specifically by the grouping type you select in Settings. Not selecting the option gives you more flexibility on the forms.

5. **Save the settings.**

REMEMBER

You need to repeat the preceding steps for each type of form (invoice, quote and sales receipt) on which you want to be able to subtotal information.

Preparing an Invoice

You enter invoices in QBO to inform customers that they owe you money for goods you sold them or services you performed for them. In QBO, you can prepare invoices and send them using email or by printing the invoice and posting it in the mail.

When you prepare an invoice, you include information about what you're selling to the customer by including items on the invoice. You create items for both services and products using the Products and Services list, as described at the end of Chapter 4.

TIP

If you have set up numerous income accounts in your Chart of Accounts, you can create an invoice and post to them directly without using items. For example, income accounts for a construction-based business may look like this:

>> Income: Machinery Hire

>> Income: Waste Disposal

>> Income: Concrete Materials

>> Income: Small Project Pool

>> Income: Major Contracts

>> Income: Renovations

This business can create an invoice to a customer and post it directly to the Renovations account without having set up products and services, because they keep no track of inventory.

To enter an invoice, follow these steps:

1. **Choose All Sales to display the Sales Transactions page.**

2. **Click the New Transaction button and, from the list that appears, click Invoice.**

3. **Choose a customer.**

   QBO displays the customer's mailing address, payment terms, invoice date, due date and Send Later option.

TIP

   If a pane appears on the right side, it displays transactions you might want to link to the invoice you're creating; you can see examples in the sections 'Preparing a quote' and 'Creating Billable Time Entries', later in this chapter.

4. **Double-check the Invoice Date, Due date and Terms, and make an appropriate selection in the Send Later check box.**

   If you want to send invoices via email, you can set up your preferences; from the QBO Home page, click the Gear button on the top right of the screen and choose Company Settings.

5. **Fill in the products and services the customer is buying:**

   a. **Click in the Product/Service column and select an appropriate item for the invoice you are creating.**

TIP

   You can type characters in the Product/Service column and QBO will help you find the item.

   b. **Optionally, edit the Description column for the selected item.**

   c. **Use the Qty, Rate and Amount columns to supply the quantity of the selected item you are selling, the rate you're charging for each item and the amount the customer should pay.**

   If you entered sales prices in for the items when you set up your inventory, these prices will appear on your screen (which you can easily override if necessary). When you supply any two of the Qty, Rate and Amount values, QBO calculates the third value.

   d. **Make the appropriate entry to the tax field by selecting the tax code that applies to the transaction or each line of the transaction (for example, GST or GST Free).**

   Make sure you choose the correct preference in the header section that advises if the values that you are entering are inclusive or exclusive of tax. Always make sure the total of the invoice, as shown in the top right of your screen, equals the exact amount that you are billing.

   e. **Repeat Steps a to d to add more items to the invoice.**

6. **To add a subtotal in the proper place on the invoice:**

   a. **Click the last line on the invoice that should be subtotalled; in Figure 6-4, we clicked the third line of the invoice.**

b. **Click the Add Subtotal button, which appears below the lines on the invoice.**

QBO adds a line that subtotals the ones above it. You can continue adding lines to the invoice, and you can add more subtotals.

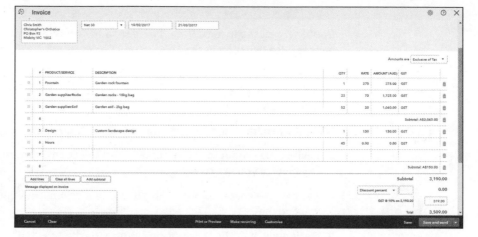

FIGURE 6-4:
Click the last line that should be part of the subtotalled group, and then click Add Subtotal.

7. **Scroll down in the Invoice window, as shown in Figure 6-5, to select a Discount Value or Percent.**

FIGURE 6-5:
Use the bottom of the Invoice window to handle discount information.

You can apply a discount to the invoice if you have turned on the company preference to display the Discount box. To the left of the Discount box, you can also type a message to the customer, type information in the Statement Memo box, which QBO transfers directly to any statement you create in the future, and attach an electronic document to the invoice.

You see the GST on invoices only if you have turned on the GST Centre feature by choosing the Navigation Menu ⇨ GST ⇨ Set up GST.

TIP

Discounts are entered exclusive of GST. GST is then applied to the invoice total minus the discount. For example, an invoice with a subtotal of $120 would attract $12 GST; however, if you apply a $10 discount to the customer's invoice, the GST would be calculated based on the invoice total minus discount. So the GST value would become $11.

8. **To attach an electronic document to the invoice, click in the Attachments box and navigate to the document or drag and drop the electronic copy into the Attachments box.**

9. **At the bottom of the window, you can**

   - **Cancel the invoice or clear the window and start again.**

   - **Click Print or Preview to print or preview the invoice.**

   - **Click Make Recurring to set up the invoice as a recurring invoice you intend to send on a schedule you specify.**

   - **Click Customise to customise the invoice form, as described in Chapter 3.**

   - **Click Save to assign an invoice number and save the invoice in QBO.**

   - **Click Save and Send to assign an invoice number, save the invoice and email a copy to the customer.** A window appears, in which you can write an email message and look at a preview of the invoice. After you send your invoice, the email time and date-stamp information appears in the header.

TIP

You can click the arrow beside Save and Send and then choose Save and New to save the invoice and start a new one, or choose Save and Close to save the invoice and close the Invoice window. The option you choose will appear the next time you display the Invoice window. In fact, in any transaction window, the choice you make appears the next time you open the window. This is called a *sticky preference*.

Recording a Customer Payment

When you receive a payment from a customer, you record it in QBO. You can display the Receive Payment window in the following ways:

>> **Click the Create menu and select Receive Payment**

- ❯❯ **Click the New Transaction button on the Sales Transactions page and select Payment**

- ❯❯ **In the Sales Transactions list, find the invoice for which you want to record a payment and click Receive Payment in the Action column**

If you use either of the first two methods, QBO displays an empty Receive Payment window. You then select a customer, and QBO displays all the customer's open invoices in the Outstanding Transactions section, at the bottom of the window (see Figure 6-6).

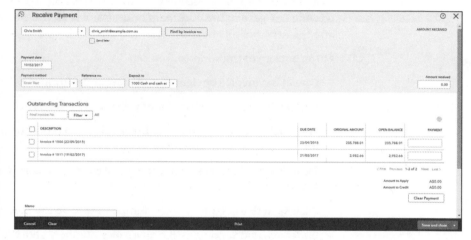

FIGURE 6-6:
The Receive
Payment window
after selecting a
customer with
open invoices.

If you choose the third method in the previous list, QBO displays the Receive Payment window, prefilled with the information for the invoice you selected in the Sales Transactions list.

At the top of the screen, select a Payment Method and select the account in which you want QBO to place the customer's payment. In the Outstanding Transactions section, place a check beside each invoice being paid by the customer's payment.

So, what happens differently if you use the third method and opt to find the invoice on the Sales Transaction list, shown in Figure 6-7, and click the Receive Payment button in the Action column? If you work from the list, QBO automatically fills in the customer name; displays and selects, in the Outstanding Transactions section, the invoice you chose in the Sales Transaction list; and fills in a proposed payment amount. The window you see when you click the Receive Payment button looks just like the window shown in Figure 6-6.

At the bottom of the Receive Payment window, click Save and New to enter additional customer payments, or click the arrow beside Save and New and choose Save and Close.

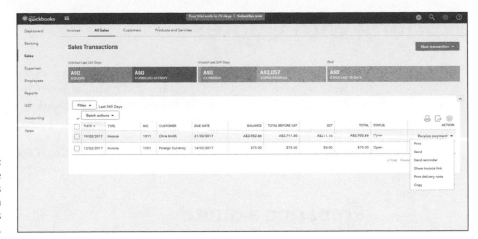

FIGURE 6-7:
You can open the Receive Payments window from the Sales Transaction list.

USING THE UNDEPOSITED FUNDS ACCOUNT

If you receive more than one customer payment in cash or by cheque on any given day, you'll find the Undeposited Funds account a convenient way to handle the money that comes into your business. If you take several cheques to your bank on a given day along with your cash, and deposit all of them as a single deposit, most banks typically don't record the individual cheques and cash amounts as individual deposits. Instead, the bank records the sum of the cash and cheques as your deposit — pretty much the same way you sum the cash and cheques on the deposit slip you give to the bank teller.

'And why is this important?' you ask. This fact is important because, when you receive your statement from your bank, you need to reconcile the bank's deposits and with-drawals with your own version of deposits and withdrawals. If you track each customer payment you receive as a deposit in your QBO Bank account, your QBO deposits *won't* match the bank's deposits.

Herald the arrival of the Undeposited Funds account in QBO, which acts as a holding tank for customer payments before you prepare a bank deposit slip. If you place cus-tomer payments in the Undeposited Funds account, you can then use the Bank Deposit feature in QBO to sum up the payments you receive and intend to deposit at your bank simultaneously. And, if you don't go to your bank daily to make deposits, there's no problem. QBO records, as the deposit amount in your QBO Bank account, the amount calculated in the Bank Deposit window, which will match the amount you actually deposit at your bank. Then your bank reconciliation process becomes quick and easy — well, okay, maybe not quick and easy, but certainly quicker and easier than if you were trying to figure out which customer payments made up various bank deposits.

See Chapter 8 for details on preparing a bank deposit and reconciling a bank statement.

Working with Quotes

You can use quotes to prepare a document that outlines what you need to charge a client to complete a project; quotes don't update your QBO accounts but do enable you to keep track of proposals you make to customers. If a customer decides to buy, based on your quote, you can copy the quote to an invoice.

WARNING

You can copy only those quotes with a status of Pending. Copying a quote to an invoice automatically changes the quote's status from Pending to Closed.

Preparing a quote

You prepare a quote in much the same way you prepare an invoice. To display the quotes window, click the Create menu and choose Quote. Or, if you prefer to work from the Sales Transactions page, choose All Sales, click the New Transaction button and, from the menu that appears, click Quote. QBO displays the Quote window (see Figure 6-8).

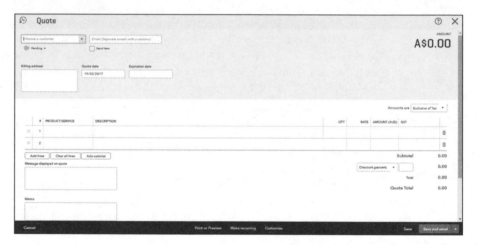

FIGURE 6-8:
Creating a quote.

Choose a customer, and QBO displays the customer's address information and the quote date. You supply the quote's expiration date and optionally select the Send Later option. You can read more about customising forms in Chapter 3.

REMEMBER

QBO sets a quote status as Pending as long as the quote is open and has not expired or been converted to an invoice. The status appears just above the customer's billing address.

NON-POSTING TRANSACTIONS

Quotes and purchase orders are two examples of non-posting transactions. Non-posting transactions don't affect your accounts in any way, but they are helpful because they enable you to enter potential transaction information you don't want to forget. In addition to the quote and the purchase order, QBO Essentials and Plus also enable you to record two other non-posting transactions: Delayed Charge and Delayed Credit.

You can use a Delayed Charge transaction pretty much the same way you use a quote. The Delayed Charge transaction records potential future revenue, and you can convert a Delayed Charge to an invoice in the same way you convert a quote to an invoice. For details, see the section 'Converting a quote to an invoice'.

The Delayed Credit transaction enables you to record a potential future adjustment note. When you prepare an invoice for a customer for whom you've entered a Delayed Credit transaction, QBO displays the Delayed Credit in the pane on the right side of the Invoice window, and you can add the credit to the invoice. A Delayed Credit transaction differs from an adjustment note transaction because an adjustment note transaction updates your accounts when you enter it, but a Delayed Credit transaction updates your accounts only when you include it on an invoice.

You fill out both forms the same way you create an invoice; for details, refer to the section 'Preparing an Invoice'.

To fill in the products and services the customer is considering for purchase, click in the Product/Service column and select an item. You can type characters in the Product/Service column and QBO will help you find the item. QBO fills in any default information stored about the item. You can change the description, quantity, rate, amount and taxable status of the item. Repeat this process to add more items to the quote.

Other features of the quote window are shown in Figure 6–9.

You can apply a discount percentage or dollar amount to the quote if you have the company preference turned on to display the Discount box, type a message to the customer, type information in the Memo box, and attach an electronic document to the quote (such as any terms and conditions).

TIP

To attach an electronic document to the quote, click in the Attachments box and navigate to the document or drag and drop the electronic copy into the Attachments box.

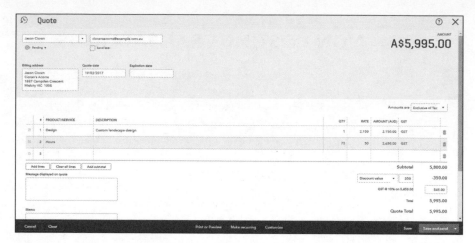

FIGURE 6-9:
Apply a discount to the quote.

At the bottom of the window, you can

>> Cancel the quote or clear the window and start again.

>> Click Print or Preview to print or preview the quote.

>> Click Make Recurring to set up the quote as a recurring quote you intend to send on a schedule you specify.

>> Click Customise to set up a custom form style for the quote.

>> Click Save to assign a number to the quote and save it in QBO.

>> Click Save and Send to assign a number to the quote, save it and email a copy to the customer. A window appears, in which you can write an email message and look at a preview of the quote. After you send your invoice, the email time and date-stamp information appears in the header.

TIP

You can click the arrow beside Save and Close and then choose Save and New to save the quote and start a new one, or choose Save and Close to save the quote and close the quote window.

Converting a quote to an invoice

When you're ready to prepare an invoice for a customer based on a quote you previously created, save yourself some time and effort and convert the quote information to an invoice. You can, if necessary, make adjustments to such an invoice by adding or removing lines. You can convert quote information to an invoice using any of several approaches.

REMEMBER

Converting a quote to an invoice in QBO automatically changes the quote's status from Pending to Closed.

First, you can open the Invoice window and select the customer with the open quote. QBO displays available documents you can link to the invoice, including any quotes (see Figure 6-10). Click the Add button at the bottom of a quote, and QBO automatically adds the quote's information to the Invoice window.

FIGURE 6-10:
Converting a quote to an invoice from the Invoice window.

Second, you can filter the Sales Transactions page to display only quotes, and click the Start Invoice link in the Action column beside the quote you want to convert (see Figure 6-11). QBO displays an invoice that contains all the lines available on the quote.

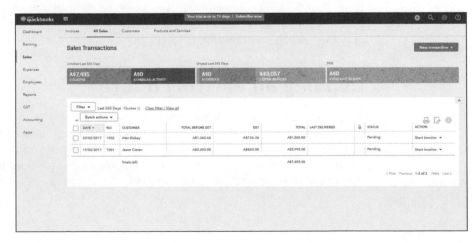

FIGURE 6-11:
Click the Start Invoice link to use quotes information on an invoice.

Third, from the Sales Transactions page, you can click the quote to open it (and review its content, if you want). In the quote window of any quote with a status of Pending, you'll find a Copy to Invoice button, as shown in Figure 6-12; click that button, and QBO displays the Invoice window containing all the information from the quote.

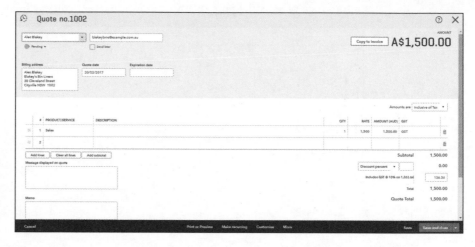

FIGURE 6-12: Click Copy to Invoice to display quotes information on an invoice.

Regardless of the method you use, after you have converted a quote to an invoice, QBO changes the quote's status from Pending to Closed. Be aware that QBO closes the quote even if you don't invoice the customer for all lines on the quote. Also be aware that you can change a quote's status from Closed to Pending, but, if you do, you are making all lines on the quote available for invoicing — and you could then accidentally invoice your customer twice for the same goods. So, if your customer buys only some lines on the quote but intends to buy other lines at a later point in time, your best bet to ensure that you have the right information available for a future invoice is to let QBO close the original quote and create another quote for only the lines the customer didn't yet buy.

Copying an existing quote

Suppose that you have an existing quote — even one you've already converted to an invoice — and you want to create a new quote using most of the information on the existing invoice. You can make a copy of the existing quote, edit the copy as needed, and then save the new quote. Making a copy saves you time because you don't need to re-enter a lot of information.

On the Sales Transactions list, click the arrow next to Print in the Action column for the quote you want to copy. Select Copy from the drop-down menu that appears. Notice that, in Figure 6-13, we've selected a quote with a status of Closed.

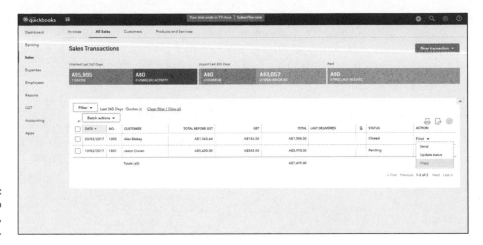

FIGURE 6-13:
Click Copy to duplicate a quote, even if it's closed.

QBO opens a new quote that already contains the information of the quote you copied. Just above the Billing Address information, you see a message that explains that the quote you're viewing is a copy and you should make any changes you need (see Figure 6-14). For example, change the customer, and QBO updates the Billing Address information. Feel free to add or delete lines as needed. When you finish making changes, click Save or Save and Send, as appropriate.

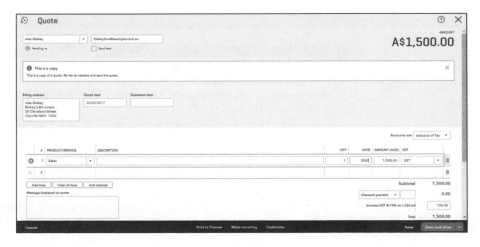

FIGURE 6-14:
Edit the duplicated quote and save it.

Working with Sales Receipts

You use invoices when you need to track money that a customer owes you but hasn't yet paid. But suppose that your customer pays you at the time you sell goods or render services. In these situations, you don't need to enter an invoice; instead, you can enter a sales receipt. And, if you're shipping the items to the customer, you can print a delivery note, which shows the quantities of the items the customer purchased without price information.

Entering a sales receipt

To enter a sales receipt, click Create⇨Sales Receipt or, from the Navigation bar, select Sales then click New Transaction⇨Sales Receipt to display the window shown in Figure 6-15.

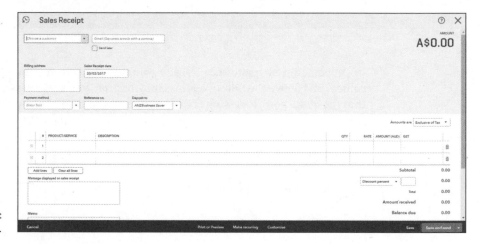

FIGURE 6-15:
A sales receipt.

The sales receipt form closely resembles other sales forms you've seen in this chapter: You select a customer — QBO fills in customer billing address information and assigns today's date to the transaction — enter a payment method and optional reference number, and select the account into which QBO should place the funds. See the sidebar in this chapter, 'Using the Undeposited Funds account', for information on selecting an account from the Deposit To list.

You fill out the rest of the Sales Receipt transaction the same way you fill out an invoice transaction; if you scroll down in the window, you find the same fields at the bottom of the Sales Receipt window as the ones that appear at the bottom of the Invoice window.

Printing sales receipts and delivery notes

You can print both the sales receipt and, if appropriate, a delivery note. To print either document, click the Print or Preview button at the bottom of the Sales Receipt window. Regardless of the document you opt to print, QBO saves the sales receipt and then displays a preview window. If you opt to print the sales receipt, QBO displays a preview window you can use to scroll through the appearance of the sales receipt. However, a better preview appears when you click the Print button (see Figure 6-16).

FIGURE 6-16:
The Print Preview window for a sales receipt.

Notice that the sales receipt displays all pertinent information, including the prices of items.

If you opt to print the delivery note, QBO again saves the sales receipt if you haven't already saved it. Then, QBO again displays a preview window you can use to scroll through the appearance of the delivery note; again, a better preview appears when you click the Print button (see Figure 6-17).

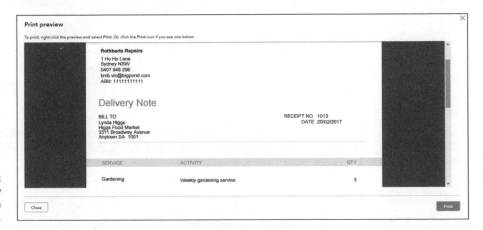

FIGURE 6-17:
The Print Preview window for a delivery note.

Notice that the delivery note identifies only what the customer bought and not how much the customer paid.

Giving Money Back to a Customer

It happens. It's a bummer, but, it happens. Occasionally, you need to return money you have received from a customer.

If a customer returns merchandise to you, issue an adjustment note. This will offer the customer a credit off their purchases. Alternatively, if you need to refund money to a customer — perhaps because goods arrived damaged and the customer doesn't want to reorder them — issue a refund receipt.

Recording an adjustment note

If a customer returns goods previously purchased or if you and your customer agree that the customer's outstanding or future balance should be reduced, record an adjustment note in QBO.

TIP

By default, QBO automatically applies adjustment notes to outstanding or future invoices. If you want to change that behaviour, open the Company Settings dialog box (choose Gear menu⇨Company Settings) and click Advanced on the left. Scroll down to the Automation section on the right, and click the Automatically Apply Credits option.

You enter adjustment notes pretty much the same way you enter an invoice; to display the Adjustment Note window shown in Figure 6-18, you can click the Create menu button and choose Adjustment Note or, from the Sales Transactions page, you can click the New Transaction button and choose Adjustment Note.

Select the customer, fill in the products or services for which you are issuing an adjustment note, fill in the bottom of the Adjustment Note window with appropriate information, and save the transaction. This transaction window is very similar to the Invoice transaction window: Refer to the section 'Preparing an Invoice' for details.

You can enter an adjustment note for a customer even if that customer currently has no outstanding invoices; when you enter the customer's next invoice, QBO will apply the adjustment note to the invoice.

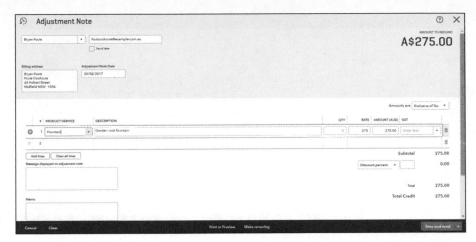

FIGURE 6-18:
Entering an
adjustment note.

When you enter an adjustment note for a customer who has outstanding invoices, QBO applies the adjustment note to an outstanding invoice; if you view the Sales Transactions list for that particular invoice, you'll notice that its Status is Partially paid (see Figure 6-19).

FIGURE 6-19:
An invoice to
which QBO has
applied an
adjustment note.

If you click the invoice to view it, you'll see the credit amount on the Amount Received line at the bottom of the invoice (see Figure 6-20).

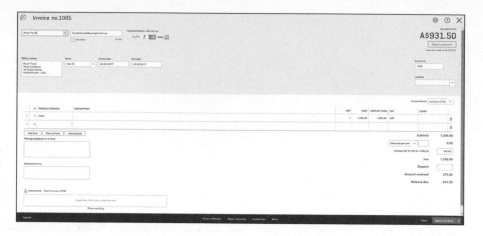

FIGURE 6-20:
By default, QBO applies adjustment notes to an existing outstanding invoice.

Issuing a refund to a customer

Use QBO's Refund Receipt transaction if you need to refund money to a customer instead of reducing an outstanding or future balance. In the following example, we issue a refund cheque to a customer, which will deduct the amount of the refund from a Bank account and reduce an Income account. The customer didn't return any items.

TIP

To account for refunds you issue when a customer doesn't return an item, first set up an account called something like Returns and Allowances and assign this account to the Category Type of Income and a Detail Type of Discounts/Refunds Given. Then set up a service on the Products and Services list and call it something like Customer Refunds or even Returns & Allowances. Do *not* select Is Taxable for the service. Assign the service to the Returns and Allowances account and don't assign a default Price/Rate.

Filling in the Refund Receipt window is very similar to filling in the Invoice window so, if you need more details than we supply here, refer to the section 'Preparing an Invoice'. To display the Refund Receipt window shown in Figure 6-21, click the Create button — the plus (+) sign — and choose Refund Receipt in the Customers column. Select a customer, and QBO fills in related customer information.

Select a payment method and an account; if you select a Bank account, QBO lists the Bank account's current balance and the next consecutive cheque number (in the cheque number field on the right) associated with the account.

In our example, the customer isn't returning any items, so we selected the Refunds & Allowances service. If your customer is returning items, select the item in the Product/Service column that the customer is returning in exchange for the refund and don't select the Refunds and Allowances service shown in Figure 6-21.

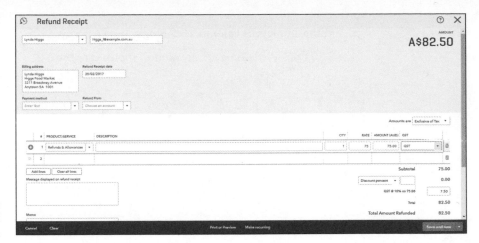

FIGURE 6-21:
Issuing a refund
cheque.

You can scroll down to the bottom of the Refund Receipt transaction window and fill in all the same information available at the bottom of an invoice.

Creating Billable Time Entries

Your employees might work directly for you on activities needed to run your company (such as preparing customer invoices or entering accounting information into QBO), and they might also perform work directly related to your customers. In the latter case, you might want to track the time employees spend on client-related projects and then bill your customers for your employees' time.

To track time, you use either the Single Time Activity window or the Weekly Timesheet window; regardless of the window you use, QBO tracks the time entered and, when you prepare an invoice for a client for whom time was recorded, QBO prompts you to add the time to the invoice.

In this section, we cover entering time using both the Single Time Activity window and the Weekly Timesheet window, and how QBO prompts you to include the billable time on a customer's invoice. Note that a time entry that you can bill back to a customer is called, cleverly, *billable time.*

Entering a single time activity

Open the Single Time Activity window using the Create plus (+) sign menu at the top of QBO. Follow these steps:

1. Click the Create plus (+) sign button to open the Create menu.

2. In the Employees column, click Single Time Activity.

QBO displays the Time Activity window shown in Figure 6-22.

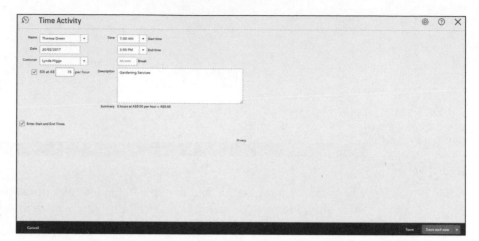

FIGURE 6-22:
The Time Activity
window.

3. From the Name list, select the employee or supplier who performed the work.

4. Enter the date the work was performed.

5. From the Customer list, select the customer for whom the work was performed.

6. Place a check in the Billable box, which changes to the Bill At box, and supply an hourly rate.

7. In the Time box, enter the amount of time spent on this activity.

You can enter start and end times, including any break time, by checking the Enter Start and End Times box; QBO calculates the time spent and displays it below the Description box.

8. Enter a description of the work that will appear, by default, on an invoice.

You can change the description after adding the time entry to the invoice.

9. Click Save to save the entry or Save and New to enter another time activity.

If you click the arrow beside Save and New, you can choose Save and Close.

Using a timesheet to record time

If you prefer to enter time in a grid format that shows the days and dates for a week, the Weekly Timesheet, shown in Figure 6-23, is for you.

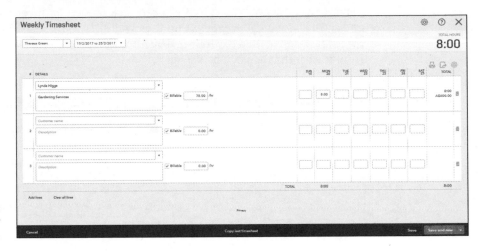

FIGURE 6-23:
The Weekly
Timesheet.

To enter time using this window, follow these steps:

1. Click the Create button — the plus (+) sign — to open the Create menu.

2. In the Employees column, click Weekly Timesheet.

3. Select the name of the person whose time you're recording.

4. Select the week for which you want to record time.

5. In the Details section, select a customer name, a service item and, if appropriate, supply a description.

6. To bill the time back to a customer, select the Billable check box and provide a rate at which to charge the time.

7. Fill in the time worked on the appropriate day.

8. Click Save, Save and New, or click the arrow beside Save and New and select Save and Close.

TIP

The weekly time sheet is great if you want to print a physical timesheet. It's also great for employees who work with several customers or at different locations on any given day.

Adding a billable expense to an invoice

You can add billable time entries to an invoice in a couple of ways. For example, if you view any customer's page, QBO displays a list of outstanding transactions, as shown in Figure 6-24. In the Action column of any billable time entry, QBO displays a Start Invoice button that you can click to start an invoice to the customer and include the billable expense on the invoice. To view a customer's page, click Sales in the Navigation bar followed by All Sales and then click a customer's name from the list that appears on screen.

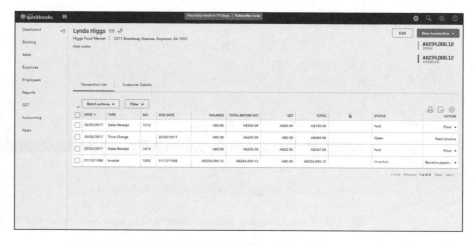

FIGURE 6-24:
Viewing a
customer's page
in QBO.

But you don't need to go looking for billable time entries. QBO prompts you to add them to any invoice you create for a customer for whom billable time entries exist. Start an invoice (from the Create menu — the plus sign — click Invoice) and select a customer. If the customer has billable time entries, they appear in the pane on the right side of the screen (see Figure 6-25).

Click the Add button in each billable time entry that you want to add to the invoice. Or, to add all the entries, click the Add All button at the top of the pane on the right. QBO enters each billable time entry's information on a line on the invoice, filling in the service, description, quantity, rate and total amount. You can edit any information on the line as needed. Fill in the rest of the invoice as described in the section 'Preparing an Invoice', earlier in this chapter, adding other lines that might not pertain to time entries.

TIP

Don't forget that you can add a subtotal for time entries, if you choose. See the first section in this chapter, 'Customising Forms to Handle Subtotals', for details.

FIGURE 6-25:
Creating an invoice for a customer with billable time entries.

Chapter **7**

Diving into Account History via the Ledger

C hapters 5 and 6 show you how to enter transactions such as cheques, sales receipts, invoices and customer payments using various QBO transaction windows. You also see ways to find and filter for certain transactions.

But transaction windows and lists aren't the only way to work with transactions in QBO. You can also use the Account History link, which essentially takes you to an account's Ledger or Register. Some people are more comfortable entering transactions, particularly cheques, directly into a ledger or register and to do this in QBO you use Account History — which we cover in this chapter.

Account History is a great way to quickly view the transactions that affect a particular account and find particular transactions, as described at the end of this chapter.

Understanding Account History

You use Account History to see every transaction that affects a particular account. Account History in QBO contains much of the same information you find in paper Ledgers or Registers that banks give you along with handwritten cheques. To view the Account History for a particular account, click Gear⇨Chart of Accounts. Another way to view your account ledgers in your Chart of Accounts and access Account History is to simply select the Accounting tab from the Navigation menu on the left. Then use the Account History link in the Action column to display the Ledgers or Registers of a particular account (see Figure 7-1).

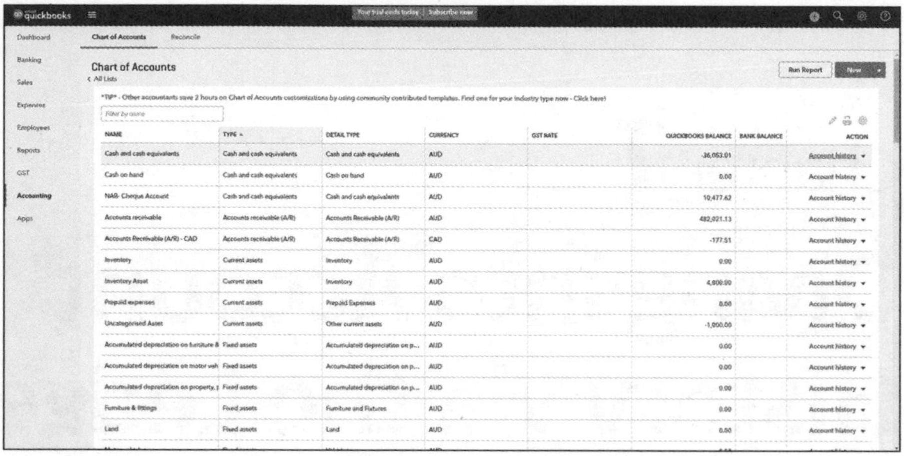

FIGURE 7-1:
Use the Chart of Accounts page to open a particular account's Ledgers via the Account History link.

When you switch to Account History, QBO assumes you want to enter a new transaction and displays a new transaction window at the top of the Account History screen. In Figure 7-2, we've closed that new transaction window so that you can see a bank account register in QBO as it appears by default.

FIGURE 7-2:
A typical Bank Account History account.

The Account History page displays the name of the account and its ending balance at the top of the Account History.

If the Bank Account History shown in Figure 7-2 is electronically connected to its counterpart at a banking institution, you also see the balance in the account as that financial institution reports it.

One rule you need to remember about Account History: They are *not* available for all accounts. You'll find that Account History is available for all *balance sheet* accounts except Retained Earnings. Balance sheet accounts fall into the following QBO account category types:

>> Bank

>> Accounts Receivable

>> Other Current Assets

>> Fixed Assets

>> Other Assets

>> Accounts Payable

>> Credit Card

>> Other Current Liabilities

>> Long Term Liabilities

>> Equity

You see these account category types when you add a new account to the Chart of Accounts or when you view the Chart of Accounts page in QBO.

TIP

If you use account numbers, typically all asset accounts begin with 10000, all liability accounts begin with 20000 and all equity accounts begin with 30000. This numbering scheme is *not* carved in stone, but most accountants recommend that you follow these guidelines when you assign numbers to the accounts in your Chart of Accounts.

Within the Account History, you see column headings that identify the information contained in each column for every transaction and, at the right edge of an Account History page, you see a running balance for the account. All the transactions in a bank account's ledgers or registers affect a bank account — along with some other account, as dictated by the rules of accounting (*double-entry bookkeeping*, a founding principle of accounting, means that every transaction affects at least two accounts). The amount shown in the Balance column is a running balance for the account as long as the Account History is sorted by date.

TIP

At the end of this chapter, in the section 'Looking at Other Account History Features', you learn how to sort the Account History so that it appears in some order other than the default transaction date order. Be aware that if you sort by any column other than the Date column, the Balance column won't display any information because the information wouldn't make any sense.

By default, the latest transactions appear at the top of the Account History but, if you prefer, you can change the appearance of the Account History to use Paper Ledger Mode, as shown in Figure 7-3. In Paper Ledger Mode, QBO lists transactions from earliest to latest — similar to the way transactions appear when you use a paper bank account register. In a paper register or ledger, you enter your transactions as they occur, so the earliest transactions appear at the top of the Account History and the latest transactions appear at the bottom.

FIGURE 7-3:
A bank account register in Paper Ledger Mode.

REMEMBER

When you switch to Paper Ledger Mode, QBO assumes you want to enter a new transaction, as described later in this chapter in the section 'Entering a transaction,' and automatically displays a new transaction window at the bottom of the register page.

To switch to Paper Ledger Mode, follow these steps:

1. **Click the Settings gear icon on the right of your screen.**

   Refer to Figure 7-3.

2. **From the drop-down menu that appears, click Paper Ledger Mode to select it.**

QBO reorders the transactions in the register so that they appear in date order from oldest to newest.

In addition, QBO displays a new transaction window at the bottom of the register.

To switch back to the register's regular appearance, repeat the preceding steps; when you remove the check beside Paper Ledger Mode, QBO reorders the transactions in the register in date order with the latest transaction at the top of the register page.

TIP

QBO remembers the setting you select for the register's appearance; if you choose to display the register in Paper Ledger Mode, the next time you display any register, QBO displays it in Paper Ledger Mode.

In addition to using Paper Ledger Mode, you can control the appearance of a register in a few other ways; you can

» Change the size of columns

» Control the number of rows on a page in your QBO company

» Reduce each register entry to a single line

TIP

QBO remembers adjustments you make in Account History, even after you navigate away from Account History. Further, if you open a different Account History, QBO applies your adjustments to that ledger or register.

To change the size of any column, slide the mouse pointer into the column heading area on the right boundary of the column. In Figure 7-4, we've resized the Ref No. Type column so it's significantly larger (check Figure 7-5 for a comparison). When the mouse pointer changes to a pair of left- and right-pointing arrows connected to a pair of vertical bars, drag the pointer. Dragging to the left makes the column narrower, and dragging to the right to makes the column wider. As you drag, a solid vertical line helps you determine the size of the column. Release the mouse button when the column reaches the size you want.

If resizing columns doesn't satisfy your viewing needs, you can save space horizontally by removing columns from the Account History. To do so, you use the options on the Table Settings gear. Click the Gear button above the Balance column (see Figure 7-5). In the Columns section, remove the checks beside any options you don't need to view; by default, QBO displays the Memo, Reconcile and Banking Status, GST and Running Balance columns. Remove the checks beside these options and QBO removes their columns from the Account History.

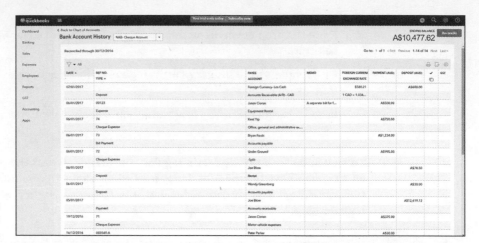

FIGURE 7-4:
Resizing a column.

FIGURE 7-5:
Options you can use to control the appearance of the Account History.

To save space vertically, place a check mark in the Show in One Line box and change the number of rows that appear on a page. You can display 50 rows, 150 rows or 300 rows. Figure 7-6 shows an Account History displaying a single line for each transaction.

By default, if you opt to show transactions on a single line in the Account History, QBO hides the Memo and the Reconcile and Banking Status columns.

REMEMBER

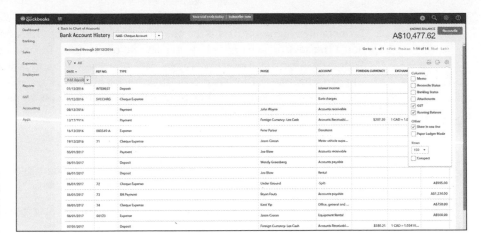

FIGURE 7-6:
An Account History displaying one line for each transaction.

Entering and Editing Transactions

Many people are comfortable using a Bank Account Ledger to enter a cheque or a bill payment; some people are also comfortable entering a bill in the Accounts Payable Ledger or an invoice in the Accounts Receivable Ledger. But, even if you're not comfortable entering transactions in a Ledger, many people find viewing a transaction in a Ledger very easy and helpful.

You open a Ledger from the Chart of Accounts page. To open the Chart of Accounts page, click the Gear button beside your company's name and, from the menu that appears, click Chart of Accounts in the Settings column. From the Chart of Accounts page (shown earlier in Figure 7-1), you click the Account History link in the Action column beside any account that displays the link to display that account's Ledger; all accounts displaying the link are balance sheet accounts.

Entering a transaction

Because cheques are the transaction most often entered using an Account History, we're focusing the discussion in this section on the Bank Account Ledger. After you click the Account History link of a Bank or Credit Card account, you can enter a transaction into the Ledger.

REMEMBER

If you need to add attachments to transactions you enter, display the Attachment column in the register; click the Gear icon above the table and check the Attachments box. You can see the open Gear Settings menu in Figure 7-5. Displaying the Attachments column automatically gives you the option to add an attachment as you enter a transaction.

By default, when you first open the Account History, QBO assumes you want to add a transaction and opens the window you use to enter the most common transaction type for that Ledger — in the case of a bank account, QBO opens the Add Cheque window. But let's suppose that you've already entered a transaction and now you want to enter another transaction. To start a new transaction and enter it, follow these steps:

1. **Click the down arrow beside the Add button.**

   The Add button, which appears just below the Date column heading, is named Add Cheque in Bank accounts and Add CC Expense in Credit Card accounts.

   After you open the list box, QBO displays the list of available transaction types (see Figure 7-7).

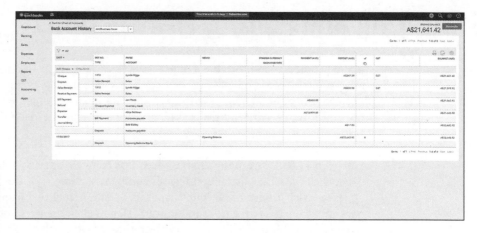

FIGURE 7-7:
Select the type of transaction you want to enter.

TIP

REMEMBER

For you keyboard fans, you can press Ctrl+Alt+N to open the Add list box.

QBO displays only those types of transactions available in the Account History Ledger you opened. For example, you can record a customer payment in a Bank Account Ledger, but you cannot enter a customer invoice. Similarly, you can record a cheque or a bill payment in a Bank Account Ledger, but you cannot enter a supplier's bill.

2. **From the list that appears, select the type of transaction you want to enter.**

   QBO fills in today's date and displays lines so that you can complete the transaction (see Figure 7-8).

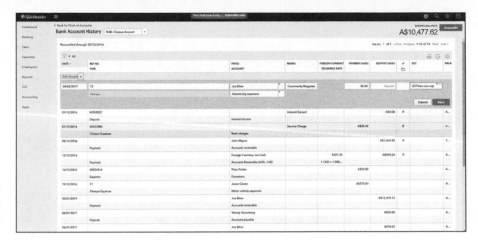

FIGURE 7-8:
Entering a
Cheque in a Bank
Account History.

3. **If necessary, change the transaction date.**

4. **Press Tab and, if appropriate, change the cheque number for the transaction.**

5. **Press Tab and supply a Payee name.**

   For example, if you're recording a payment you received from a customer, select the customer's name. If you're writing a cheque, select the cheque recipient's name.

6. **Press Tab and, in the Memo column, supply any memo information you want to record for the transaction.**

7. **Press Tab and, in the appropriate column, provide the amount of the transaction.**

   In a Bank Account Ledger, record a payment you're making in the Payment amount box and an amount you're depositing in the Deposit amount box.

8. **Press Tab.**

   QBO places the mouse pointer in the Reconcile and Banking Status column. This column displays a character representing the status of the transaction: C for Cleared or R for Reconciled. When the column is blank, the transaction is neither cleared nor reconciled. Typically, this column is updated when you download or reconcile transactions.

   If the account is also connected electronically to your financial institution, this column also indicates whether a transaction was added or matched when transactions were downloaded via the account's bank feed.

WARNING

Don't be tempted to adjust the reconciliation status of a transaction from this screen, because doing so adjusts the account's reconciled balance but the adjustment doesn't show up on reconciliation reports. You'll have a mess on your hands if you modify the reconciliation status outside the reconciliation process.

TIP

Priscilla uses the cleared feature on accounts that are not electronically linked. If she does a printout of that account, she clears the transactions that appear on her printout so she knows what's still due to come in or go out in between reconciliations.

9. **Press Tab.**

QBO's placement of the insertion pointer depends on the type of transaction you're entering. For example, if you're entering a Sales Receipt, a Receive Payment, a Bill Payment or a Refund transaction, QBO places the insertion point in the area where you can save the transaction.

If, however, you're entering a Cheque, a Deposit, an Expense, a Transfer or a Journal Entry transaction, QBO places the insertion point in the Account column. Select the other account affected by the transaction (in addition to the account for the Account History you have opened). For example, if you're entering a cheque, select an Expense account. If you enter an account and press Tab, you can enter a memo for the transaction.

TIP

To add an attachment to the transaction, click the Add Attachment button in the lower left corner of the window. QBO opens a standard 'Open' dialog box, where you navigate to the electronic document you want to attach to the transaction. Once you find it, click it and click Open to attach it to the transaction.

10. **Click the Save button that appears in the transaction.**

Keyboard fans, press Ctrl+Alt+S.

QBO saves the transaction and starts another of the same type. You can click Cancel to stop entering transactions.

Editing a transaction

You can edit the transaction in the Account History by clicking the transaction and then making changes. Or, if you prefer to use the transaction window for the type of transaction you selected, click the Edit button. For example, if you opt to edit an Expense transaction in an account Ledger, QBO displays the transaction in the Expense window. If you opt to enter a Cheque transaction, QBO displays the transaction in the Cheque window. See Chapter 5 for examples of transaction windows.

Looking at Other Account History Features

Account History wouldn't be all that useful if you could only add and edit transactions. You need to be able to find transactions easily. And it's always helpful to be able to print an Account History register.

Sorting transactions

After a while, the number of transactions in an Account History Ledger can make the Ledger page very long, especially in a bank account. Looking for a transaction by skimming through the Account History — or *eyeballing* — can be a nonproductive way of finding a transaction. Instead, sort to help you find a particular transaction.

You can sort by any column in the Account History simply by clicking that column heading. In Figure 7-9, the transactions are sorted by date, in descending order from latest to earliest; note the downward-pointing arrow in the Date column.

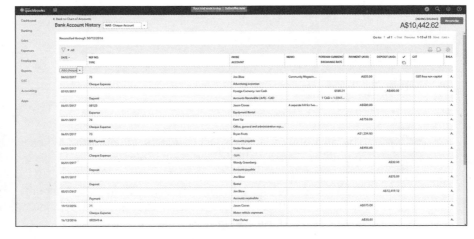

FIGURE 7-9:
Sorting transactions by date, from latest to earliest, is the default order QBO uses to display transactions.

To sort the transactions by date from earliest to latest, click the Date column; the arrow changes direction and points upward. Or suppose you want to search for transactions for a particular payee. You can click the Payee column heading to sorting transactions in alphabetical order by payee, and you can click the column heading a second time to sort in reverse alphabetical order.

WARNING

You can sort by any column heading *except* the Account, Balance, Memo and Attachment columns. And if you sort by any column other than Date, the Balance column won't display any information because the information wouldn't make any sense.

Filtering transactions

When sorting seems like the long way to find a transaction, try working with filters. Click the Filter button that appears just above the Date column, and QBO displays a variety of ways you can filter register transactions (see Figure 7-10).

FIGURE 7-10:
Displaying
available filters.

TIP

The current filter appears just beside the Filter button. When you haven't selected any filters, you see All beside the Filter button.

If you're looking for a transaction of a certain dollar amount, enter the amount, making sure that you don't forget the currency symbol. When you filter by amounts, use these examples as a guideline:

» 1234 will find all cheques or reference numbers with 1234.

» $500 will find all transactions that equal $500.

» >$25 will find all transactions with amounts over $25.

To display transactions for a specific transaction date, use the All Dates box to select one of the predefined date ranges (such as Last Week) or use the Date From and To dates to view transactions only within that timeframe.

You also can filter by a transaction's reconciliation status, transaction type, or payee.

Any transactions that meet the criteria you specify in the Filter window appear in the Account History after you click Apply. In addition, the selected filter appears beside the Filter button (see Figure 7-11). You can click the Clear Filter/View All link to clear the filter and redisplay all transactions in the Account History.

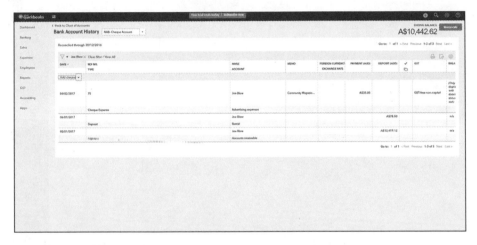

FIGURE 7-11:
A list of transactions QBO found based on criteria specified in the Filter window.

Printing an Account History

When doing research, many people find it easiest to print the information that appears in the Account History. To do so, click the Print button beside the Ledger table Gear button (at the right edge of the Account History, just above the Balance column). QBO displays the Print tab, with your Account History formatted for printing (see Figure 7-12).

Select the printer you want to use and make any other necessary selections, such as the pages to print, the number of copies and the layout orientation. When you finish selecting settings, click Print. When the report finishes printing, you can close the Print tab to redisplay your Account History in your QBO company.

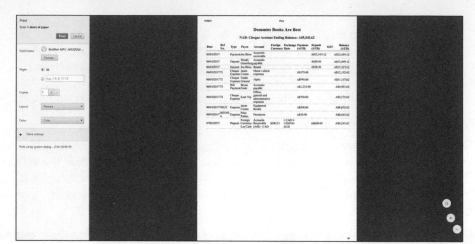

FIGURE 7-12:
Printing an
Account History.

IN THIS CHAPTER

» **Managing the order and appearance of Bank accounts**

» **Connecting QBO Bank and Credit Card accounts to accounts at financial institutions**

» **Downloading and using activity information**

» **Entering bank deposits**

» **Reconciling a Bank account**

Chapter **8**

Handling Bank and Credit Card Transactions

The real title of this chapter should be 'Handling Bank and Credit Card Transactions and Other Banking Tasks', but our editors said that title, although accurately descriptive, was too long.

So, in a nutshell, this chapter covers the ways you can connect Bank and Credit Card accounts in QBO to their counterparts at financial institutions. You also find out how to make bank deposits and reconcile your bank statement.

Controlling the Appearance of Bank Accounts

Before diving in to using Bank accounts, let's take a look at a few things you can do to make your life easier while working with Bank accounts.

Bank accounts (and Credit Card accounts) appear on the QBO Home page and also on the Bank and Credit Cards page. You can control the order in which your accounts appear on these pages. For example, perhaps you'd like your accounts to appear in alphabetical order. Or maybe you'd like them to appear in most used order. Whatever works for you.

On the QBO dashboard, click the pencil that appears to the right of Bank Accounts. The pencil changes to the Save button. Then using the icon that appears to the left of an account, drag up or down to move the account (see Figure 8-1). Once the accounts appear in the order you want, click the Save button. Changes you make will appear on both the Home page and on the Bank and Credit Cards page.

FIGURE 8-1:
Drag accounts to place them in the order you want.

In addition to changing the order of accounts, you can, to some extent, control the information that appears in the table on the Bank and Credit Cards page. For example, you can opt to

>> Display cheque numbers

>> Display Payee names

>> Make the date field editable so that you can change it if necessary

>> Display more detailed information about a transaction by displaying information provided by the bank

>> Copy bank detail information into the Memo field

TIP

You can display the Memo field in an individual bank ledger; refer to Chapter 7 for details.

To display the Bank and Credit Cards page, choose Banking from the Navigation menu on the left. To make changes to the page's appearance, click the Gear button that appears just above the Action column (see Figure 8-2).

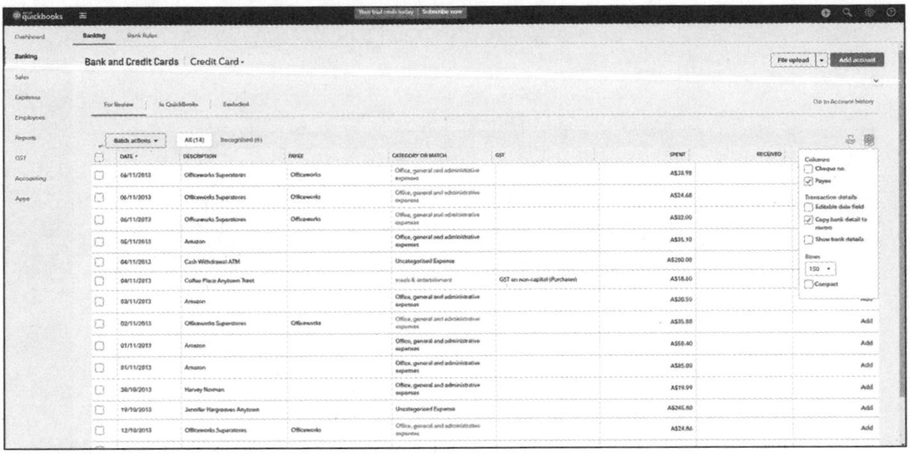

FIGURE 8-2:
Use the table Gear button to make changes to the Bank and Credit Card page table.

You also can make adjustments to the column widths in the table on the Bank and Credit Cards page, and QBO will remember any column width adjustments you make, even after you sign out of QBO and then sign back in.

Connecting QBO Accounts to Financial Institutions

QBO offers two main ways to connect QBO Bank and Credit Card accounts to corresponding accounts at financial institutions:

» Connect directly if your bank supports a direct connection.

» Download transactions from your online bank account and import transactions stored in an Excel or CSV file to QBO.

You have a third option: You don't have to connect at all. If you choose this option, skip to the end of this chapter, where we discuss making bank deposits and reconciling bank statements. If you aren't sure whether to connect, read through this section until you make up your mind.

CONNECTING AS A FORM OF DATA ENTRY . . . NOT!

Don't be tempted to use connecting as a method for entering information into QBO. You might think you'll save time because you won't have to fill out transaction windows in QBO but, in reality, you won't save time. As you see later in this chapter, you need to review every downloaded transaction and confirm that it is properly assigned in QBO. And, even if you review transactions daily, you won't have an up-to-date version of your accounting information, because you won't know about transactions that have not yet cleared your financial institution. That means that the account balances in QBO won't really be up-to-date unless you enter transactions in QBO and use connecting as a method of confirming that your QBO balances match financial institution balances. Long story short: It's safer to enter transactions and use connected account information to confirm QBO balances.

Connecting . . . or not connecting

We don't think Shakespeare would mind if we paraphrased Hamlet: 'To connect or not to connect, that is the question'.

In QBO, you might be able to directly connect QBO Bank and Credit Card accounts to their counterparts at financial institutions. We say 'might' because not all financial institutions support directly connecting to QBO; however, most of the larger and more common banks do. If you bank at an institution that doesn't support a direct connection, you can export transactions from your financial institution's online portal into QBO.

Before we dive into connecting, it's important to understand that you *don't have to connect.* You can work along quite happily in QBO without ever connecting an account at a financial institution to one in QBO. You simply enter transactions that affect the appropriate account and, monthly, you reconcile the accounts.

So, why connect? Most people connect to accounts at financial institutions so that they can electronically verify (by matching) the transactions recorded in QBO with the ones recorded at the financial institution. Connecting is, therefore, primarily a matter of convenience.

Connecting Bank or Credit Card accounts

When you add a new Bank or Credit Card account, you can opt to connect it to a financial institution — or you can choose not to connect to a financial institution, as you read in the preceding section. The method you choose to add a new account depends on whether you want to connect it to a financial institution.

REMEMBER

Just a reminder: See Chapters 5 and 6 for details on entering transactions that affect a Bank account. You typically use an Expense transaction to record credit card purchases and Credit Card Credit to record refunds to a credit card.

Adding but not connecting

In Chapter 3, we show you how to create a new Bank account in QBO. The technique we use in Chapter 3 assumes that you do not want to connect the QBO Bank account to its corresponding account at a financial institution. If you want to set up and not connect a Credit Card account, you use the same technique. For example, follow these steps to set up a Credit Card account that you don't intend to connect to a financial institution:

1. **Click the Gear button beside your company's name and, from the left side of the menu that appears, choose Chart of Accounts.**

    Alternatively, you can select the Accounting tab from the Navigation menu on the left.

    QBO then displays the Chart of Accounts page.

2. **Click the New button on the Chart of Accounts page to open the Account dialog box (see Figure 8-3).**

3. **Open the Category Type list and choose Credit Card.**

4. **If you're using account numbers, supply a number for the new account.**

5. **Optionally, you can enter your account's balance as it appears on the last statement.**

WARNING

    If you enter a balance, QBO updates both the account balance and the Opening Balance Equity account, and your accountant probably won't be happy with you. We suggest that you not enter a balance.

6. **Click Save and Close.**

    QBO redisplays the Chart of Accounts page and your new account appears in the list.

REMEMBER

You need to enter expense transactions that have occurred since you received the last statement for this credit card account.

FIGURE 8-3:
The dialog box
you use to create
an account.

Adding and directly connecting

If, on the other hand, you want to create an account that is connected to a financial institution, you can do so if your financial institution offers the option to connect directly to QBO accounts. Gather up the user ID and password you use to log in to the financial institution online and follow these steps:

1. **In the Navigation bar, choose Banking.**

   QBO displays the Bank and Credit Cards page.

2. **In the upper right corner, click Add Account (see Figure 8-4).**

   QBO starts a wizard that helps you connect to a financial institution.

3. **On the first wizard page, shown in Figure 8-5, you either provide your financial institution's website address, or you click your financial institution's name if it appears on the page.**

   TIP

   To expand the search for banks, click the Search Global Banks option at the right edge of the website address box.

   The screen that appears next depends on whether you typed a web address or clicked one of the popular banks onscreen.

4. **Supply your user ID and password and click the Log In button.**

   Follow any additional onscreen prompts you see to finish setting up the account.

FIGURE 8-4:
Adding an
account
connected to a
financial
institution.

FIGURE 8-5:
Identify your
financial
institution.

Downloading Bank Activity

Once you've connected a Bank or Credit Card account to QBO, you download activity from the bank so that you can compare transactions you've entered in QBO with those the bank has cleared. The method you use to download activity depends on the method you use to connect to your financial institution.

DIRECTLY CONNECTING AFTER THE FACT

Suppose that you originally decided that you didn't want to connect a Bank or Credit Card account to a financial institution, but now you've decided that you do want to connect, and your bank supports direct connection. You're not out of luck.

If you follow the steps outlined for setting up an account that is connected to a financial institution, you end up with two accounts on your QBO Chart of Accounts for the same account. And that's okay because you can then merge the accounts so that the connected account ends up containing all the transactions from the unconnected account.

But we think you'll find it easier to connect after the fact by following these steps, which don't involve merging accounts; instead, you get the opportunity to identify accounts at your bank that should correspond to accounts in QBO:

1. **Choose Banking from the Navigation menu on the left.**

2. **Click the Add Account button.**

   QBO displays the page shown previously in Figure 8-5, where you select the bank with which you want to connect.

3. **Select your bank, supply the user ID and password you use to sign in to your bank's website, and click Log In.**

   A page appears, listing the accounts you can connect and, for most banks, the number of historical transaction days you would like to import (such as 90, 30 or 7).

4. **Select the accounts you want to connect to QBO and choose Connect.**

   You're then given the option to select accounts in QBO to tie to the selected online accounts.

Downloading information for a directly connected account

This is kind of a silly heading for the book, but we need a way to get your attention. You see, if you connect your account directly to a financial institution as described in the preceding section, transactions download automatically whenever

>> You sign in to QBO

>> You manually update connected accounts to check for new transactions

>> You're working in QBO, because the bank can automatically downloads periodically

>> You create or change an *auto-add rule* (you can read more about auto-add rules later in this chapter, in the section 'Establishing rules to accept transactions')

So, if you connect your account directly to a financial institution, you don't need to take any action to download transactions.

You can view downloaded transactions by choosing Banking from the Navigation menu on the left, which then displays the Bank and Credit Cards page. From here you can compare transactions and resolve any issues. Later sections in this chapter cover more about using the Bank and Credit Cards page to review and, if necessary, resolve any questions.

Manually downloading banking information

If you can't connect your account directly to QBO, perhaps because your financial institution doesn't yet support QBO, you're not out of luck. Instead, you can manually download transactions from your financial institution's website to your computer, and then upload the downloaded transactions from your computer to QBO.

Most banks support downloading transactions to a CSV format (a *comma-separated values* format that can be read by Excel). This means you can download your banking activity to a CSV format and then import it into your QBO Bank account. First, log in to your bank's website and save your banking transactions. QBO can import CSV files formatted in either three or four columns, as shown in Tables 8-1 and 8-2.

TABLE 8-1

An Acceptable Three-Column Format

Date	Description	Amount
1/1/2019	Example payment	-100.00
1/1/2019	Example deposit	200.00

TABLE 8-2

An Acceptable Four-Column Format

Date	Description	Credit	Debit
1/1/2019	Example payment		100.00
1/1/2019	Example deposit	200.00	

WARNING

Because this process does not encrypt files, you should not use a public computer to download information.

Here's how to manually download transactions from your bank:

1. **Log in to your financial institution's website and look for a link that enables you to download a CSV file.**

2. **Select the dates for the transactions you want to download.**

   If you download transactions with dates that precede the opening balance you entered for the account in QBO, the account's opening balance will change.

3. **Save the file to a location on your computer where you'll be able to find it later.**

   Many people download to the Downloads folder or to their Windows desktop.

Importing transactions via Excel

Once you've manually downloaded transactions in a CSV format from your bank (refer to preceding section), open your CSV file using Excel and make sure it matches one of the formats listed in Tables 8-1 or 8-2; if necessary, edit it. The most common edit required would be to the date column. If this is the case, highlight the entire column in your spreadsheet and reformat the date. Then, to upload the file to QBO, follow these steps:

1. **Log in to QBO and, in the Navigation bar, choose Banking.**

   QBO displays the Bank and Credit Cards page.

2. **At the right side of the page, click the File Upload button (see Figure 8-6).**

   QBO starts the Upload Bank File wizard and displays the screen shown in Figure 8-7.

3. **Click the Browse button, navigate to the location where you saved your CSV file of transactions, and select the downloaded file.**

4. **Click Next.**

   QBO displays a screen where you select the QBO account into which you want to upload the transactions.

5. **Select the account into which you want to import transactions and click Next.**

6. **On the Map CSV Columns screen that appears, match the fields in QBO to the fields in your CSV file and then click Next.**

   Figure 8-8 shows the fields you need to match up.

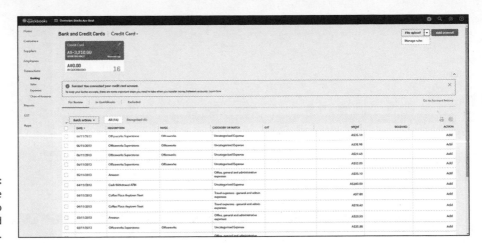

FIGURE 8-6:
Click the File Upload button to start the Upload Bank File wizard.

FIGURE 8-7:
Use this screen to navigate to the transactions you download from your financial institution.

7. **Click Next.**

   QBO displays the number of transactions that will be imported and asks if you want to import the transactions.

8. **Click Yes to import the transactions.**

   When QBO finishes importing the transactions, a confirmation screen appears.

9. **Click Finish.**

   The Bank and Credit Cards page appears, and the transactions you imported appear on the New Transactions tab.

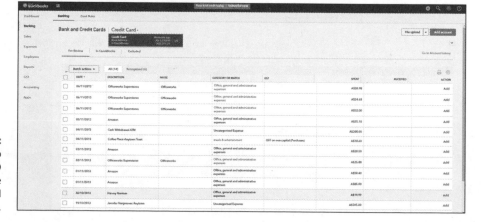

FIGURE 8-8:
Match QBO fields to the fields in your CSV file.

Handling Downloaded Activity

After you manually download transactions, you evaluate each transaction and, as appropriate, use them to update QBO. From the Bank and Credit Cards page, you match, exclude or add transactions downloaded from a financial institution to your QBO company.

REMEMBER

Don't worry; if you make a mistake, you can fix it, as described later in this chapter in the section titled (what else?) 'Fixing mistakes'.

To start updating in QBO, go to Banking on the Navigation menu to display the Bank and Credit Cards page (see Figure 8-9) and, if necessary, select an account by clicking it at the top of the page.

FIGURE 8-9:
Use this page to specify how QBO should handle each downloaded transaction.

TIP

You match transactions the same way for bank accounts and for credit card accounts.

Just below the accounts, QBO displays three transaction status tabs:

» If you click For Review, transactions appear that you have downloaded but have not yet specified how you want to handle.

» If you click In QuickBooks, transactions appear that you have downloaded and added to QBO.

» If you click Excluded, transactions appear that you have downloaded and decided not to include in QBO.

To view the transactions you need to consider, click For Review. QBO displays a button you can use to take batch actions — we discuss that button in the following section — and two additional tabs:

» The All tab lets you view all downloaded transactions for the selected account.

» The Recognised tab displays downloaded transactions that QBO thinks it knows how to handle.

Both the All tab and the Recognised tab display the same information; think of the Recognised tab as a filtered version of the All tab.

In the Category or Match column, QBO suggests a way to assign each transaction. Using both information from other businesses like yours and your past behaviour, QBO tries to identify downloaded transactions that potentially match transactions you entered in QBO. If you have previously accepted a transaction from a supplier, QBO assumes that you want to assign the same category to subsequent transactions for that supplier. And, if you change the payee on a transaction, QBO will suggest that same change the next time a transaction appears for that payee.

TIP

Although the suggestions are helpful, after a while, you might find yourself wishing that QBO would stop suggesting and just record the transaction — and you can use *auto-add rules* to accomplish that behaviour. See the section 'Establishing rules to accept transactions', later in this chapter, for details.

When QBO finds no matches, the words 'Uncategorised Expense' or 'Uncategorised Income' appear in the Category or Match column. When QBO finds only one possible match, QBO assumes the match is accurate and assigns the transaction accordingly; transactions like these appear in green in the Category or Match column; you can still make changes to the transaction before you accept it. If QBO finds multiple possibilities, QBO doesn't actually assign information to the transaction but notifies you of possible matches by displaying the match information in the Category or Match column in grey.

Read on to learn how to handle these situations.

Excluding transactions

Here we examine the Batch Actions button. As you evaluate new transactions, you need to decide first whether they belong in QBO. We suggest that you identify transactions to exclude and then exclude them before you deal with transactions you intend to include in QBO. That way, you eliminate transactions that need no further consideration. When might you exclude a transaction from QBO? Suppose that you accidentally used a business credit card to pay for groceries. This transaction is not a business expense and shouldn't be part of your QBO transactions. So, you can exclude the transaction from QBO. (Keep in mind, however, that if you used a business or company credit card to make the purchase, the transaction should be recorded as a personal expense — refer to Chapter 3 for more information.)

REMEMBER

When you reconcile your statement, remember that the statement balance will include all transactions, not just those you included in QBO.

To exclude a transaction, follow these steps:

1. **On the For Review tab, select the check box beside each transaction you intend to exclude.**

2. **Click the Batch Actions button above the list of transactions.**

3. **From the menu that appears, click Exclude Selected.**

QBO moves the selected transactions to the Excluded tab.

Including transactions

The remaining transactions fall into two categories: Those that don't have an obvious matching transaction in QBO and those that do. You can identify the category into which a transaction falls using the Action column. If you see Add in the Action column, QBO couldn't find an obvious matching transaction; if you see Match in the Action column, QBO did find a potentially matching transaction (refer to Figure 8-9). QBO makes its best guess for adding or matching transactions, but it isn't perfect.

When QBO guesses correctly . . .

You need to confirm or change each transaction before you include it in QBO. If the listed transaction information is correct, you don't need to individually add or match transactions as described in the rest of this section. Instead, you can follow the steps in the 'Excluding transactions' section except, in Step 3, click Accept Selected.

If you need to make the same change to a number of transactions, select those transactions and choose the Modify Selected option in the Batch Actions list.

When QBO doesn't know . . .

QBO might not know how to handle a transaction (for these transactions, QBO displays the words 'Uncategorised Expense' or 'Uncategorised Income' in the Category or Match column), or QBO might simply guess wrong. In these cases, you need to change the transaction before you accept it.

When you click any transaction that you intend to add to QBO, QBO expands the transaction information so that you can change the details of the transaction (see Figure 8-10). For example, you can use the option buttons above the transaction information to specify whether you want to add the transaction, search for a matching QBO transaction or transfer the transaction information to another account. You also can change the category QBO suggests to one you deem more appropriate, and you can click the Split button to distribute the transaction among multiple categories. After you make your changes, you can click the Add button to add the transaction to QBO.

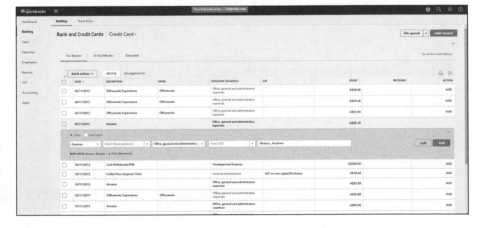

FIGURE 8-10: When you click a transaction, QBO displays transaction details.

TIP

If you're working with a bank account transaction, you can change the cheque number if needed.

If you change the transaction's category, QBO will assume in the future that all transactions for the selected supplier should be assigned to the category you choose. You can change this behaviour by clicking the Edit This Setting link just below the supplier name. When you click the link, you can choose to leave future transactions uncategorised or to create a custom rule; we talk about rules in the next section.

You also can add attachments to any transaction using the Add Attachment link at the bottom of the expanded transaction information window.

When you click a downloaded transaction that QBO suggests you match to an existing QBO transaction, QBO displays a different set of details (see Figure 8-11). You can select the correct matching transaction, search for other matching transactions, add the transaction (and supply account information for it) or transfer the transaction to a different account. After you make your choices in this window, you can click the Match button at the right edge of the window.

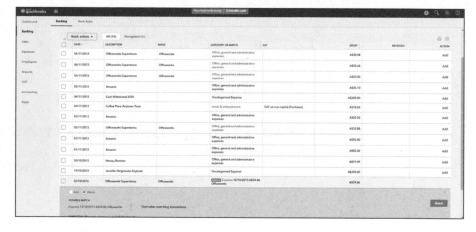

FIGURE 8-11:
The transaction details QBO displays when you click a transaction you plan to match to an existing QBO transaction.

Repeat the process of adding and matching until you've handled all downloaded transactions.

Establishing rules to accept transactions

As explained earlier in this chapter, QBO tries to learn your habits as you review downloaded transactions; you can help the process along by establishing rules for QBO to follow. When you set up rules, you speed up the review process because, effectively, you tell QBO in advance how to treat certain types of transactions.

THE ORDER OF RULES

The order of the rules you establish matters. QBO uses your rules in the order they appear on the Rules page and applies only one rule to any particular transaction. To ensure that QBO applies the correct rule to a transaction, you can reorder the rules. Drag the waffle icon that appears to the left of the rule on the Rules page.

Suppose that you set up two rules in the following order:

- Rule 1: Categorise all transactions under $10 as Miscellaneous Expenses.

- Rule 2: Categorise all McDonald's transactions as Meals & Entertainment.

If a $12 dollar transaction from McDonald's appears, QBO applies Rule 2. But if a $7.50 transaction from McDonald's appears, QBO applies Rule 1.

How rules work

Suppose, for example, that you purchase fuel for business-use cars from Shell petrol stations and you always pay using a credit card you've connected to a financial institution in QBO. Effectively, you want to categorise all transactions at Shell stations to your Fuel expense account. (Keep in mind, of course, you may need to split some transactions if you purchase other goods along with your fuel, such as food and drinks.)

You can manually assign the category to one of these transactions and wait for QBO to 'learn' your preference, or you can set up a rule for QBO to follow. When you establish a rule, you specify information such as the accounts and the types of transactions (money in or money out) to which the rule should apply.

TIP

You can create a rule that affects all accounts or a rule that affects specific accounts.

You then identify criteria that individual transactions should meet before QBO acts on the transactions. Last, you stipulate the information QBO should assign to transactions that meet the criteria. For example, you can specify a transaction type and a category.

The rules you establish can work in one of two ways:

» QBO can use your rule to suggest changes to downloaded transactions that you then review and approve.

» You can opt to have QBO automatically apply the rule to all transactions that it determines match the rule's conditions and add those transactions to QBO.

When you use the first approach, QBO identifies, on the For Review tab of the Bank and Credit Cards page, transactions for which it finds and expects to apply a rule. You can identify these transactions because, in the Category or Match column, they display a Rule icon, as shown in Figure 8-12.

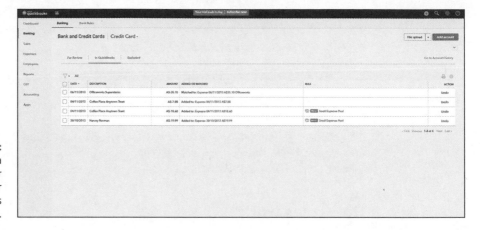

FIGURE 8-12:
QBO displays a
Rule icon for
transactions for
which it finds
a rule.

TIP

QBO uses different icons to identify transactions matched by rules but not yet added to your company and transactions added automatically by rules; you can read more about these icons in the section 'Fixing mistakes'.

The second approach might seem risky, but it really isn't. Even though QBO automatically applies the rule, you can still make changes to transactions that QBO automatically accepts.

Creating a rule

You set up either type of rule — the one that suggests changes and you must review them, and the one that automatically adds transactions based on a rule — using the same steps. You only do one step differently; we point out that step when we get there.

Here's how to create a rule:

1. **Choose Banking from the Navigation menu on the left.**

   The Bank and Credit Cards page appears.

2. **On the right side of the page, click the down arrow beside the File Upload button and choose Manage Rules.**

   QBO displays the Manage Rules page. You can also get to the Manage Rules page by clicking Manage Rules at the top left of the banking feed page (to the right of the Navigation bar).

3. **Click the New Rule button in the upper right corner of the Rules page (see Figure 8-13).**

   QBO displays the Rule dialog box shown in Figure 8-14.

4. **Assign the rule a name — one that will be meaningful to you.**

5. **Identify whether the rule applies to money coming into QBO or money flowing out of QBO, and select the accounts to which you want the rule to apply.**

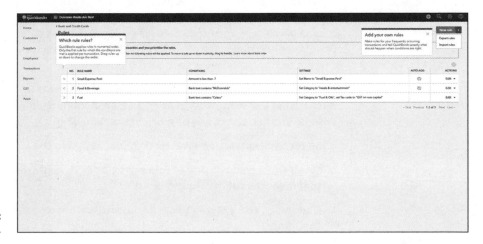

FIGURE 8-13:
The Rules page.

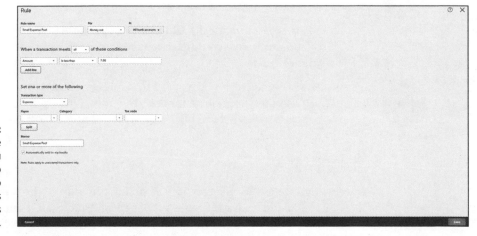

FIGURE 8-14:
Set the information you want QBO to apply to transactions when it uses the rule.

6. **Use the 'When a Transaction Meets' section to set criteria QBO should use when examining downloaded transactions to determine whether to apply the rule to them.**

   You can set multiple criteria using the Add Line button, and you can specify that a transaction should meet all or any of the criteria. Specifying 'all' is more stringent and QBO is more selective about applying the rule.

   The first list box in the section enables you to specify whether QBO should compare the transaction description, the bank text or the transaction amount to a condition you set. For those inquiring minds out there, Description (the transaction description) refers to the text that appears in the Description column of the Bank and Credit Cards page. The Bank Text option refers to the Bank Detail description the bank downloads; you can view the Bank Detail description if you click any downloaded transaction.

7. **At the bottom of the Rule dialog box, shown in Figure 8-14, set the information you want QBO to apply to transactions that meet the rule's criteria. You can select one or more of the following:**

   a. **Select the Transaction Type QBO should assign to the transaction.**

   b. **Select the Payee and one or more categories to apply to transactions that meet the rule's conditions.**

   c. **Optionally, add a Memo to each transaction that meets the rule's conditions.**

      See the sidebar, 'The Memo field and transactions rules' for a way you might want to use the Memo field.

   d. **Select the Automatically Add to My Books check box if you want QBO to automatically add transactions that meet the rule's conditions to your company.**

      This is the 'different' step we refer to in the introduction to these steps. If you select this box, you don't need to approve transactions to which QBO applies this rule. But you can always make changes to automatically added transactions.

8. **Click Save.**

Once you create a rule, you can use the Actions column of the Rules page to copy it (so that you don't have to create similar rules from scratch) and to delete rules you no longer want. And, if you need to edit a rule, click the Edit button in the Actions column to reopen the Rule dialog box and make changes.

Accountants, you can help your clients and save some time if you export and import rules between QBO companies. See Chapter 15 for details.

THE MEMO FIELD AND TRANSACTION RULES

QBO uses different special icons to identify transactions added using rules and transactions automatically added using rules. These icons follow the transactions into QBO registers. But, at the time of writing, you can't filter a register to show you only those transactions added by a rule (automatically or not).

You can, however, filter registers using the Memo field. So if you anticipate needing to filter a register for transactions added by rules and transactions added automatically by rules, use the Memo field in the Rule dialog box to distinguish them. You might include text such as, 'Added by Rule' and 'Added Automatically by Rule' to appropriate rules.

Fixing mistakes

You can easily identify transactions to which QBO has applied rules. In Figure 8-12, you see that the Rule icon appears in the Rule column when QBO finds a transaction to which QBO wants to apply a rule. And you can see how QBO handles each downloaded transaction in your company when you click the In QuickBooks tab on the Bank and Credit Cards page (see Figure 8-15).

FIGURE 8-15:
Use the In QuickBooks tab to find transactions you've accepted into QBO.

REMEMBER

QBO uses different icons to identify transactions added by rules and transactions added automatically by rules.

Suppose that you accidentally include a transaction in QBO that you meant to exclude. Or suppose that QBO assigned the wrong category to a transaction. You can easily correct these mistakes using the In QuickBooks tab on the Bank and Credit Cards page.

REMEMBER

The method used to match and add a transaction — manually through a rule or automatically through a rule — doesn't matter. You can make changes to any downloaded transaction. Be aware, though, that QBO treats downloaded transactions as having cleared your bank, so if you edit a downloaded transaction in the ledger, QBO will ask you if you're sure.

If you include a transaction in QBO that contains mistakes — for example, the transaction was automatically added by a rule to the wrong category — you can undo the action. Undoing an accepted transaction places it back on the For Review tab, where you can make changes and accept it again as described earlier in this chapter in the sections 'Excluding transactions' and 'Including transactions'.

To undo an accepted transaction, click the In QuickBooks tab on the Bank and Credit Cards page. Find the transaction and click the Undo link in the Action column. QBO displays a message explaining that it will place the transaction on the For Review tab, where you can click it, edit it and accept it again — or, you can exclude it from QBO, if appropriate.

Making a Bank Deposit

In Chapter 6, we show you how to record payments from customers, and we suggest that you use the Undeposited Funds account as you record a Receive Payment transaction. So, after receiving a customer payment and placing it in the Undeposited Funds account, your Bank account — where the money will eventually show up — hasn't yet been updated. That updating happens when you prepare a bank deposit.

As we explain in Chapter 6, you can think of the Undeposited Funds account as a temporary holding place until you prepare a bank deposit. 'So why use the Undeposited Funds account?' you ask. 'Why not just place the customer payments into the Bank account where they belong?'

Excellent questions. And the answers revolve around making sure that the bank deposits in QBO match the ones at your bank, because if the deposits match, bank statement reconciliation — everybody's least favourite task — becomes quite easy. But if they don't match . . . well, you don't want to go there.

TIP

If you have great customers and most of them pay you directly into your account via EFT, you can post the payment directly to the account that the money was deposited into as soon as you see that it has come in or receive a remittance.

If getting paid by EFT is not so common for your business and you receive more than one customer payment on any given day via cash or cheque, you take several cheques to your bank each day along with your cash. And you probably deposit all of them as a single deposit. Using the Undeposited Funds account helps you ensure your QBO deposits match the bank's deposits. (Refer to Chapter 6 for more on this.)

So, assuming that you're following our advice and using the Undeposited Funds account before you prepare a bank deposit slip, you then use the Bank Deposit feature in QBO to sum up the payments you receive and intend to deposit simultaneously at your bank. QBO records, as the deposit amount in your QBO Bank account, the amount calculated in the Bank Deposit window, which will match the amount you actually deposit at your bank. Then your bank reconciliation process becomes quick and easy — okay, maybe not quick and easy, but certainly quicker and easier than if you were trying to figure out which customer payments make up various bank deposits.

To set up a bank deposit, follow these steps:

1. **Click the Create button — the plus (+) sign — and, from the Create menu, select Bank Deposit.**

    QBO displays the Deposit transaction window shown in Figure 8-16. You can use the lines in the Add New Deposits section to add a new payment transaction that is not associated with an outstanding invoice.

WARNING

    Don't try to record a payment from a customer for an outstanding invoice in the Add New Deposits section. QBO is unlikely to match the line on the Deposit transaction to the outstanding invoice. Instead, record the Receive Payment transaction; the transaction will then appear in the Select Existing Payments section of the Deposit transaction window.

2. **At the top of the window, select the account into which you plan to deposit the payments.**

3. **In the Select Existing Payments section, click the check box beside each transaction you want to include on the deposit.**

4. **For each transaction you intend to deposit, select the Payment method.**

TIP

    If you have a merchant facility, credit card companies often deposit merchant transaction receipts into your Bank account, and most of them make a daily deposit. Most businesses only have one merchant account, but if you have more than one, we have a suggestion to keep your bank statement reconciliation as simple as possible: Record separate QBO deposits for each merchant account. You can group the cheques and cash payment methods on the same deposit.

5. **Optionally, you can supply a memo and a reference number.**

The total of the selected payments — and the amount you intend to deposit unless you add entries in the Add New Deposits section — appears below the Select Existing Payments list.

6. **Scroll down the Deposit transaction window.**

Optionally, supply a memo for the deposit.

Optionally, supply a cash back amount — money from the deposit total that you don't intend to deposit — along with an account in which to place the cash back amount and a memo to describe the purpose of the cash back amount.

Optionally, you can attach an electronic document to the deposit, such as a scanned copy of the deposit ticket you take to the bank.

TIP

To attach an electronic document to the deposit, click in the Attachments box and navigate to the document or drag and drop the electronic copy into the Attachments box.

7. **Click Save and Close.**

QBO moves the deposited amount from the Undeposited Funds account to the account you selected in Step 2.

All that's left to do is take a trip to the bank.

FIGURE 8-16: Use the Deposit window to select payment transactions to deposit.

Reconciling a Bank Account

Most people's least favourite task is reconciling the bank statement. However, if you're diligent about entering transactions in QBO and recording bank deposits as described in the preceding section, reconciling your bank statement should be a fairly easy process.

To reconcile an account, follow these steps:

1. **Click the Gear button beside your company name and, from the Tools portion of the menu that appears, select Reconcile.**

Alternatively, you can select the Accounting tab in the Navigation menu and switch between tabs at the top left of the screen — that is, from Chart of Accounts to Reconcile.

2. **From the Reconcile page that appears, select the account you want to reconcile and click the Reconcile Now button.**

QBO displays the Start Reconciling dialog box shown in Figure 8-17.

3. **Enter the ending date and balance found on your bank statement, and then click OK.**

QBO displays the Reconcile page shown in Figure 8-18.

4. **Select each transaction that appears on your bank statement and in the Reconcile page.**

By selecting a transaction, you're marking it as having cleared the bank. Your goal is to have the Difference amount at the top of the Reconcile window equal $0.

TIP

If you have lots of transactions, make sure that a check appears in the Hide Transactions After the Statement's End Date check box (upper right corner of the window). Hiding those transactions can help you find transactions to clear. If the Difference amount isn't $0, then deselect the box to look for additional transactions to mark as cleared.

5. **When the Difference amount equals $0, click the Finish Now button.**

QBO redisplays the Reconcile page that appeared in Step 2 but wasn't shown. The reconciliation you just performed now appears in the History and Reports part of the screen (see Figure 8-19).

FIGURE 8-17:
Enter information found on your bank statement.

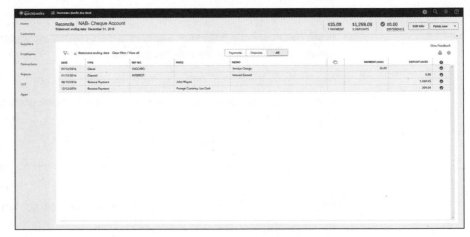

FIGURE 8-18:
Match transactions found on your bank statement with those shown on the Reconcile page in QBO.

FIGURE 8-19:
A history of reconciliations for the selected account appears on the History and Reports page.

You can click any reconciliation on this page to see its Reconciliation report, which resembles the one shown in Figure 8-20.

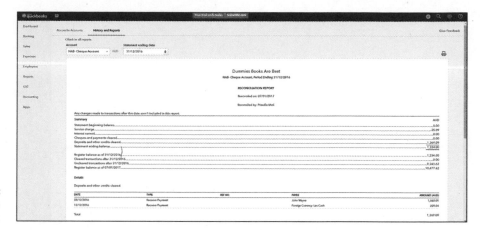

FIGURE 8-20: A Reconciliation report.

You can drill down to view any transaction in the window where you created it; just click the transaction. And to produce a paper copy, click the Print button in the upper right corner of the report window.

TIP

If you are using bank feeds and have matched transactions, you will notice that some entries in your reconciliation screen have a green icon which looks like a note of money. Transactions that haven't gone through the bank feeds but have been entered into QBO will not have this icon.

IN THIS CHAPTER

» Turning on payroll and setting payroll preferences

» Adding in employees

» Fine-tuning employee records and setting up their opening balances

» Processing payruns

» Reporting PAYG and superannuation

Chapter **9**

Paying Employees

This chapter is all about using QBO to quickly and seamlessly pay your employees. You discover how to set up (and fine-tune) your payroll preferences, how to enter employees and, of course, how to actually create payruns. You can also learn more about the many payroll-related reports QBO can help you generate.

In the Australian version of QBO, payroll is provided by a third party called KeyPay, so this chapter starts with a quick explanation on how this arrangement works.

Understanding the Connection between QuickBooks and KeyPay

When you take out a QBO subscription, the KeyPay payroll software is fully integrated into it; however, because KeyPay is a separate program, during the set-up process you may be asked to again enter information you've already provided. A minor annoyance but unavoidable.

The good news is the KeyPay standard package included in your QBO subscription allows you to pay up to 10 employees per month at no extra cost. If you want to add any further employees, you're simply charged an additional $4 for each one (which is why, when setting up payroll, KeyPay will also ask for credit card details).

QBO defaults to QuickBooks Payroll Standard automatically. KeyPay also offers QuickBooks Payroll Advanced as an enhanced package (see Figure 9-1 for comparisons), but this advanced option doesn't allow for any free employees per month, with each employee being charged out at $6 per month.

FIGURE 9-1: Selecting a KeyPay payroll plan.

This chapter sticks to outlining the features available through the QuickBooks Payroll Standard subscription, because this covers most users' needs. If you do need to change your KeyPay subscription preference, go to Employees ⇨ Payroll Settings ⇨ Business Management ⇨ Subscription (see Figure 9-2).

TIP

You can click the Payroll Support button on the right side of your screen for further help whenever you are working within payroll. This links you directly to KeyPay support.

For more information on KeyPay, visit www.keypay.com.au.

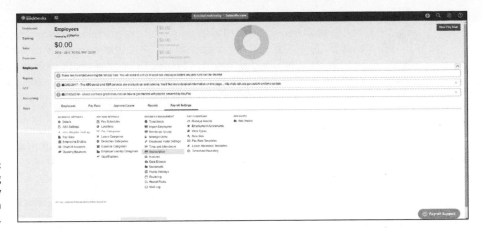

FIGURE 9-2:
Changing
your KeyPay
subscription
preference.

Turning on Payroll

The payroll section in QBO can be found under the Employees heading of the Navigation bar on the left of your screen.

If you have already created some employee profiles in QBO, those names will come across to KeyPay. You can also import a list of employees from a CSV file or other payroll software by going to Employees ⇨ Payroll Settings ⇨ Business Management ⇨ Import Employees (see Figure 9-3).

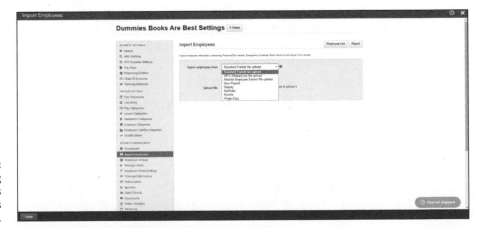

FIGURE 9-3:
Importing
employee details
via the Business
Management tab.

Getting started with QBO Payroll

From the Navigation section on the left of your screen, select Employees and, once the page loads, head over to the top right side and click on the Turn on Payroll button. The Payroll set-up wizard pops up to confirm your business details.

The Payroll set-up wizard also asks you to confirm when your pay periods begin — that is, Monday or Sunday and so on — and the number of hours in your business's average working day. This is for the purpose of calculating leave; however, calculations are based on the default value and you are able to adjust this information for individual employees from within their profiles.

Once you have confirmed the information within the set-up wizard, select the Sign Up button on the right of your screen. A pop-up will appear advising you that you are signing up to KeyPay (see Figure 9-4).

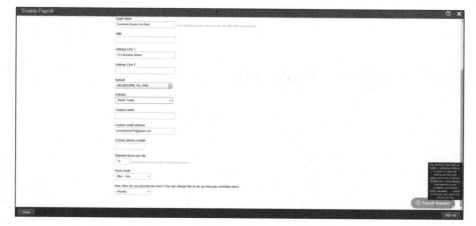

FIGURE 9-4:
Signing up to KeyPay via the Payroll set-up wizard.

KeyPay tells you about any notifications via yellow boxes on the top of the screen. If you find this a bit distracting, you can close down notifications by clicking the X on the right side of each box (refer to Figure 9-2 for examples of these notifications).

Fine-tuning your payroll preferences

Besides updating your subscription and importing employees, you may also want to further fine-tune other payroll settings. To access payroll settings, head to Employees ⇨ Payroll Settings. You have numerous settings to choose from and play with (and knock yourself out if you have the time), but this section concentrates on the 10 areas most users like to adjust.

ABA Settings

ABA (Australian Bankers Association) files can be used to bulk pay your employees via internet banking. You can set up more than one ABA account and then choose which account should be used for each pay schedule. From the Business Settings column on the left, select the ABA Settings option. Once the page loads, click the Add button on the right side of your screen. Enter the bank details for the account from which you would normally pay your employees, as well as any other requested information (see Figure 9-5).

ATO Supplier Settings

Linking your software to the Australian Tax Office (ATO) means you can electronically lodge Tax File Number Declaration Forms and Payment Summaries for employees. To set up this link, go to the Business Settings column on the left and select the ATO Supplier Settings option. Scroll to the bottom of your page and click on the Copy From Business Settings button to prefill the information.

REMEMBER

Even after setting up your link to the ATO, you still need to make a very quick telephone call to the ATO. (They have a designated line for this so you usually won't be kept waiting long.) They ask you for your company details to identify you and then for your software ID so that they can link it to your company profile. You don't need to scramble around for any of this info — the software ID is displayed on your screen, as is the contact number for the ATO (see Figure 9-6).

Payslips

To customise your employees' payslips, navigate to the Business Settings column on the left and select Pay Slips. From here, you can add your business logo, select what details to show on the payslips, enter an email address (which your employees will see when receiving payslip notifications) and set any custom messages that will display on payslips by default (see Figure 9-7).

FIGURE 9-6:
Linking your
KeyPay software
to the ATO.

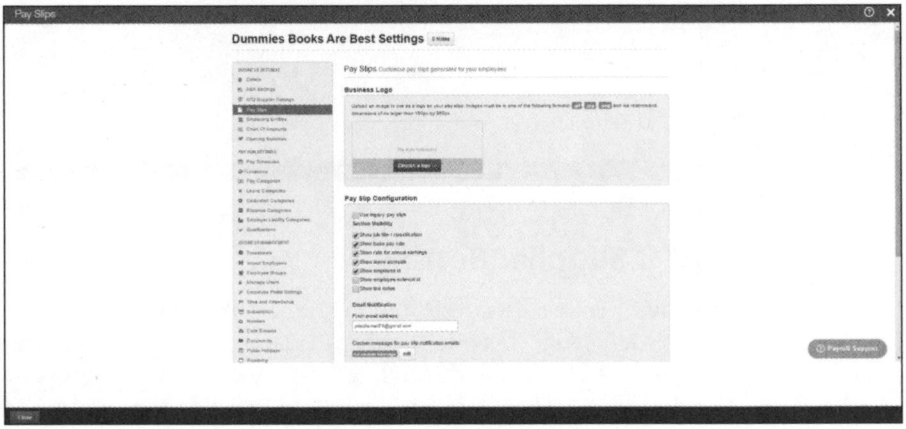

FIGURE 9-7:
Customising your
payslips.

Chart of Accounts

One of the most important settings to fine-tune is your Chart of Accounts, because this is what links the KeyPay information to your QBO accounts. A great example of the kind of information you want to carry across to your QuickBooks accounts are any superannuation contributions you pay to an employee — you want that information to be posted to the Superannuation Payable Liability in QBO.

To map your Chart of Accounts, head to the Business Settings column on the left and select Chart of Accounts. Click on each subheading starting with Default Accounts. The KeyPay payroll category is shown on the left and the QBO category is to the right within a drop-down menu. Map each KeyPay category to the relevant QBO category (so, as per the preceding example, superannuation contributions are mapped to Superannuation Payable Liability). Check with your accountant if you're unsure on which category should be mapped where.

TIP

To import additional QBO accounts, click the Import Accounts button on the top right of your screen. Under the Import column on the left, select whether to include each individual account from QBO into KeyPay. If no suitable QBO category exists, you will need to close down payroll and go back into QBO to add a new account in QBO via QBO's Chart of Accounts (see Chapter 13).

Pay Schedules

By default, a weekly pay schedule is automatically set up when you activate payroll. You can create other pay schedules, such as fortnightly or monthly, by heading to the Payrun Settings column and selecting Pay Schedules. Click the Add button on the right and give your pay schedule a name, select its payment frequency and also any employees that default to this pay schedule (see Figure 9-8).

FIGURE 9-8:
Setting your pay schedules.

REMEMBER

Once you begin creating payruns, you are also able to make one-off payments to employees without the need to set up another pay schedule.

Deduction Categories

To add deductions such as Child Support, navigate to the Payrun Settings column and select Deduction Categories. You will see pre-populated deductions such as a general Pre Tax and Post Tax deduction category, but you can create additional specific deductions by selecting the Add button on the right. Give your deduction a name and select whether this deduction comes out of the employee's wage pre-tax or post-tax (see Figure 9-9).

FIGURE 9-9:
Adding deduction categories.

Employer Liabilities

On top of the most common liability, superannuation, some businesses need to pay additional amounts on behalf of their employees. Superannuation is dealt with separately and you don't need to include it within this section, but you will need to include any liability paid to a fund or scheme on behalf of your employees, such as portable long service leave or redundancy. If you're not sure whether this applies to your business, you should check your award or EBA agreement. (For more information on awards and agreements visit `www.fairwork.gov.au/awards-and-agreements`.)

Employee Portal Settings

When you're adding employees to payroll, you can opt to give them access to their own portal where they can view their accumulated payslips and request leave (among other things). To select what options you want to allow your employees to have access to within their portal, go to the Business Management column and click on the Employee Portal Settings option. Select the settings that you're happy for each employee to be able to edit, such as their personal details or bank accounts.

Public Holidays

Each state in Australia has its own schedule of public holidays (even though, of course, many are shared across all states). To select which apply to you, head to the Business Management column and select Public Holidays. From the drop-down box on the right, select your state. Alternatively, you can click on an individual day within the calendar and manually enter a description.

Pay Rate Templates

The QuickBooks Payroll Advanced subscription automatically links to awards, but with the QuickBooks Payroll Standard subscription (which, as mentioned at the start of this chapter, covers most users) you need to enter this information in manually. You do this by going to the Pay Conditions column and selecting Pay Rate Templates.

TIP

If you have numerous award categories to set up, the easiest way to do so is by downloading an Excel template, filling in the details and importing the completed template. To do this, click the Export button on the top right of your screen in Pay Rate Templates. From the drop-down box, select whether to export an Excel or CSV template and then click Download. Fill in your data and save your file. (If you need further information on awards and agreements, visit www.fairwork.gov. au/awards-and-agreements.) Go back to the Pay Conditions column and select Pay Rate Templates. This time click the Import button on the top right of your screen. Browse to find your file and upload. *Note:* You can also select to upload only updated rates at a future stage.

To enter in pay rate templates without using a spreadsheet, go to Pay Rate Templates and select the Add button on the top right of your screen. Give the template a name or use your award category — for example, Construction worker Level 1 or ECW1. From the drop-down list select what this Pay Category relates to (the most common being Casual Ordinary Hours or Permanent Ordinary Hours). Enter the hourly rates for pay, including regular hours, overtime hours and leave. Select whether superannuation is to be applied to each. Enter in any rates for allowances such as Travel Allowance, which will be calculated in units. When done, click the Save button.

Setting Up Employees

In KeyPay you have the option of adding individual employees or uploading a list of employees. You can also import a list of employees from a CSV file or other payroll software by going to Employees ➪ Payroll Settings ➪ Business Management ➪ Import Employees and downloading a template (refer to Figure 9-3). If you created any employee profiles in QBO prior to activating payroll, these employees will come through into KeyPay, but you may need to add additional information.

Adding employees

To add new employee profiles, select Employees from the QBO Navigation menu on the left of your screen. Once the page populates, select the Add Employee button on the right of the page.

TIP

The Add Employee button also has a drop-down menu where you can select to export or import lists of employees.

Once the Add Employee button is selected, a set-up wizard opens. Here you can enter basic details for your employees. This provides the system with enough information for you to create a payrun — such as your employee's name, address, bank details and tax file number. You then need to expand on each employee's details later to include emergency data, deductions and any further relevant information. To do this, select an employee by clicking on their name from the main menu and scroll down through the Navigation menu on the left of your screen, elaborating on the information in each category (see Figure 9-10, which shows the Opening Balances page where you can add leave balance details).

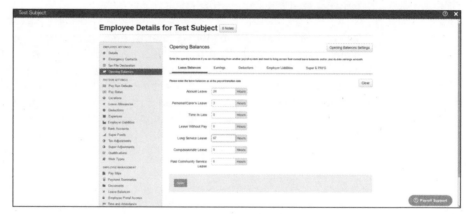

FIGURE 9-10:
Expanding on an employee's details on file.

Fine-tuning employee details

One of the most useful categories to fine-tune in your employee profiles is the Pay Rates category because this screen allows you to select the earnings you want to appear automatically in each payrun for individual employees. For example, a few of your employees may receive an allowance for First Aid. In this case, you can choose to show this allowance in all payruns for the individual employees who receive it and not show it for those who don't.

WARNING

An important section relating to tax that the employee wizard doesn't cover is whether your employee has a HELP or HECS debt. To include this information in your employee's profile — and ensure an appropriate amount of tax is deducted — open your employee's profile by clicking on their name from the main menu and select the Tax File Declaration option from the Navigation menu on the left. Select any relevant information under the Additional Information section by marking the applicable checkboxes.

TIP

After fine-tuning your employees' tax information, you may also choose to lodge the information electronically with the ATO via the Lodge with ATO button on the bottom of your screen.

If the employee would like you to withhold additional tax from their pay, select the Tax Adjustments option in the Navigation menu on the left and complete the required details.

Entering Payroll History

If you've been using another payroll system and are coming over to using KeyPay/QBO mid-year, you can enter in any existing balances by going to Employees⇨Payroll Settings⇨Business Settings⇨Opening Balances. Here you can configure the year-to-date figures for PAYG, gross earnings and super as well as opening leave balances for your business. The easiest way to do this is by exporting a template, filling in the details and re-importing. The other option is to enter opening balances for each employee manually. This section runs you through both options.

WARNING

Your accountant may have already included existing payroll balances in the opening balance journal when setting up your file, so you may want to make sure the information hasn't already been entered; otherwise, your figures will double up.

Exporting and importing your business's payroll opening balances

To import existing payroll balances, you first need to export a template to fill out. You do this by navigating to Business Settings⇨Opening Balances and selecting the Export button on the top right of your screen. From the Data Type drop-down box select the type of template you wish to export — that is, containing employee information or blank template. You then select the format of the file you wish to export — Excel or CSV. When done, click the Download button. Fill in opening balances for each employee in the template and save your file. When done, return to the Opening Balances screen and select the Import button on the top right. Browse to your completed spreadsheet and upload.

Entering payroll opening balances manually for each employee

Even if you have or have not needed to enter in your business's opening balances, you will need to enter them for each individual employee so that their first payslip reflects their accumulated entitlements, deductions and income to date. If you have a list of employees already set up, select each employee by clicking on their name and then scrolling down to Opening Balances from the Navigation menu on the left of your screen under the Employee Settings heading. Enter in opening balance values for leave, wages, deductions, employer liabilities and super and tax (refer to Figure 9-10).

Paying Employees Using Timesheets

QBO offers three timesheet options. The first is used to invoice customers for time incurred by your employees. Although this option doesn't allow you to bring your employees' hours over to payroll, it is useful none the less. The second option is to use the Time Sheet function within KeyPay Payroll, while the third (and for most businesses, the best) option is to use WorkZone, an app available for both iOS and Android devices. This section runs through all three options.

Invoicing customers for time incurred

If you use QBO Plus, you can set certain employees up as Time Tracking users. This allows these employees to log in with limited privileges that enable them to complete timesheets (and do nothing else).

To add an employee as a Time Tracking user, follow these steps:

1. **Click the Gear button beside your company name and, from the menu that appears, click Manage Users.**

2. **Click the New button and, from the window that appears, click Time Tracking Only.**

3. **Click Next and select the employee (or supplier/subcontractor) you want to fill out timesheets.**

4. **Supply the employee's (or supplier/subcontractor) email address.**

5. **Click Next and then click Finish.**

QBO sends the user an email containing a link the user needs to click to complete the Time Tracking Only set-up process. If the user already has a QBO sign-in name and password, they can use it. Otherwise, they need to create a sign-in name and password.

Once a user has signed in, the Single Activity Time Sheet screen appears; if the employee prefers to use the Weekly Timesheet screen, they can click the tab at the top of the screen. Because most employers don't pay their employees based on hours reported on timesheets — employers instead use timesheets to bill clients for time spent on client projects — refer to Chapter 6 for details on entering time.

TIP

You can view hours entered on timesheets by time-tracking employees. Before you start payroll, click the Create (+) button at the top of QBO, select Weekly Timesheet, and then select the employee. If you prefer, you can print information: Run a Time Activity by Employee report (click the Reports link in the Navigation bar and then search for 'Time Activities by Employee Detail'). Then, customise the report to display the payroll timeframe. For information on reports, see Chapter 11.

Using KeyPay's Time Sheet function

Using the Time Sheet function within KeyPay Payroll doesn't allow for hours to be billed to customers; however, this function does allow you to review the time your employees are claiming and approve that time prior to producing a payrun. To activate this feature, go to the Employee section of the QBO Navigation menu, go to the Business Management heading and select the option for Time Sheets. Then you can adjust the preferences for your business.

Next, select an individual employee from the main payroll screen and scroll to Time and Attendance in the Navigation menu on the left. You will see a user ID and a pin number, which you'll need to pass on to the employee. The employee then uses these credentials to log into Clockme In — software available via the iTunes App Store.

WARNING

The Clockme In app is only available for use on iPad only. See the following section for more information on an app that works on both iOS and Android devices.

Allowing employees to use WorkZone

An alternative to the Clockme In app is the WorkZone app — and this is available for both iOS and Android devices. WorkZone allows the user to bypass the KeyPay employee portal and still view their payroll details, including payslips, payment summaries and superannuation information. Using their own mobile telephone or tablet, each employee can also view their submitted timesheets and see their status — that is, rejected or approved. When entering in timesheet information, the employee can also add notes and select a location.

TIP

At the time of writing, getting employees on WorkZone is the option that works best for most business, because of the range of options available and the ease of use for all involved. For further information on the WorkZone App see keypay. com.au/introducing-workzone-ios-android-smart-phones.

Creating New Payruns

Payruns can be created weekly, fortnightly or monthly, depending on your chosen payrun schedules. The software also allows users to generate one-off payruns. You can even overlap payrun dates and delete payruns if necessary — without undoing anything bar the particular payrun you need to remove. You can also amend payruns and refresh values sent to QBO from KeyPay via journal. You also have the option of printing draft payslips for review prior to finalising a payrun, and of downloading ABA files.

To create a new payrun, select the Employees tab of the QBO Navigation menu and then click the New Payrun button on the top right of your screen. Select the pay schedule and, because this will be your first payrun, enter in the date that the pay period ends and the date your payrun will be paid. This information will then roll over to future payruns. When done, click on the Create button.

Select an employee's name to open up their window (see Figure 9-11). To add additional earnings lines, adjust PAYG or super, or to include leave and deductions, select the Actions button on the bottom right. This button can also be used to import timesheets if that is a preference that you have selected for the company and the individual employee — refer to the preceding section for more on this.

FIGURE 9-11:
Looking at payrun details for each employee.

In the Notes for This Payrun section, you can add in any personal notes for the particular employee. Any notes to be included for all employees can be added via the Payrun Actions button at the top and then going to Add Message. The Payrun Actions button will also allow you to import timesheets for all employees, as well as add in any other employees who don't already appear in the payrun and adjust the pay period if needed.

Once you are satisfied with the earnings you have entered for each employee, select the Finalise Payrun button on the top left. This will export journals to QBO and allow you to download payslips and ABA files. Once you select to finalise the payrun, a pop-up window will appear asking you to confirm when you would like payslips to be published and whether you would like your employees notified once this is done (see Figure 9-12).

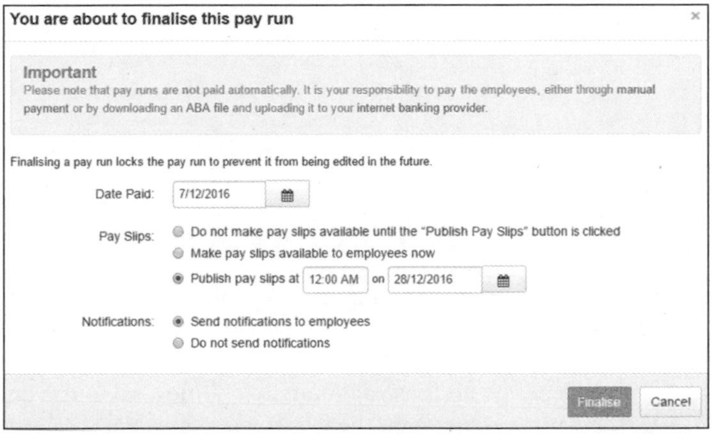

You are about to finalise this pay run   ×

Important
Please note that pay runs are not paid automatically. It is your responsibility to pay the employees, either through manual payment or by downloading an ABA file and uploading it to your internet banking provider.

Finalising a pay run locks the pay run to prevent it from being edited in the future.

Date Paid: 7/12/2016   📅

Pay Slips: ○ Do not make pay slips available until the "Publish Pay Slips" button is clicked
      ○ Make pay slips available to employees now
      ⦿ Publish pay slips at   12:00 AM   on   28/12/2016   📅

Notifications: ⦿ Send notifications to employees
      ○ Do not send notifications

Finalise   Cancel

FIGURE 9-12:
Finalising the payrun.

TIP

A list of payruns can be viewed by going to the Employees section of the Navigation menu on the left of your screen and selecting the Payruns tab.

To delete a particular payrun (perhaps you want to start again or perhaps it was a duplicate), open the payrun and from the Payrun Actions drop-down list, select the option to Unlock the Payrun. Here you can choose to make any adjustments or updates. Once complete, select Finalise, which will update the journal entry posted to QBO. If you want to delete the payrun, simply select the button marked Delete from your options at the top of the payrun screen.

Taking Advantage of Payroll-Related Reports

Via KeyPay, QBO allows you to generate numerous payroll reports (see Figure 9-13). You can also group these reports for simplicity. This section covers the five most frequently run reports.

FIGURE 9-13:
Working through
the Payroll
reports offered
by QBO.

Employer Liability Report

As covered in the 'Fine-tuning your payroll preferences' section, earlier in this chapter, employer liabilities other than superannuation — such as portable long service leave or redundancy fund contributions — can be set up for your employees. To run a report on these additional liabilities, go to the Employees section of the QBO Navigation menu on the left of your screen and select the Reports tab. In the first column under the Payroll heading, select the Employer Liabilities Report to view a breakdown of employer liabilities over a given period of time.

A pop-up window will appear that allows you to filter the information you wish to view in the report — such as date range, pay schedule, location, employee name or specific liability name. Once you've made your selections, click the Run Report button on the bottom right to view the report on your screen. Alternatively, you can select the option to view the report as a PDF or Excel/CSV spreadsheet.

PAYG Withholding Report

To run a PAYG report, go to the Employees section of the QBO Navigation menu on the left of your screen and select the Reports tab. In the first column under the Payroll heading, select PAYG Withholding Report to view a breakdown of the Pay As You Go Tax Withheld per month for a given date range.

A pop-up window will appear. Click the Run Report button on the bottom right to view the report on your screen or select the option to view as a PDF or Excel/CSV spreadsheet.

Payroll Tax Report

QBO (via KeyPay) automatically calculates the Payroll Tax Liability for the state your business operates in. Should you wish to exclude an employee from this, you may do so by going into the employee's profile and selecting the Payrun Defaults section of the Navigation menu on the left. Scroll to the bottom of the screen and mark the No Payroll Tax is Incurred for Paying This Employee checkbox under the Payroll Tax heading.

To generate a Payroll Tax Report, including wage and superannuation payments for the purpose of reporting to each state's revenue department, go to the Employees section of the QBO Navigation menu on the left of your screen and select the Reports tab. In the first column under the Payroll heading, select Payroll Tax.

A pop-up window will appear where you can filter the information that you wish to view by month or financial year, according to how you report Payroll Tax. You can also further filter the report by location. Click the Run Report button on the bottom right to view the report on your screen, or select the option to view as a PDF or Excel/CSV spreadsheet.

Super Contributions Report

The Super Contributions report allows you to view superannuation contributions payable to funds over a period of time, and can be filtered by fund or by employee. To run a Super Contributions report, go to the Employees section of the QBO Navigation menu on the left of your screen and select the Reports tab. In the first column under the Payroll heading, select Super Contributions.

A pop-up window will appear where you can filter the information that you wish to view in the report — including date range, pay schedule, location, employee name or specific contribution such as Super Guarantee or Salary Sacrifice. Select the Run Report button on the bottom right to view the report on your screen or select the option to view as a PDF or Excel/CSV spreadsheet.

Payment Summaries

QBO also allows the generation and printing of payment summaries for employees over a given financial year. To run a Payment Summary report, go to the Employees section of the QBO Navigation menu on the left of your screen and select the Reports tab. Under the ATO Reporting heading, select Payment Summaries.

A pop-up window will appear where you can filter by location and financial year. Next, click the Show Payment Summaries button (see Figure 9-14).

To the right of each employee's name is an Actions button, where you can choose to edit, view, download or publish individual payment summaries.

TIP

The Actions button at the top of the Payment Summaries screen enables you to publish payment summaries for all employees. Once published, you can choose to download the payment summaries and send notification to your employees advising that the payment summaries are available in their portal.

You can download payment summaries as either PDF or Excel documents by selecting either of the buttons to the right of the Actions button. You can also automatically lodge the Payment Summaries report with the ATO or create an EMPDUPE file to lodge with the ATO via the Business Portal (see Figure 9-14).

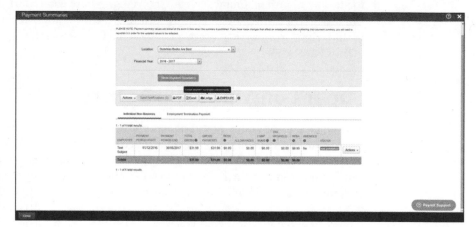

FIGURE 9-14:
Payment summaries — printing and lodging options.

IN THIS CHAPTER

» **Working out your GST liability**

» **Managing PAYG in instalments**

» **Working with ATO Running Balance accounts**

» **Recording — and paying — your annual income tax liability**

» **Adding in extra tax codes and groups**

Chapter **10**

Reporting Taxes

P aying taxes is by far the most unsatisfying part of business; however, they are unavoidable — all business must pay taxes. At least QuickBooks Online makes the tedious task of reporting taxes quick and simple. This chapter runs you through the most common tasks you need to complete as a business owner or manager, including tallying up your GST liability, completing your BAS, recording PAYG and paying income tax. You can also learn more about specific topics such as using Running Balance accounts and adding extra tax codes and groups.

TIP

At the time of writing, the Australian Tax Office (ATO) was getting ready to roll out simplified GST and BAS reporting requirements, which may create changes in QBO's GST centre — in particular, the listed tax codes. Watch this space!

Getting Up and Running

Chapter 3 shows you how to set up your business to report on GST (so skip back to that chapter if you need some pointers). Once you've been working in QBO for a while, you've probably entered in numerous transactions. But don't jump straight into working out your GST and Business Activity Statement (BAS). First make sure all bank accounts have been reconciled (and any incorrect entries removed) prior to reporting taxes (refer to Chapter 8 for more on this). Then you're ready to get started — and this section shows you how.

REMEMBER

Although your business's tax obligations can be viewed via the Chart of Accounts, and then the respective liability accounts, this chapter explores the GST section of the Navigation menu. To access this, go to the Navigation menu on the left of your screen, and click the GST tab (see Figure 10-1).

FIGURE 10-1: Opening the GST Centre.

Understanding your GST liability at a glance

Once you're on the GST screen, the balance shown on the top in the middle indicates your current liability for the GST period you are in. If the value is negative, you're owed a refund (yay!). The balances below indicate the value of GST you have collected from customers (included through your invoicing) as well as the amount of GST you have paid to suppliers via your purchases. This area also indicates any changes that have taken place in prior GST periods — such as any transactions that have been modified or deleted after you have lodged your GST. The value of these changes is shown as Adjustments (refer to Figure 10-2).

Running Business Activity Statement reports

You can run two main reports prior to lodging your BAS: A Summary report and a Details report. Both of these are pretty self-explanatory but this section takes you through a couple of extra tricks, and runs through the third report offered — the Amendment Details report, which relates to those adjustments mentioned in the preceding section.

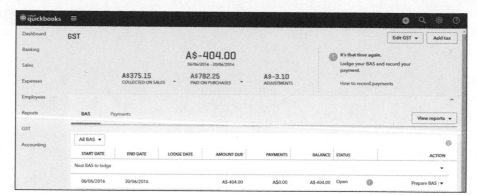

FIGURE 10-2:
Adjustments to
previously
lodged BAS.

BAS Summary report

From the GST Centre, you can select the View BAS Summary in the Action column of the BAS period you want to run a report for. If you select the drop-down arrow to the right of the BAS period, you will be given the option of running the following reports:

>> View BAS details

>> View amendment details

>> View payments

(See Figure 10-3 for how these options are listed.) Select to view the BAS Summary. From the top right, select your date range and your reporting basis (that is, Cash or Accrual). Headers can be edited and reports can also be customised to include notes. The icons on the right of the report allow you to view, print, save, export and forward reports.

TIP

The BAS Summary report has the added benefit of including the codes that relate to each respective field on your BAS form or online portal.

BAS Details report

The BAS Details report groups all transactions within a specified date range by tax code. So this report is a big help when you need to confirm that the correct tax codes have been entered for all transactions within your BAS period prior to reporting.

To access this report from the GST Centre, select the drop-down arrow to the right of the Run Reports link and select the View BAS Details option. From the top left, select your date range and your reporting basis (Cash or Accrual).

FIGURE 10-3:
Viewing BAS reports.

Headers can be edited and notes can also be added. You are also able to view, print, save, export and forward reports as per the BAS Summary report.

Reviewing the Amendment Details report

Whenever a transaction is changed or deleted in QBO after the BAS for that period has been lodged, QBO calculates the difference between what was reported and the change, and includes that information within the next BAS period.

TIP

You don't need to go back and adjust a previously lodged BAS if changes have been made to transactions within that BAS period because QBO automatically reflects that change for you in the next BAS period.

The accumulated value of these changes or adjustments appears in a separate column when you are completing your BAS.

To view the Amendment Details report from the GST Centre, select the drop-down arrow to the right of the select BAS period and choose the option for the Amendment Details report. From the top left, select your reporting basis (Cash or Accrual).

Headers can be edited and notes can also be added. You are also able to view, print, save, export and forward reports as per the BAS Summary report.

Completing BAS

Once you've run a few reports and are satisfied you've entered all data correctly, you can now prepare your BAS. To get started from the GST Centre, click the Prepare BAS link to the right of the new BAS period and ensure the frequency (that is, monthly, quarterly and so on) and your dates for the BAS period to be lodged are correct.

REMEMBER

If you have any Amendments for this BAS, a column with their value will appear in between the tax codes and amount columns.

The report will prepopulate with values for this period, including:

>> Total sales

>> Capital purchases

>> Non-capital purchases

>> Total salary, wages and other payments

>> Amount withheld from payments

>> GST on sales

>> GST on purchases

TIP

To view more detail on a specific value within your BAS, simply click on the amount and a report will populate detailing how that amount is made up.

You can manually record adjustments by selecting the Record link on the right (see Figure 10-4). For example, you may need to record adjustments for:

>> Wine equalisation tax

>> Luxury car tax

>> PAYG tax withheld

>> PAYG tax income tax instalment

>> FBT instalment

>> Fuel tax credit over claim (do not claim in litres)

>> Wine equalisation tax refundable

>> Luxury car tax refundable

>> Credit from PAYG income tax instalment variation

>> Credit from FBT instalment

>> Fuel tax credit (do not claim in litres)

REMEMBER

When manually recording adjustments, be sure to match the adjustment with the correct bank, liability or expense account.

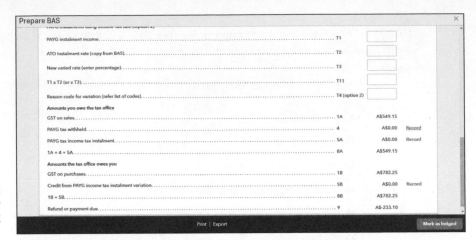

Prepare BAS				
PAYG instalment income		T1		
ATO instalment rate (copy from BAS)		T2		
New varied rate (enter percentage)		T3		
T1 x T2 (or x T3)		T11		
Reason code for variation (refer list of codes)		T4 (option 2)		
Amounts you owe the tax office				
GST on sales		1A	A$549.15	
PAYG tax withheld		4	A$0.00	Record
PAYG tax income tax instalment		5A	A$0.00	Record
1A + 4 + 5A		8A	A$549.15	
Amounts the tax office owes you				
GST on purchases		1B	A$782.25	
Credit from PAYG income tax instalment variation		5B	A$0.00	Record
1B + 5B		8B	A$782.25	
Refund or payment due		9	A$-233.10	

Print | Export   Mark as lodged

FIGURE 10-4:
Manually
recording
adjustments.

Prior to marking BAS as lodged, the buttons on the bottom of your screen give you the option of printing or exporting the report for further checking (if needed). When you are satisfied with the BAS report, select the Mark as Lodged button on the bottom right of your screen to close off the BAS period. This also saves a snapshot of your return.

REMEMBER

Once you've closed the BAS period in QBO, you still need go to the ATO website to lodge online. To do so, simply copy the amounts from your QBO return and paste them into your BAS in the ATO portal.

Viewing your BAS History

Underneath the current BAS period you will see a list of previously recorded BAS. From the drop-down menu on the right of each period you can choose to view BAS details or Amendment details as well as view any recorded payments and record any refunds.

Recording Monthly IAS Payments for PAYG Withholding

If the value of a business's wages to employees exceeds a certain amount per annum, the business is required to report and complete Pay As You Go (PAYG) on a more frequent basis, usually monthly. If this is the case for your business, along with making the payment you also need to adjust your QBO account to ensure everything lines up and plays nice. This section takes you through the adjustments needed.

One click PAYG

From the Payments tab of the GST Centre, select the Record PAYG Payment button on the right (see Figure 10-5). Select the bank account you are paying from and make entries to the Adjustment Date and the Payment Date fields. The adjustment date typically reflects the last day of the period for which the payment is for. The last step is to enter the amount you are paying and a memo as a description of the payment you are making (see Figure 10-6).

FIGURE 10-5:
The link to make PAYG payments.

FIGURE 10-6:
Entering the data relating to your PAYG payment.

Manually creating a PAYG payment

As the Record a PAYG Payment is a relatively new feature, we've also given those of you whose files have not yet been upgraded a workaround.

To manually adjust your QBO account when lodging PAYG in monthly instalments, you first need to run a PAYG Withholding Report (refer to Chapter 9). This report gives you the value of PAYG withheld as well as the total value of wage payments for the period.

Once you have the PAYG value to be reported, create an expense transaction (refer to Chapter 5). Select the ATO as your supplier and select the bank account that the PAYG payment will be paid from. Choose Out of Scope as your tax code. In the accounts section, select the PAYG Withholding account and enter details of the period that you are paying for in the Description field. Save the transaction and your liability account will be reduced and a payment will be noted in the bank account ledger.

TIP

If you are not paying PAYG from a bank account but are assigning it to the Running Balance account, select the ATO RBA account as the payment account (provided you have created this RBA account as a cash and cash equivalent account — see 'Using Running Balance Accounts', later in this chapter). If you can't see an option for selecting the RBA account or if you know that you created your RBA account as a liability account, make the payment from your suspense account. In this instance, you will need to create a secondary transaction to balance your suspense account back to zero. To do this, record a journal entry between your suspense account and your RBA account. (For more on journal entries refer to Chapter 3.)

Ensuring Quarterly BAS reflects manual monthly PAYG payments

REMEMBER

If you've been recording your PAYG monthly payments in QBO using the Record PAYG Payment feature, QBO automatically reduces the PAYG liability on your quarterly BAS to reflect the final month remaining to be lodged. You do not need to make any further adjustments to your BAS.

Once you've manually recorded your PAYG payments for the past two months (refer to preceding section), in the last month of the quarter you need to include your PAYG obligation in your BAS to marry your accounts up with your paper documentation or online portal requirement.

If you've manually recorded your PAYG payment, a problem emerges when you create your BAS in QBO — you see a PAYG value for the entire period even if you have been reducing the liability by way of monthly IAS instalments.

To reflect a true BAS value, you need to manually record the PAYG adjustment for the past months' Instalment Activity Statement (IAS) payments in the BAS, leaving only the current month's obligation in the BAS. Here's how to make this adjustment:

1. **In the Complete BAS screen, scroll down to the Amounts You Owe the Tax Office heading on the left.**

2. **Select the Record link to the right of the PAYG Tax Withheld row.**

3. **Enter the PAYG Withholding Payable liability account as your adjustment account.**

   This is the same account that QBO will post to under BAS Account, which means the adjustment will go in and out without upsetting your liability balance — because this liability was already recorded at the time the IAS was lodged (refer to the preceding section for more on this).

4. **In the Amount field, enter in a negative value equalling the total amount that has already been reported and paid.**

   For example, if your IAS for January was $4,750 and your IAS for February was $5,250, enter **–$10,000** in the Amount field.

5. **Add a memo to the transaction and click Save.**

   The memo can include information on the period the adjustment is for.

Figure 10-7 shows an example of the PAYG adjustment.

FIGURE 10-7: Manually adjusting BAS to reflect PAYG instalments.

Using Running Balance Accounts

Running Balance accounts are a reflection of the accounts that the tax office establishes for your business on their system. The two main accounts you should keep an eye on are:

>> ICA (Integrated Client Account)

>> Income Tax Account

The ICA is where your BAS and PAYG payments are posted to, along with any penalties relating to failure to lodge on time. The Income Tax Account (not to be confused with the PAYG side of things) is used to record the tax your business owes to the tax office, based on its recorded profits each year as declared in the business's tax return.

TIP

If you always pay your tax obligations in full by the due date, you may not need to set up a RBA account for ICA; however, you may need one for paying your annual income tax, unless you also pay that outright when due.

The most popular way of setting up these ATO accounts in QBO is to create them as liability accounts — because that's predominantly what they are. They then can be reconciled through the ledger or via the Reconciliations feature in QBO (refer to Chapter 8) when statements become available.

WARNING

The downside of setting up these accounts as liabilities is that you can't automatically make payments from these accounts, because you can't create expenses or write cheques from a liability account. As such, some people prefer to enter these accounts in as bank accounts. If you choose this option, just be aware that if you owe money to the tax office, the bank account will indicate a negative balance — just like it would in the case of an overdraft facility.

Whatever option you choose, you can create your RBA accounts as per the instructions for updating your Chart of Accounts provided in Chapter 3.

REMEMBER

RBA accounts should be periodically reconciled just like bank or credit card accounts.

Entering and Paying Income Tax

If you don't already have an Income Tax Liability account in your Chart of Accounts in QuickBooks Online, you first need to create one before you can enter the details of tax paid (refer to Chapter 3 for more on setting up new accounts).

Once you know the value of your income tax liability for the previous financial year, you can then enter its value in the Income Tax Payable liability account — either directly in the accounts ledger or by creating a journal transaction — and offset the value of the Income Tax Liability with the Income Tax Expense account (see Figure 10-8).

To create a journal, select the Create (+) button from the top right of your screen and from the Other column, select the option for Journal Entry.

REMEMBER

Re-visiting your Chart of Accounts around this time to make sure your income tax value is posted correctly into your income tax liability account is good practice.

FIGURE 10-8: Offsetting the value of the Income Tax Liability with the Income Tax Expense account via a journal entry.

TIP

If you're paying your income tax in one transaction prior to its due date, you can enter the payment as an expense to the tax office from your bank account and post it to the Income Tax Payable liability account with the GST code listed as Out of Scope (see Figure 10-9). If you're not, speak to your accountant or bookkeeper to ascertain whether or not you should create an RBA.

If you want to post the income tax liability to the RBA account for payment at a later stage, after entering its value in the Income Tax Payable liability account, create a transaction that offsets this account (DR Income Tax Payable and ATO RBA account — see Figure 10-10). This transfers the liability from the Income Tax Payable account to the RBA account for reconciliations.

When paying your income tax, use the same expense transaction, as if making the payment in full from your bank account, except, in the Account section, enter the respective RBA liability account rather than the Income Tax Payable account (see Figure 10-11).

FIGURE 10-9:
Paying your
Income Tax
obligation with an
expense
transaction.

FIGURE 10-10:
Transferring
income tax
liability from the
Income Tax
Payable account
to the RBA
account.

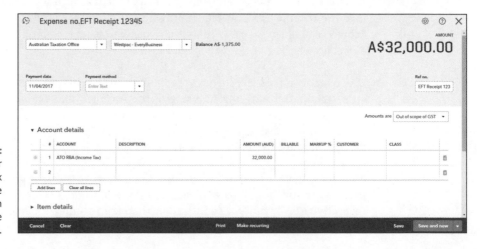

FIGURE 10-11:
Paying your
income tax
obligation in the
RBA with an
expense
transaction.

Creating Additional Taxes and Special Transactions

Depending on the type of business that you operate, you may need to create additional taxes — for example, taxes specific to the tobacco, hotel or petrol industries. To set up additional taxes, go to the GST Centre and click the New Tax button on the top right, select the Add Tax button and then select the option that best suits the tax you would like to create (see Figure 10-12). This section runs through the three options on offer, and explains when you might need to use special transactions.

FIGURE 10-12: Adding taxes.

Additional tax rate

If the rate for an existing tax changes, adding an additional tax rate is a better option than changing the existing one.

To create an additional tax rate, enter the name of the new tax and select whether you would like the tax to apply to sales, purchases or both. You may also enter a description in the field provided.

Additional group rate

If you want to combine two taxes and apply them at the same time, you can set up a group rate with a single code. Both taxes are calculated and charged together, but they're still tracked in their own separate accounts.

To create an additional group rate, enter the name or tax code that will be used on reports to identify the tax, and then select a current tax rate from the drop-down list provided. Select whether it should be applicable to the net amount, tax amount or both. Continue to do this for each tax that you would like to include in your group. If you need to group more than two taxes, select the Add Rate link.

Custom tax

You may need to add a tax specific to your industry — for example, a tax specific to the tobacco, hotel or petrol industry, or an environmental levy. *Note:* Custom taxes must be a percentage.

To create a custom tax, enter a name for the tax and select the lodgement frequency and reporting basis (that is, Cash or Accruals). Choose whether the tax applies to sales, purchases or both and enter a description (optional). If the tax applies to purchases and can be reclaimed as Input Tax (GST) credit, also select the Purchase Tax is Reclaimable checkbox. Select Next to move to the next screen and enter a rate for the tax.

Taxes requiring special transactions

In some instances, special transactions are required to accurately reflect taxes payable. These transactions can be created and saved as templates for future use to ensure the correct reporting technique is used — since they may occur infrequently (refer to Chapter 5 for more on setting up recurring transactions).

An example of where a special transaction may be required is for a business that imports goods from overseas. This business may receive a bill that is 100 per cent GST. In this case, you would assign a transaction to the applicable account for the same value as the GST to be paid. In the example shown in Figure 10-13, an expense is entered for the Purchases account to the value of $2,000 with the 100% tax code — which means tax to the value of $2,000 will also be added to the transaction. However, leaving the transaction there would incorrectly bring the total transaction to a figure of $4,000. This means a negative entry also needs to be made on the next line against the Purchases account, with the Out of Scope or GST

Free tax code applied (depending on what the transaction line allows). This creative transaction essentially removes any value posted against the Purchases account but keeps the tax value in place.

WARNING

It is important to ensure that Exclusive of Tax is selected in the Amounts Are drop-down list on the right (see Figure 10-13).

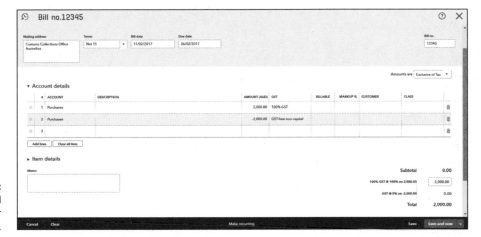

FIGURE 10-13:
Creating a special
transaction for
GST on imports.

Chapter **11**

How's the Business Doing?

No big surprise here: To help you measure and evaluate your business's health, you use reports. The reports reflect the information in QBO, so keeping QBO up to date with your daily activities helps ensure that accurate information appears on the reports you run. This chapter takes you through the main reports to focus on.

Quickly Review Income and Expenses

When you click Reports on the Navigation bar, you see a page like the one shown in Figure 11-1.

The graphic at the top of the page shows profit and loss information and is interactive; for example, if you click anywhere in the graphic — on the Net Income number, on either the Income or the Expenses number, or on any of the bars in the chart — QBO displays the Profit and Loss report shown in Figure 11-2. This version of the Profit and Loss report breaks down income and expenses by week for the period of the graphic.

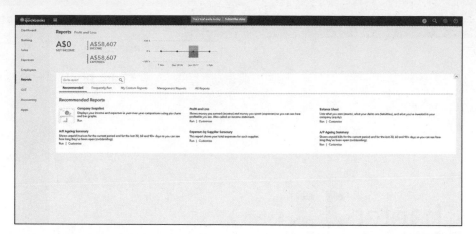

FIGURE 11-1:
The Reports page.

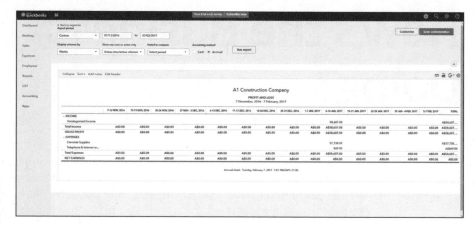

FIGURE 11-2:
A Profit and Loss
report by week.

You can click Reports in the Navigation bar to redisplay the Reports page shown in Figure 11-1, or you can click your browser's Back button.

TIP

Don't want the income and expense numbers displayed onscreen? Click the upward-pointing arrow at the bottom right edge of the graphic on the Reports page, and QBO hides the graphic.

Finding the Report You Want

Reports in QBO are organised into five categories:

» Recommended Reports

» Frequently Run Reports

>> My Custom Reports

>> Management Reports

>> All Reports

These categories appear on the Reports page below the graphic and function as tabs; that is, you click a tab to see the reports in that category.

Examining recommended reports

QBO lists reports on the Recommended tab of the Reports page based on features you use in QBO, preferences and add-ons (refer to Figure 11-1). Remember, the reports we display in the figure might differ from the ones you see when you review your recommended reports.

Looking at frequently run reports

No surprise here: On the Frequently Run tab, QBO lists the reports you run most often. When you first start using QBO and haven't run reports yet, the Frequently Run tab doesn't contain any reports. Instead, it contains a message that describes what you'll see after you start running reports.

Finding reports you customise

The My Custom Reports tab lists reports you have printed — whether to your display or to a printer — customised and saved, either as single reports or in a report group. Like its cousin, Frequently Run reports, the My Custom Reports tab remains empty until you print, customise and save a report (as described later in this chapter in the section 'Saving a customised report'). In that section, we also show you how to place a customised report into a group, and you get a look at the My Custom Reports page after it contains a report saved to a group.

TIP

If you're a former QuickBooks desktop user, be aware that saving a report in QBO is the equivalent of memorising a report in QuickBooks desktop, and saving a report to a group in QBO is conceptually the same as creating a memorised report group in QuickBooks desktop.

Taking a look at management reports

The Management Reports tab, shown in Figure 11-3, lists three predefined management report packages you can prepare and print by clicking the View link in the Action column. Each package contains a professional-looking cover page, a table of contents and several reports that relate to the report package's name:

» The Sales Performance management report contains the Profit and Loss report, the A/R Ageing Detail report and the Sales by Customer Summary report.

» The Expenses Performance management report contains the Profit and Loss report, the A/P Ageing Detail report and the Expenses by Supplier Summary report.

» The Company Overview management report contains the Profit and Loss report and the Balance Sheet report.

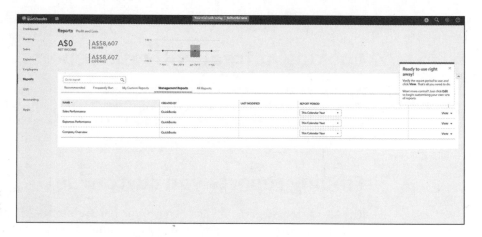

FIGURE 11-3:
The Management
Reports page.

The management report appears in its own window, where you can scroll through and print it. You can also customise these reports; click the downward-pointing arrow beside a report to see your choices.

TIP

If you opt to edit a report package, you can add more reports to the package and you can include an executive summary and end notes to the package.

Exploring all QBO reports

The All Reports tab gives you a way to find any QBO report. The page lists a series of categories for reports, such as Business Overview and Manage Accounts Receivable.

TIP

Once you select a category, you can redisplay the All Reports page by clicking the All Reports link that appears above the report category name.

Searching for a report

You don't need to use the tabs to find a report. Instead, you can click in the Go to Report box; when you do, QBO displays all reports, listed alphabetically, in a drop-down list (see Figure 11-4).

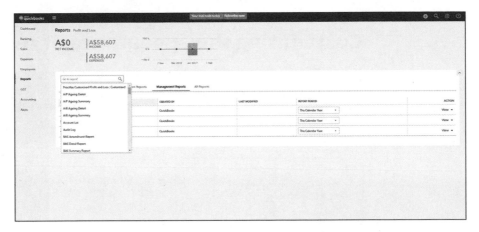

FIGURE 11-4:
Searching for a report.

If you see the report you want, you can click it, and QBO displays it onscreen. If you don't see the report you want, you can type some keywords into the Go to Report box, and QBO narrows the reports displayed in the drop-down list to those with names that contain the keywords you typed.

Generating a Report

To generate any report, simply click the report's title. QBO automatically displays the report with a standard set of settings. To redisplay reports, click Reports in the Navigation bar.

On most reports, you can *drill down* to view the details behind the report's numbers. For example, from the Profit and Loss report, you can click any Income or Expense account value, and QBO displays the transactions that make up the number on the Profit and Loss report.

To redisplay the original report, you can click the Back to Summary Report link on the left side of the report page.

TIP

If you want to keep the original summary version of the report open and also view the details from drilling down, duplicate the tab containing the summary version of the report before you drill down to view details. When you finish working with the details, you can close the tab containing the details. To duplicate a tab in Chrome, right-click the tab and select Duplicate. To duplicate a tab in Firefox, press and hold down the Ctrl key as you click the browser refresh button, which appears at the right edge of the address bar.

Customising the appearance of reports

If you click the Customise button in the upper right corner of the report (refer to Figure 11-2), you see additional customisation options that let you control the column and row data on the report, set period comparisons and more (see Figures 11-5 and 11-6).

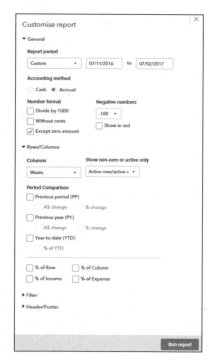

FIGURE 11-5: The Customise Report dialog box that appears when you customise a report.

Customising a report

You can *customise* most reports in a variety of ways. For all reports, you can change the date range covered by the report by opening the Transaction Date list box and making a selection or by setting specific dates in the From and To boxes. After you make your selection, click the Run Report button to refresh the report and display information only in the date range you selected.

To set more detailed custom settings, click the Customise button at the top of the report. QBO displays the Customise Report dialog box shown in Figure 11-6; from this dialog box, you can make changes that affect the information QBO displays on the report.

FIGURE 11-6: The Customise Report dialog box in further detail.

First, although you see arrows down the side of the dialog box, the Customise Report dialog box contains one long list of settings you can control. The tabs help you scroll down quickly to a particular type of setting.

Second, it's important to understand that the settings that appear in the Customise Report dialog box vary, depending on the report you are customising. Figure 11-5 shows the settings in the General section of the Customise Profit and Loss dialog box. From this section, you can, for example, opt to display the report using the accrual basis of accounting rather than the cash basis.

From the Rows/Columns section of the Customise Profit and Loss dialog box (see Figure 11-5), you can control the columns and rows that appear on the report as well as the order in which they appear. You also can add a variety of comparison columns.

Figure 11-6 also shows the Filter settings, and if you click Header/Footer on the left side of the dialog box (or you scroll down in the dialog box), you see the rest of the report header and footer settings.

Printing, exporting and emailing reports

When you're finished customising the report, click Run Report, and QBO displays the report onscreen using your customised settings. With the report onscreen, you can click the Print button to print the report to paper or to a PDF file. Or, you can click the Email button to email the report or the Excel button to export the report to Excel.

From within the My Custom Reports tab, you can click the down arrow in the Action column beside the report where you can perform any of the following actions:

>> Edit the report

>> Export the report to Excel

>> Export the report to PDF

>> Delete the customised report by clicking Delete

To print the report from the My Custom Reports tab, you select the name of the report, and once the report opens, select the Print button to print or download the report. As per Figure 11-7, you can also export the report to Excel.

REMEMBER

You can email the report or export it to Excel from the Customise dialog box, but we suggest that you use the Run Report button to display the report onscreen first and make sure that what you see is what you want to send.

When you use Chrome to export a report to Excel, a button with the title 'report1. xls' appears in the bottom left corner of the screen; click that button to open the report in Excel. Be aware, too, that QBO automatically saves a copy of the report to the local hard drive, usually in the Downloads folder. If you don't delete the reports, QBO increments the report name for subsequent reports you export to Excel.

TIP

To find the folder where QBO stores the report, click the down arrow on the right side of the report's button in the lower left corner of the QBO screen and choose Show in Folder.

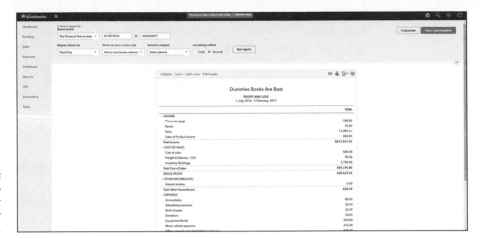

FIGURE 11-7:
Use these tools to print, email or export your reports.

Saving a customised report

Once the report looks the way you want, you might want to save it so that you don't need to apply the same customisations each time you run the report. Click the Save Customisations button at the top of the report page to display the Save Report Customisations dialog box shown in Figure 11-8.

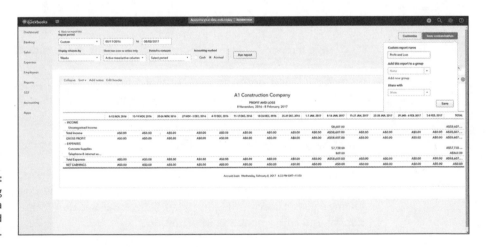

FIGURE 11-8:
Use this dialog box to save a customised report.

Supply a name for the customised report; you can use the QBO name for the report, but you'd be better off including some information in the name that helps you remember the customisations — unlike the one we use in the figure, which really doesn't tell us much other than the report is a Profit and Loss report.

You can add the report to a group you create; creating a group is useful if you want to email several reports simultaneously.

Once you save your settings in the Save Customisations dialog box, the saved report appears on the My Custom Reports tab of the Reports page. And, if you created a group, the report appears in that group. In Figure 11-9, Priscilla's customised version of the Profit and Loss report appears.

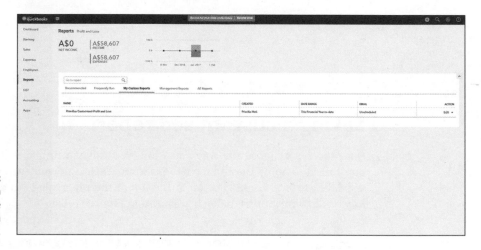

FIGURE 11-9: The My Custom Reports page after creating a custom report.

TIP

To change a report's name or group, click the Edit link beside the report.

If you click Delete at the bottom of the Report Group Settings page, you delete the report group and all custom reports the group contains.

WARNING

Auto generate reports

If you select the Edit link in the Action column beside a report group, you can set an email schedule for the report group; QBO displays the Custom Report Group Settings page shown in Figure 11-10. Select the Set Email Schedule check box to display and edit scheduling information.

If you select Attach the Report as an Excel File, QBO sends the report in Excel format; if you don't select this option, QBO sends the reports in HTML format.

Fill in the Email Information; QBO will use the same subject each time it emails the report group. By default, QBO chooses monthly as the email interval, but QBO does let you customise the email schedule.

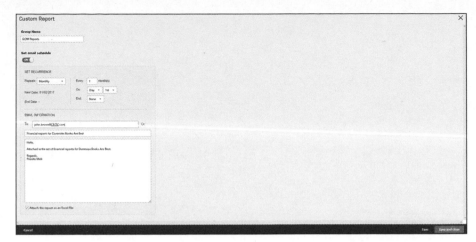

FIGURE 11-10:
Set an email
schedule for a
report group.

Running Reports for Individual Accounts

As we touched on in earlier chapters, you are able to print a report for individual accounts from the Chart of Accounts screen (to access this screen, go to the Navigation bar➪Accounting). For example, if you want to see the transactions associated with your Office expense account or perhaps a loan account, you can go directly to that account and run a report via Chart of Accounts (see Figure 11-11).

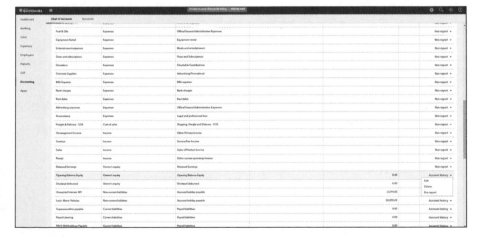

FIGURE 11-11:
Run a report
directly from your
Chart of
Accounts.

Chapter **12**

Preparing a Budget in QBO

Q uickBooks Online (QBO) supports preparing budgets that help you monitor, track and compare expected income and expenses with actual income and expenses. When you prepare a budget, you typically prepare it for a financial year, and you can opt to supply budget amounts or use historical amounts from QBO. You also can opt to subdivide your budget based on customer, location or class. This chapter takes you through preparing budgets and your various options.

REMEMBER

QBO uses pop-up windows to help you prepare budgets. If you have your browser set to block pop-ups, you should make an exception for QBO.

Checking Financial Year Settings in QBO

Before you start to prepare your budget, you can double-check your financial year settings by following these steps:

1. **Click the Gear button on the top right of your screen.**

2. **From the drop-down menu that appears, click Company Settings in the Settings column. See Figure 12-1.**

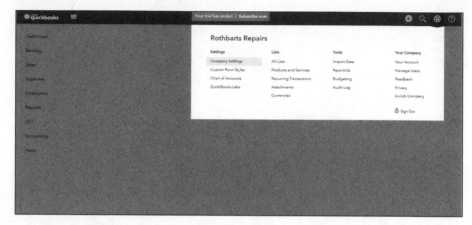

FIGURE 12-1:
The Company
Settings option.

3. **Click Advanced on the left side of the dialog box, as shown in Figure 12-2.**

FIGURE 12-2:
The Advanced
category.

4. **In the Accounting section, double-check that the first month of your financial year is correct.**

If necessary, you can change the first month of the fiscal year by clicking it.

5. **Click Done.**

Budgeting with QBO

The ability to work with budgets is only available in QuickBooks Online Plus. You can create a budget within QBO either by Class, Location or Customer, but not by two or all three. Budgeting in QuickBooks Online was designed to only create budgets one year at a time, and the budgets in QBO are designed to subdivide by only one category per budget. QBO also does not have the capability to do budget forecasting. If a new budget is created, existing budgets will not be superseded or affected. (See Figure 12-3 for an overview of the budgeting screen.)

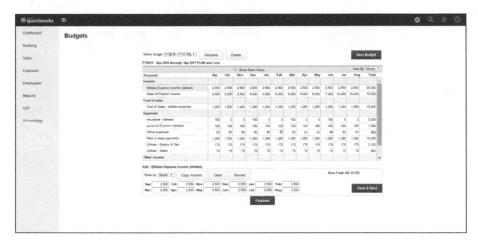

FIGURE 12-3:
The Budgeting
Screen.

Using the Budget Wizard

REMEMBER

To prepare a budget in QBO, you use a four-page wizard that helps you set up the Budgets page, where you then provide budget values. Follow these steps:

1. **Click the Gear button on the top right of your screen.**

2. **From the drop-down menu that appears, click Budgeting in the Tools column.**

   The Creating a Budget wizard — a four-page wizard — starts. The first page of the wizard explains what you'll do as you create a budget.

3. **Select the New Budget button from the top right of your screen.**

TIP

   If you have not enabled pop-ups, at least for QBO, a prompt appears asking you to disable your pop-up blocker. Click OK and disable your pop-up blocker or list the QBO web address as an exception to blocked pop-ups.

   The second page of the Budget wizard interview appears, as shown in Figure 12-4.

The second page
of the Budget
wizard interview.

4. **Click an option to specify how you intend to establish budget amounts.**

   In our example, we have chosen to create a budget using actual amounts from the last financial year.

5. **Click Next.**

   The third page of the interview appears, shown in Figure 12-5.

FIGURE 12-5:
The third page of
the interview.

6. **Specify how you want to subdivide your budget.**

   You can opt not to subdivide your budget, subdivide by customer or, if you have locations and classes enabled, subdivide by location or class.

7. **Click Next.**

The last page of the interview appears.

8. **Select a financial year and provide a name for the budget.**

9. **Click Finish. See Figure 12-6.**

QBO displays the Budgets page; the actual appearance of the page depends on the choices you made as you walked through the interview. The following steps outline what the Budgets page looks like when you don't subdivide.

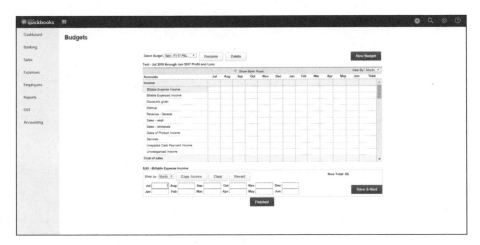

FIGURE 12-6:
The Budgets page.

10. **Click a line in the top part of the window and type in amounts.**

QBO displays monthly boxes at the bottom of the window for the selected line. This is where you enter your amounts. After you enter them, select the Save and Next option on the right and the values will be populated in the budget screen above.

You can also type an amount and click Copy Across to copy the amount from one box to all the rest of the boxes. To enter quarterly or yearly values, change the Enter By drop-down field from the default monthly preference to the preference of your choice. QuickBooks Online averages out the quarterly or annual values over a given number of months.

11. **Repeat Step 10 for each budget line.**

You don't have to provide budget amounts for every line of the budget, and you can select or de-select the button at the top of your budget that's labelled Show Blank Rows to consolidate or expand what appears in your budget.

12. **Click Finished when you complete your budget.**

Finding your budgets

Your budgets are stored in the Reports Centre and you can choose to view either a Budget vs Actuals report or simply a Budget Overview. To view a list of your budgets, firstly make a selection between which of the two reports you prefer (see Figure 12-7).

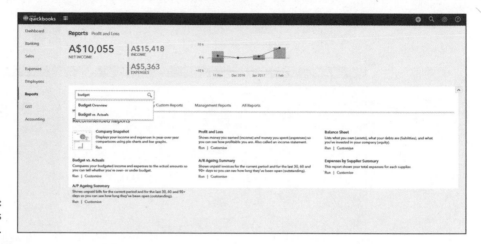

FIGURE 12-7:
The Reports Centre.

If you have multiple budgets for any given period, select the budget you want to view from the Budget drop-down box on the left of your screen, as per Figure 12-8.

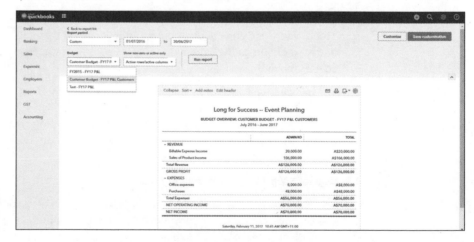

FIGURE 12-8:
Working with multiple budgets.

From the options that appear above the budget report you can:

>> Collapse the report

>> Sort

>> Enter Notes

>> Edit heading

>> Email

>> Print

>> Export to Excel

>> Download to PDF

By clicking the Customise button on the top right of your screen, you can further modify the appearance of your report (see Figure 12-9). Some of the customise options include removing any cents from your amounts, viewing negative figures in red and adding a logo to your Budget report.

FIGURE 12-9:
Customising the
look of your
budget.

3

Working in QuickBooks Online Accountant

Examine the QBOA interface, set up QBOA users, and work with the QBOA client list, free company and sample company.

Learn how to add clients to the Client List, including importing desktop QuickBooks companies.

Become familiar with working with a client QBO company from QBOA.

Learn how to use notes and tasks to keep track of information, and how to communicate with clients from within their QBO companies.

Use tools available to accountants to manage client QBO companies.

IN THIS CHAPTER

» **Setting up a QBOA account, and signing in and out**

» **Understanding the QBOA front-end interface**

» **Setting up multiple users in a QBOA account**

» **Using the Client List page**

» **Working with the free QBOA company and the sample company**

» **Understanding Wholesale Billing**

Chapter **13**

Setting Up Shop in QBOA

Parts 1 and 2 of this book cover the details of QBO, and QBO is the product you use to enter transactions into a company.

Because accountants need to work in multiple QBO companies, they use Quick-Books Online for Accountants (QBOA). QBOA provides a front-end interface that acts as a portal you use to open client QBO companies. When you open any particular client's company, you have available to you the features for the client's subscription level: Simple Start, Essentials or Plus.

REMEMBER

As you see in this chapter, the interface for a client QBO company opened in QBOA varies slightly from the interface your client sees when opening the company.

Signing Up for and into QBOA

Setting up a QBOA subscription account is free, and your QBOA subscription remains free for life from the day you sign up. You can sign up for the Intuit

Wholesale Pricing program and receive discounted rates for each client subscription you manage; contact Intuit for details.

TIP

When you sign up for a QBOA subscription account, you get, as one of the perks, a free QBO company that you can use for your own company — that is, to manage the books for your own business. You can read more about this company later in this chapter, in the section 'Understanding and Using the Free QBOA Company'.

To create a QBOA account, open your browser and navigate to www.intuit.com.au. Choose the Accountants & Bookkeepers tab at the top of the screen and make your selection. You will be directed to another page with additional information relating to the QBOA product for you to review; once there, select the green 'Get Started' button (see Figure 13-1).

FIGURE 13-1:
Navigating to the QBOA sign-in page.

This will take you to the Sign Up page (see Figure 13-2) where you will need to provide the requested information, including your email address (which will become your User ID), and also where you will set up your password. Once completed, go ahead and click the Continue button.

REMEMBER

Just as you'd expect, by clicking the Continue button, you're agreeing to Intuit's Terms of Service, the End-User License Agreement and the Privacy Policy for QBOA.

Your new company is created and the Home page in QBOA appears. In addition, the 'Take a Tour' video, lasting less than two minutes, provides some tips to get you started. When the video finishes, you'll see that your Client List page is empty except for links to two other 'getting started' videos and to a PDF version of the 16-page QuickBooks Accountant Welcome Guide, which you can use to help you work in QBOA.

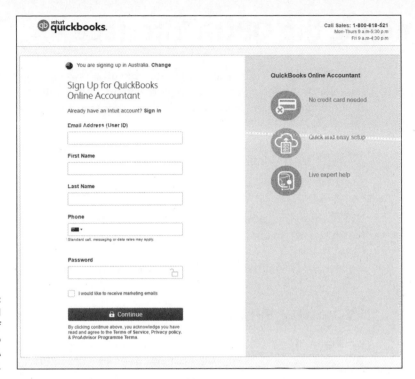

FIGURE 13-2:
Provide a limited
amount of
information to
create a QBOA
account.

Once you've created a QBOA account, you use the same page to log in to your QBOA account that your client uses to log in to QBO. Navigate to www.intuit.com.au to view the web page shown in Figure 13-3 and supply your login credentials.

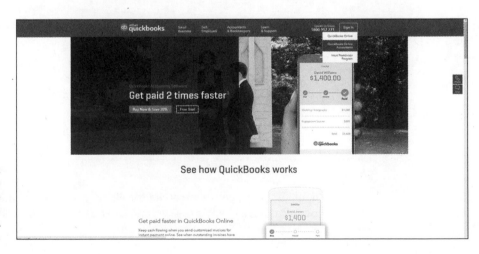

FIGURE 13-3:
The page you use
to sign in to
QBOA after you
set up a QBOA
account.

Examining the QBOA Interface

The QBOA interface focuses on giving accountants access to tools they need to manage multiple clients. Although the view in the QBOA interface changes, depending on where you're working, two common elements appear in the QBOA interface:

>> The Navigation bar runs down the left side of the page.

>> The QBOA toolbar (green) runs across the top of the page.

You use the Navigation bar to display the various pages in QBOA. The Navigation bar contains two choices that display different views and affect the choices in the QBOA toolbar: The Your Practice and Your Books views. The following two sections explore the Navigation bar and the QBOA toolbar in each of these views.

Working with the Your Practice view

By default, the QBOA Home page displays, in the Navigation bar, the links for the Your Practice view and the Clients page, as you see in Figure 13-4.

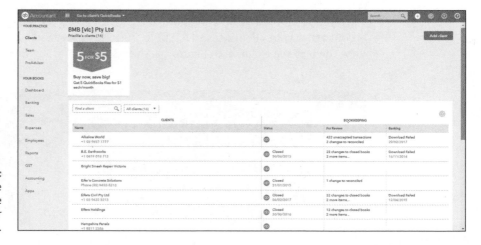

FIGURE 13-4:
The Your Practice view of the Navigation bar in QBOA.

On the Client List page, you can search for a client, see overview information about each client, and open a client's QBO company. You can also control the appearance of the Client List page. See the section 'Controlling the Appearance of the Client List,' later in this chapter, for details on working with the Client List page.

When you click Team in the Navigation bar, you can set up the users in your firm that will have access to various client companies. For more information, see the later section 'Setting Up Your Team'.

When you click ProAdvisor, you see information about the Intuit ProAdvisor program.

Across the top of the interface, you find a toolbar with the following buttons, from left to right:

- » **The Accountant button:** This button contains the QuickBooks logo and offers you another way to display the Client List shown in Figure 13-4.

- » **The Go to Client's QuickBooks button:** You can use this list box to display a list of your clients; clicking a client name opens the client's company.

- » **The Search box:** When you click in this box, a list of recent transactions or reports appears; you can type in the box to search for the transaction or report of your choice or you can click an item in the list.

- » **The plus sign (+) icon:** This button displays the Create menu, which you use to create a client or a user.

- » **The Gear button:** Click this button to display the Gear menu (see Figure 13-5). The Gear menu shows the settings you can establish for your own company, your client's company, and your QBOA account.

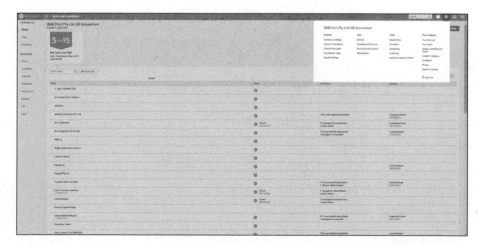

FIGURE 13-5:
The choices available from the Gear menu.

REMEMBER

You also can open the QBO sample company from the Gear menu; read more about opening and working in the sample company later in this chapter, in the section 'Working with the Sample Company'.

» **The Profile button:** The profile button allows you to modify the information Intuit displays about your practice in its 'Find an Expert' section targeted to clients. This is a great way of promoting your firm free of charge. Your profile also displays the number of page views and leads that your firm has received as a result of the 'Find an Expert' link.

» **The Help button:** Click this button to open the Help menu so that you can search for help on any topic. Help in QBOA is context sensitive and available from all screens. When you open the Help menu from a transaction screen, for example, the suggested choices that appear are based on the type of transaction you were viewing when you clicked Help.

Working with the Your Books view

When you work with any of the buttons under the Your Books section of the Navigation bar, you are viewing your own QBO company details (see Figure 13-6). At the time of writing, the Navigation bar in QBOA had not been upgraded to match that of the QBO program, so some things may be slightly different — for example, in QBOA you have a Client button in the Navigation menu whereas in QBO you have a Sales button, which links to your clients. Similarly, in QBOA you have a Suppliers button, while QBO displays an Expenses button, which links to your suppliers.

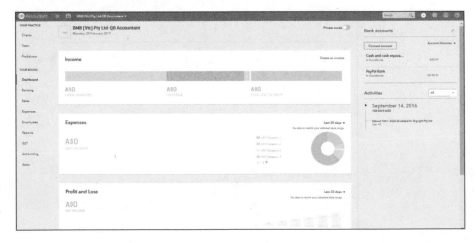

FIGURE 13-6:
The view of a QBO company from QBOA.

The view when you open your own company's books in QBOA matches the view you see when you open any client's QBO company; the only difference onscreen is the name of the company that appears on the QBOA toolbar.

The Home screen of a company displays overview income, expense, and profit and loss information in interactive filters; you can click part of any graphic on this page to display the details that make up that part of the graphic. In Figure 13-6, we haven't entered any data into the company, so there's no reason to click anything.

The QBOA toolbar in a QBO company changes somewhat when you display the Your Books view. In particular, beside the Accountant button, you see a suitcase button that we call the Accountant Tools button; you can click this button to display, well, tools accountants need frequently when working in a client's company (see Figure 13-7). See Chapter 17 for details on these tools.

FIGURE 13-7:
The tools available to accountants while working in a client company.

The List Box button beside the Accountant Tools button displays the name of the currently open QBO company; when you click Your Books, your company's name appears.

The Create button (the plus sign), the Search box, the Gear button, the Profile button and the Help button all work the same way in the Your Books view as they do in the Your Practice view.

REMEMBER

While any company is open, you can use the QBOA toolbar to open the list box displaying the company's name to switch to a different client company. Also, you can redisplay the Client List page at any time by clicking the Accountant button on the QBOA toolbar.

Setting Up Your Team

If your accounting firm has more than one person who needs access to client QBO companies, the person who creates the QBOA account — called, in QBOA parlance, the *Master Administrator* — can set up the other users. The other users get their own login credentials and access to those clients that the Master Administrator specifies; for those clients, the user can access the Accountant Tools described in Chapter 17. The Master Administrator also specifies the user's level of access to the firm's information; a user can have basic, full or custom access.

TIP

Using separate QBOA login information helps maintain security in QBOA, because a lot of financial information (product subscriptions and billing information, for example) is tied to login information.

So, what's the difference, status-wise, between basic, full and custom access? Here's a rundown:

» Those users with full access can open and work in the firm's books as well as in client QBO companies, and can access the Team page and make changes to any user's privileges.

» Those users with basic access can access only client QBO companies.

» Those users with custom access have nothing more than basic or full access with at least one privilege set differently from QBOA's defaults for basic or full access.

To set up multiple users in a QBOA account, the Master Administrator or any firm member with full access privileges to QBOA sets up other members of the firm; during the process, QBOA sends an email to the other firm members whom, for this discussion, we'll call *invitees*. Once an invitee accepts the invitation, QBOA prompts the invitee to set up his own QBOA login credentials. Follow these steps to set up a new user in a QBOA account:

1. **Log in to QBOA.**

2. **Click Team in the Navigation bar.**

   The Team page appears (see Figure 13-8).

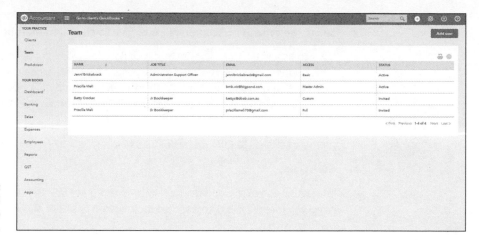

FIGURE 13-8:
View, edit and add members to your QBOA team.

3. **Click the Add User button.**

   The Add User wizard begins.

4. **On the first page of the Add User wizard (see Figure 13-9), fill in the name, email address and title of the team member you want to add.**

   The team member's title is optional.

5. **Click Next.**

   The second page of the Add User wizard appears. On this page, you identify the privileges related to your firm that you want to provide to the team member.

FIGURE 13-9:
Provide basic profile information for the invited users.

6. Select the type of access you want to give to the team member.

You can assign Basic, Full or Custom access; a description of each type of access appears on the right side of the page. Assign Full access to those team members who should have access to your own company's books. Assign Basic access to give a team member access to QBO client companies only.

You can make changes to individual settings; if you do, QBOA sets the team member's access to Custom by default.

7. Click Next.

The last screen of the Add User wizard appears (see Figure 13-10). On this page, you identify the clients for whom the team member should be able to perform work.

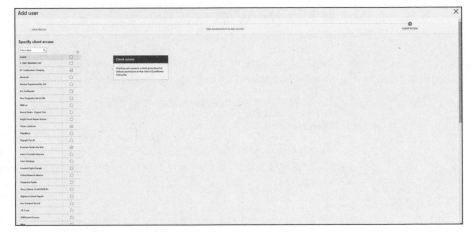

FIGURE 13-10:
You can provide a team member access to your firm's clients on a selective basis.

8. Deselect clients as needed.

9. Click Save.

QBOA adds the new user to your team and assigns a status of Invited to the user. In addition, the Status column on the Team screen indicates that QBOA sent an email invitation to the user, inviting the user to join your team. After the user responds to the QBOA invitation, the user's status changes to Active on the Team page in QBOA.

The email invitation that QBOA sends looks like the one shown in Figure 13-11.

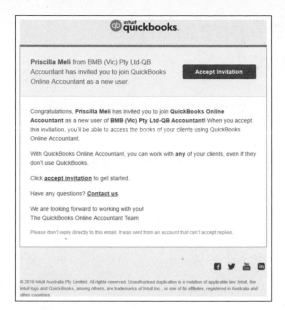

FIGURE 13-11:
An email invitation to use a QBOA account.

The recipient clicks the Accept Invitation button and, assuming the invitee doesn't already have login information for QBOA, the page shown in Figure 13-12 appears. The invitee then sets up QBOA login information by providing a user ID (which does not need to be an email address) and a password. Once the invitee clicks Create User, QBOA confirms that the user ID is available, sets up the login information and displays a page on which a Sign In button appears. Clicking the Sign In button signs the user into QBOA with the user's assigned privileges.

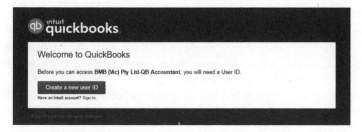

FIGURE 13-12:
An invited team member sets up her own login information.

To log into QBOA in the future, the team member navigates to www.intuit.com.au and makes the QuickBooks Online Accountants selection from the sign in button on the top right of the page and supplies their login credentials. These team members can bookmark the login screen for easy access.

Controlling the Appearance of the Client List

You can use the Client List page to open any client's QBO company, and you can control the appearance of the Client List page, shown in Figure 13-13.

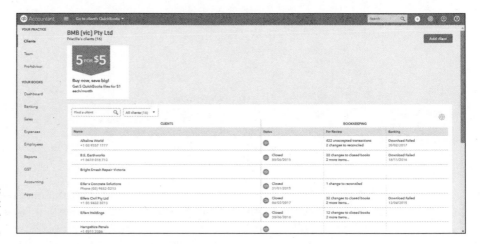

FIGURE 13-13: Select a client from your client list.

To open any client's QBO company, click the QuickBooks logo in the Status column of the Client List page. Or, if you prefer, open the Go to Client's QuickBooks list box on the QBOA toolbar to select the QBO company you want to open.

REMEMBER

If you click a client's name — rather than the QuickBooks logo — you don't open the client's company. Instead, you see overview details about the client.

You can control the appearance of the Client List page. For example, you can control the number of clients listed on the page by limiting the number of rows that appear. You also can specify the columns of information that appear on the Client list page. And, you can opt to hide or display inactive clients; for more information on making a client inactive, see the section 'Removing clients from your Wholesale Billing subscription', later in this chapter. Click the Gear button that appears just above the list of clients and make choices from the list that appears (see Figure 13-14).

REMEMBER

QBOA actually contains multiple Gear menus. One of them appears on the QBOA toolbar and is visible from most QBOA pages, even while you work in a client's QBO company; you use that Gear menu to provide information about your QBOA account, establish settings, view lists and access tools — to, for example, import data. On the QBOA Clients page, the other Gear menu appears on the right side just above the list of clients, and you use it to control the information that appears on the page.

FIGURE 13-14:
Control the number of rows and the information appearing on the Client List page.

Understanding and Using the Free QBOA Company

As mentioned at the beginning of this chapter, QBOA users get one free company to use for their own books. To open the company reserved for you, click the — yep, you guessed it — Your Books link in the Navigation bar, and QBOA opens your company.

The Sample company name appears on the Client Home page as 'Long for Success -- Event Planning'. No name appears beside the Gear button on the QBO company toolbar.

You can use the free QBOA company to enter your own company's information using transactions or, if you've been tracking your business in desktop Quick-Books, you can, with some limitations, import information from your desktop QuickBooks company. To enter information using transactions, you can read the chapters in Part 1 of this book, because you as a QBOA user and your clients as QBO users enter transactions in the same way.

REMEMBER

Be aware that the Your Books company is not intended to house a client's data. The Your Books company ties into QBOA and updates as clients are added to QBOA. So, if you use it to store a client's data, that data will be messed up as you add other clients.

Working with the Sample Company

If you've been a desktop QuickBooks user, you know that desktop QuickBooks comes with a variety of sample companies that you can use to test company behaviour. Like its desktop cousin, QBOA also comes with a sample company.

To open the sample company, follow these steps:

1. **Click the Gear button on the QBOA toolbar.**

QBOA opens the Gear menu.

2. **In the Your Company section, click Sample Company.**

QBOA displays a warning message that you will be logged out of QBOA if you continue.

3. **Click Continue.**

QBOA signs you out of your company and opens the sample company (see Figure 13-15). When going into the sample company 'Long for Success -- event planning' from QBOA, the interface changes and it becomes a normal QBO company. It does not provide the QBOA interface you see when opening a client's company from QBOA. When in the Sample company, for example, the upper left corner shows the Intuit QuickBooks icon, not the Accountant button.

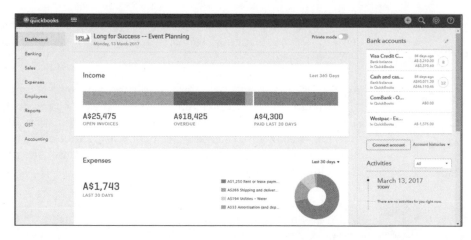

FIGURE 13-15:
'Long for success -- event planning', the QBO and QBOA sample company.

Closing Companies and QBOA

You don't close companies in QBOA the way you might using desktop QuickBooks. When you switch from one client QBO company to another, you automatically close the first client's company.

TIP

To work in two client QBO companies simultaneously, you can use two different browsers or two instances of a single browser (like setting up Chrome as two separate users). *Note:* Simply opening two tabs of a single browser doesn't allow users to work in two QBO companies simultaneously. Besides the option of two different browsers, users can use the desktop app for one QBO company and a browser for another QBO company. (For details on using Chrome, see Chapter 18.)

To close QBOA, click the Gear button on the QBOA toolbar and choose Sign Out (see Figure 13-16).

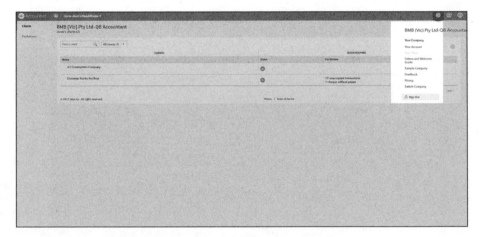

FIGURE 13-16:
Exit from QBOA
by signing out.

Working with Wholesale Billing

As we mentioned in Chapter 2, if you are an accounting professional, you can sign up for the free Wholesale Pricing program and also use QBOA for free. If you both create a client's company and manage the client's subscription as part of the Wholesale Pricing program, Intuit sends you the bill for the client's subscription. It is your responsibility to bill the client for the QBO subscription. The bill you receive from Intuit is a single consolidated bill for all the QBO subscriptions you manage. We provide some details on the Wholesale Pricing program here; for more information, contact Intuit.

REMEMBER

You don't have to enrol clients as part of the Wholesale Pricing program, but if you do, you might be able to get QBO for your clients at a reduced price. The Wholesale Pricing program is often referred to as the Wholesale Billing program; for this discussion, the two terms are interchangeable.

Signing up for Wholesale Billing

Accounting professionals are automatically signed up for the free Wholesale Billing program when they log in to QBOA for the first time. But the Wholesale Billing program doesn't become active until the accounting professional enters billing information into the Billing Profile in QBOA.

To enter information in the QBOA Billing Profile, follow these steps:

1. **From the QBOA Client list, click the Gear button located in the top right corner of the page.**

2. **From the drop-down Gear menu that appears, select Your Account under Your Company.**

The Your Account page appears, as shown in Figure 13-17.

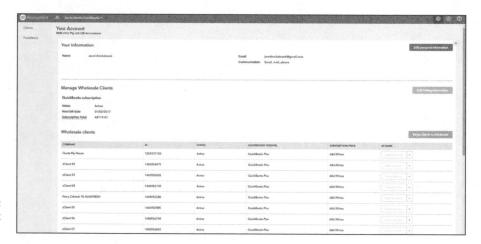

FIGURE 13-17:
The Your Account page in QBOA.

3. **Click the Edit Billing Information button.**

4. **Fill in all Payment Information fields.**

5. **Click Subscribe.**

The Your Account page reappears, and the Wholesale Billing Status will be active.

LIMITATIONS ASSOCIATED WITH THE WHOLESALE BILLING PROGRAM

You don't have to add a client to your Wholesale Billing subscription; you can still work with clients who pay their own QBO subscription costs. Enrolling a client into Wholesale Billing can save the client money on the cost of the QBO subscription but also makes you responsible for collecting subscription costs. And the Wholesale Billing program might not be right for all QBO clients. In particular:

- Companies created through the wholesale model have the ability to transfer Master Administrator rights. However, *no* accountant can be removed from the company as long as it is part of the Wholesale Billing program, including an accountant who is not associated with the firm housing the company in the Wholesale Billing program.

- If an accounting professional creates a QBO company through QBOA, the company does not come with a 30-day free trial. Instead, at the time the accounting professional creates the company, she must provide a payment method to ensure uninterrupted service.

Each month, you receive a bill from Intuit that covers the subscription costs of the clients you add to your Wholesale Billing subscription.

Adding clients to your Wholesale Billing subscription

A client QBO Wholesale Billing subscription stays active for as long as you maintain a valid form of payment in the QuickBooks Billing Profile. Wholesale QBO companies do not expire.

So, just how do you go about adding a client to your Wholesale Billing subscription? Make sure that the client appears in your Client List in QBOA; for details on adding a client to your client list, see Chapter 14. To add a client to your Wholesale Billing subscription, follow these steps:

1. **Click Clients in the Navigation bar.**

2. **Click the Gear icon in the top right corner of the QBOA toolbar.**

3. **From the drop-down menu, under Your Company, select Your Account.**

   The Your Account window appears.

4. **In the Wholesale Clients section, click the Move Clients to Wholesale button above the Actions column.**

   The Move Clients to Wholesale Billing page appears, displaying only those clients not currently part of your Wholesale Billing subscription. If you find you cannot select a particular client to add to your Wholesale Billing subscription, see the sidebar 'Why can't I migrate a client?'

5. **Click the check box beside each client you want to move and click Next.**

6. **Review your selections and, when you're satisfied they are correct, click Move Clients.**

   A page appears that identifies clients that migrated correctly and clients whose migration failed.

Removing clients from your Wholesale Billing subscription

Sometimes, things just don't work out between you and a client. If you have previously added that client's QBO company to your Wholesale Billing subscription and you need to part ways, you'll want to remove the client from your subscription. Follow these steps:

1. **Display the QBOA Clients page.**

2. **Click the Gear icon in the top right corner of the QBOA toolbar.**

3. **From the drop-down menu, under Your Company, select Your Account.**

   The Your Account window appears.

4. **Scroll down to the Wholesale Clients section and find the company you want to remove from your Wholesale Billing subscription.**

5. **In the Actions column, click Remove from Wholesale.**

Be aware that your Wholesale Billing subscription needs to be active to enable you to manage client QBO subscriptions.

REMEMBER

Once you remove a QBO company from your Wholesale Billing subscription, that QBO company will no longer be eligible for the wholesale discount, and all previous discounts will be removed as well. The client QBO subscriber will be billed the standard rate for his subscription unless the client establishes a relationship with another QBOA user. In this case, the client regains the discounts starting from the Wholesale Billing activation date.

Be aware that removing a client from your Wholesale Billing subscription doesn't remove the client from your Client List. And you can't delete QBO clients. But you can make them inactive, using these steps:

1. **Click Clients in QBOA to display your Client List.**

2. **Click the name of the client you want to make inactive.**

REMEMBER

It's very important to click the client's name in the Name column; clicking anywhere else on the client's line won't work.

A page like the one shown in Figure 13-18 appears.

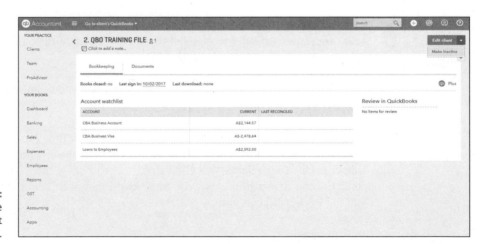

FIGURE 13-18:
The page you use to make a client inactive.

3. **Click the down arrow beside the Edit Client button.**

4. **Click Make Inactive.**

   QBOA asks if you're sure you want to make the client inactive.

5. **Click Yes.**

   QBOA redisplays the page shown previously in Figure 13-18, but '(deleted)' appears beside the client's name and the Edit Client button becomes the Make Active button.

6. **Click Clients in the Navigation bar.**

   The client no longer appears on the Clients page.

TIP

You can change the client's status back to Active if you opt to display inactive clients on the Clients page. Click the Gear button above the table on the Clients page and select the Include Inactive option (refer to Figure 13-14 to see the list). QBOA displays all your clients, both active and inactive. To make an inactive client active again, repeat the steps in this section, clicking the Make Active button in Step 4.

Stop using Wholesale Billing

So you've decided that you really don't want to participate in the Wholesale Billing program and manage QBO subscriptions for your clients. Although you can't cancel your Wholesale Billing subscription, you can stop using it. Nothing is stopping you from working with clients who manage their own QBO subscriptions.

REMEMBER

You can't cancel your Wholesale Billing subscription because that action would also cancel the QBO subscriptions of the clients assigned to your Wholesale Billing subscription.

First, you need to remove all the clients currently in your subscription using the steps in the preceding section.

After you have removed all companies from your Billing Profile, Intuit will no longer bill you because you won't have any QBO clients in your Wholesale Billing subscription. Your clients will then need to enter their own payment details to continue the subscriptions, so you and your clients can also continue accessing and using the QBO companies.

Chapter **14**

Adding Companies to the QBOA Client List

After signing up for QBOA and logging in (the topic of the previous chapter), the next step for the accountant is to populate the Client List with QBO clients, which can happen in a couple of ways. In addition, you might be helping a client set up a QBO company, either by creating a new company or by importing information into the QBO company.

This chapter shows you how to add client companies to the Client List and talks about data conversion considerations.

TIP

Need to remove a client from your Client List? Refer to Chapter 13 for details on making a client inactive.

Adding a Client's Company to the Client List

You can add a client company to the Client List in two ways:

>> By letting your client create the company and then inviting you (as their accountant or bookkeeper) to access the company

>> By creating a client's company for the client

If you create a client's company for the client and you participate in the Intuit Wholesale Pricing program (also called the Wholesale Billing program), you can opt to manage the client's subscription for them. In this case, Intuit bills you for the client's subscription and you then bill your client (refer to Chapter 13 for more information on the Wholesale Pricing program). Alternatively, the client can opt to manage their QBO subscription. At the time this book was written, Intuit was running specials on QBO through its main website. In addition, Intuit was offering discounts for QBO companies created by accountants using QBOA, regardless of whether the accountant or the client ultimately managed the client's QBO subscription.

TIP

The method you choose for creating a client company doesn't permanently affect the method chosen to manage the subscription; if you belong to the Intuit Wholesale Pricing program, you can always change subscription management later.

If you plan to manage your client's subscription as part of the Intuit Wholesale Pricing program, consider creating your client's company for them. For details on signing up for the Intuit Wholesale Pricing program, contact Intuit.

Adding a company created by a client

If a client creates her own company, she retains billing responsibility for the company. Even so, your client can invite you to access the company using the Invite Accountant process in QBO. Your client should follow these steps:

1. **Have the client open her company in QBO and click the Gear button on the top right of your screen.**

   QBO displays the client's Gear menu in QBO (see Figure 14-1).

2. **In the Your Company column, have your client click Manage Users.**

   The Manage Users page appears. This page identifies the company's Master Administrator, enables the client to add users to the QBO subscription (assuming it's not a Simple Start subscription), and also displays accounting firms the client has invited to access the QBO file (see Figure 14-2).

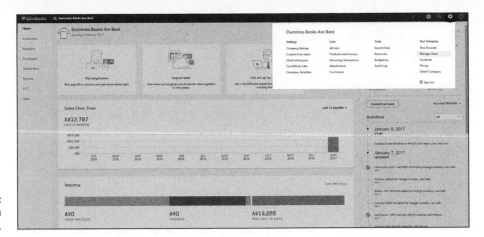

FIGURE 14-1:
The Gear menu in QBO.

FIGURE 14-2:
The Manage Users page.

3. **Have your client click the Invite Accountant button.**

TIP

If your client hasn't allowed pop-ups in the browser, she might see a message indicating that a pop-up was blocked. Have your client enable pop-ups for qbo.intuit.com.

The window shown in Figure 14-3 appears.

4. **Have your client provide your email address and click next.**

The Finish Inviting Account page appears, explaining that, when the client clicks Finish, an email will be sent to the accountant that invites the accountant to sign in to the client's company.

5. **Click Finish.**

The email message is sent and the Manage Users page is updated to indicate that the accountant has been sent an invitation.

Enter Accountant's email Address   Page 6 of 7

Accountant's email address

Confirm email

Name (Optional)
First   MI   Last

Your accountant will be sent an email that contains a link for signing into your company.

Your accountant will be asked to create a user ID before signing in the first time, unless they already have an account with Intuit.

Until your accountant signs in, their status on the Manage Users page is "Invited." After accepting the invitation, their status changes to "Active."

By default, your accountant will be given "Company Administrator" privileges for performing tasks like closing your books for prior periods. To change these privileges, click Edit on the Manager Users page.

Cancel   < Back   Next >

Privacy

FIGURE 14-3:
The client fills in the accountant's email information.

When you receive your client's email, it will look something like the one shown in Figure 14-4.

Dummies Books Are Best has invited you to access their QuickBooks as an accountant user.

Accept
Invitation

Dummies Books Are Best has invited you to access their QuickBooks Online company as an accountant user. When you accept this invitation, you'll be able to access Dummies Books Are Best's books using QuickBooks Online Accountant.

With QuickBooks Online Accountant, you can work with **any** of your clients, even if they don't use QuickBooks. Even better, it's free for accounting pros like you.

Click **accept invitation** to get started.

Have any questions? **Contact us**

We are looking forward to working with you!
The QuickBooks Online Accountant Team

Please don't reply directly to this email. It was sent from an account that can't accept replies.

FIGURE 14-4:
A sample email an accountant might receive when invited to access a client's QBO company.

Click the Accept Invitation link, and your default browser opens to the QBOA login page. Fill in your QBOA email or user ID and password, and QBOA opens; the new client appears in your list on the Client List page. Use the Team tab in the Navigation menu to identify the additional people in your firm who should have full access to the Client's QBO books. Select any member of your team followed by the Client Access tab and mark the check box alongside each company that you wish to give the team member access to (see Figure 14-5).

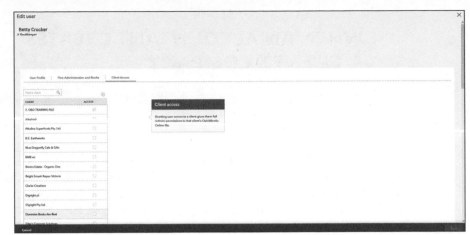

FIGURE 14-5:
After you accept
an invitation from
a client, use the
Client Access
page to identify
the members of
your firm who
should have
access to the
client's books.

QBO displays the Clients page and the new client appears in the list.

Creating a QBO company for a client

You, the accountant, can create a new QBO company for a client instead of having the client create the company. If you have signed up for the Intuit Wholesale Pricing program, billing responsibility for the QBO company you create becomes a matter of choice:

>> You can pay for the client's subscription and then bill the client back for the cost of the subscription.

>> You can transfer billing responsibility to the client.

At the time of writing (and this could change in the future), if a QBO client wants to remove an accountant, the firm managing the client's Wholesale Billing subscription must first remove the client from Wholesale Billing, even if the accountant the QBO client wants to remove is not affiliated with the firm managing the client's QBO subscription.

To remove a client from your Wholesale Billing subscription, follow these steps:

1. **In QBOA, click Gear ⇨ Your Account.**

   Your Account appears in the Your Company column of the Gear menu.

2. **In the Your Account window, scroll down to the Wholesale clients section and click the company you wish to remove from Wholesale Billing.**

3. **From the Actions column drop-down, click Remove from Wholesale.**

WHEN AN ACCOUNTANT CREATES A CLIENT'S COMPANY

If you create a company for a client through QBOA, it's important to understand that the QBO company does not get a 30-day trial period. However, ProAdvisor discounts can be applied to companies created through a trial period offer.

Further, things have changed concerning the way the Master Administrator role is assigned for clients who will be part of your Wholesale Billing subscription. You used to be assigned the Master Administrator role as you created the client's QBO company. Now, however, that restriction no longer exists. Whether the client will be part of your Wholesale Billing subscription or the client will be assuming billing responsibility, you can opt to be the Master Administrator or to assign that role to the client. For clients who want to be part of your Wholesale Billing subscription and assume the role of Master Administrator, you must be an invited accountant in the client's company.

If you retain the Master Administrator role, you can, at some later time, transfer Master Admin privileges back to the client. See the section 'Transferring Master Administrator rights back to your client', later in this chapter.

To create a company for your client, follow these steps:

1. **Open QBOA.**

2. **Click Clients in the Navigation bar to make sure you're displaying the Client List page.**

3. **From the Client List page, click the Add Client button in the upper right corner above the list.**

   The Add Client wizard begins, and you see the Client Contact Information page (see Figure 14-6).

4. **Provide a name for the new company.**

5. **Optionally, supply other information on this screen.**

6. **Select a QBO product for the client.**

   The Billing Choices list box appears. You can choose Simple Start, Essentials or Plus.

7. **Click the Billing Choices list box and select who will pay (see Figure 14-7).**

   A check box allows you to select if you want to be Master Admin or not; however, even if leaving the check box unticked (meaning you don't want to be Master Admin), you won't be asked for a Master Admin email address.

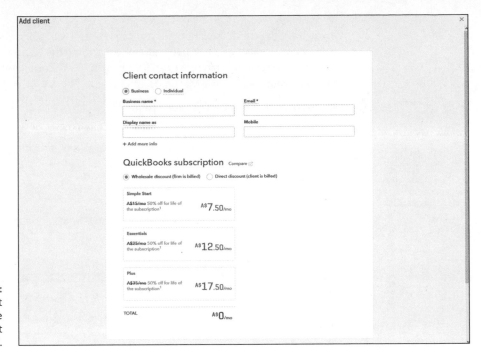

FIGURE 14-6:
The Client
Contact Info page
of the Add Client
wizard.

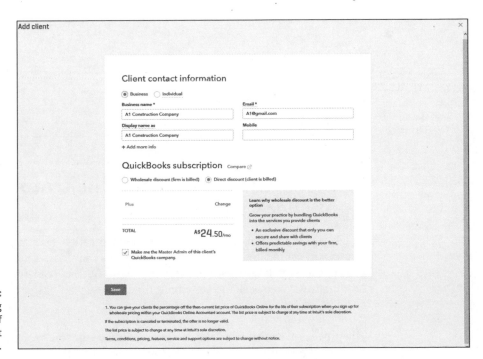

FIGURE 14-7:
The Billing
Choices page of
the Add Client
screen.

If you leave the check box unticked, you can proceed with subscribing. After that, add your client as a company administrator onto the file, and then transfer the Master Admin role to your client in order to complete the setup of having your client as the Master Admin.

8. **Assign permission levels for your team.**

QBOA displays the members of your team, and you can select who should have full administrative permissions when accessing the books of the client you're adding.

You can change access privileges later.

9. **Click Save.**

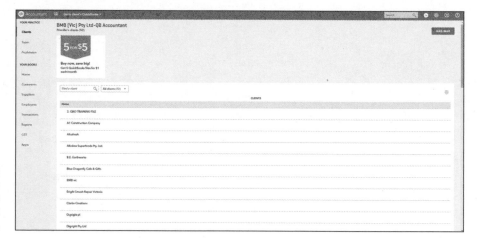

QBOA does some work and creates the company, which appears in the list of companies on the Client List page (see Figure 14-8).

FIGURE 14-8:
The new company appears on the Client List page.

Transferring Master Administrator rights back to your client

As you see in the preceding section, when you create a company for a client, you can assign yourself as the Master Administrator; in this case, QBOA also assigns you as the Accountant user for the company. But you can transfer the Master Administrator role back to your client; this process won't affect your status as the Accountant user.

The process of transferring the Master Administrator role to a client involves first inviting the client to become a Company Administrator. After the client accepts the invitation to become a Company Administrator, you can transfer the Master Administrator role to the client — again, using an invitation process.

Inviting the client to become a Company Administrator

As the first part of the process, create a Company Administrator for the new company. Follow these steps:

1. **Open the client company using the Go to Client's QuickBooks list on the QBOA toolbar.**

   TIP

   The first time you open a client QBO company, the Welcome to QuickBooks wizard walks you through some basic set-up steps, where you fill in the client's contact information, industry and legal organisation as well as some additional basic information, and QBO creates a Chart of Accounts for you.

2. **Click the Gear button on the QBOA toolbar and choose Manage Users.**

   QBO displays the Manage Users page (see Figure 14-9).

FIGURE 14-9:
The Manage Users page for a company created for a client by a QBOA user.

3. **Click Add User in the Manage Users section to add a new Company Administrator user.**

   A wizard starts.

4. **On the Choose User Type page, shown in Figure 14-10, select Company Administrator and click Next.**

5. **On the Enter User's Email Address page, shown in Figure 14-11, provide the client's email address (and optionally, name) and click Next.**

   The Finish Adding User page appears and explains that QBO will send an email invitation to the user to sign in to the company. The email explains that he must create a QBO user ID unless he already has one. In most cases, if you set up a company for a client, the client doesn't yet have a QBO login.

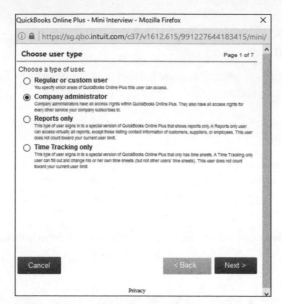

FIGURE 14-10:
Select Company
Administrator.

FIGURE 14-11:
Identify the user
you want to set
up as a Company
Administrator.

6. **Click Finish.**

The new user appears on the Manage Users page in Pending status (see Figure 14-12).

When the client receives the email invitation to become the Company Administrator, the invitation looks something like the one shown in Figure 14-13.

FIGURE 14-12:
The Manage
Users page after
successfully
sending a
message to a
client to become
a Company
Administrator.

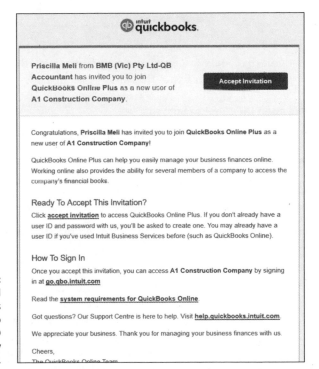

FIGURE 14-13:
The sample email
a client receives
when invited to
become a QBO
Company
Administrator.

When the client clicks the Accept Invitation button in the email to accept the invitation, a QBO login screen appears. Typically, the client doesn't have a QBO login yet and so goes through the process of creating a new one; when he finishes, he's logged in to QBO and receives a message indicating that he successfully accepted the invitation.

Transferring the Master Administrator role to the client

In the meantime, you, the QBOA user, can use QBOA to open the client's QBO company. On the Manage Users page, you can see that the status of the client's Company Administrator role is no longer Pending, but you are still listed as the Master Administrator (see Figure 14-14).

Now that you've established a Company Administrator for the client company, you can follow these steps to transfer the Master Administrator role to the client:

1. **In QBOA, open the client's company.**

2. **Click the Gear button on the QBOA toolbar and choose Manage Users.**

   The Manage Users page still lists you as the Master Administrator.

3. **Click Transfer Master Administrator.**

   The Transfer Master Administrator Role page appears (see Figure 14-15).

4. **Select a user who should assume the Master Administrator role.**

5. **Click Finish.**

QBOA sends an email invitation to your client to become the Master Administrator; the email looks very much like the one shown in Figure 14-16, and the client can accept or decline. Assuming the client accepts, he's prompted to log in to QBO. Once he does, he sees a page that explains that the Master Admin role has been successfully transferred to him and that an email explaining such has been sent to the former Master Administrator — and that's you.

If you once again use QBOA to open the client's company and view the Manage Users page, you'll notice that you no longer appear in the Manage Users section and your client is the Master Administrator for the company.

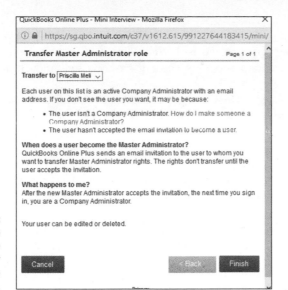

FIGURE 14-15:
Use this page to transfer the role of Master Administrator to your client.

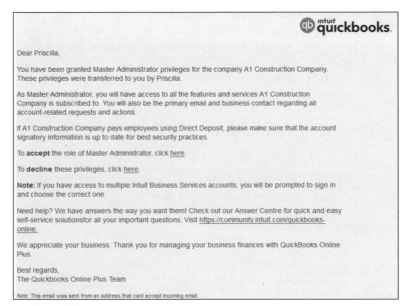

FIGURE 14-16:
A sample of the email the client receives when you invite them to become the Master Administrator.

General conversion considerations

QBO does allow you to import your company data into your new QBO file. Before you dive into converting your data, however, stack the odds in your favour by doing some homework. First, decide whether your current software file should be converted to QBO. If you are not 100 per cent satisfied with the integrity of your current file and suspect some gremlins may be lurking within, eating up your account balances, then perhaps it would be better to start off with a fresh file and simply import your customers, suppliers, chart of accounts and products and services over.

In this section we show you how you can enter open bills and invoices into QBO as part of an opening balance journal entry, as well as how you can enter that information in via the expenses and sales sections to ensure that the current invoice number and ageing periods are reflected in your new file.

If you do want Intuit to convert your current data to QBO (note that there are limitations to what information comes across), see the Appendix.

TIP

QBO allows users to enter multiple accounts payable and accounts receivable lines within a journal transaction, provided you associate a customer or supplier to that entry.

The benefit of entering Trade Debtors and Trade Creditors via journal entries is that the process is very quick and simple. The customers and suppliers appear in their respective screens alongside their balance payable or receivable. The downside to this approach is that invoice and bill numbers will start from 1001 and the date of the journal entry will determine the date of the invoices and bills — so you won't get accurate ageing information. You also won't know what they have bought, as the amount they owe gets offset against an income account directly and not through your products and services. Figure 14-17 shows a typical journal entry.

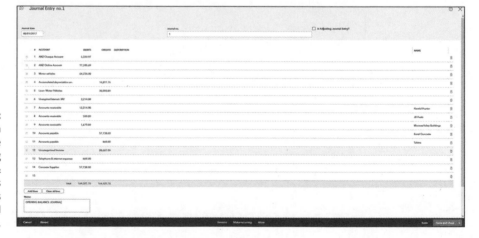

FIGURE 14-17:
Creating an opening balance journal including Trade Debtors & Creditors (Accounts Payable and Receivable).

The alternative is to exclude Trade Debtors and Creditors (Accounts Payable and Receivable) from your opening balance journal and enter their information in separately.

You may also like to activate the 'Custom Transaction Numbers' feature from the Company Settings section of the Gear Menu by clicking on the Sales tab. This will allow you to replicate the transaction's original invoice number when entering into QuickBooks (see Figure 14-18). You can de-activate this setting so that QBO automatically assigns invoice numbers that can't be accidently duplicated after this process.

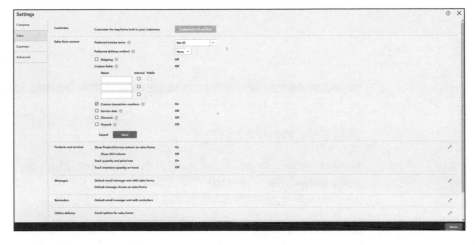

FIGURE 14-18: Activating the Custom Transaction Number feature.

Figures 14-19 and 14-20 show examples of manually entering invoices and bills. For instruction on entering invoices and bills, see Chapters 5 and 6.

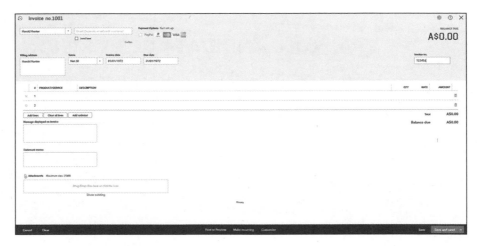

FIGURE 14-19: Manually entering open invoices for clients.

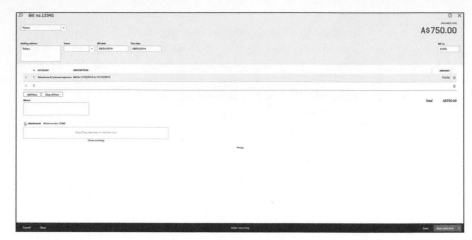

FIGURE 14-20:
Manually entering bills to pay to suppliers.

After converting . . .

After conversion finishes, you need to double-check things to make sure your data looks the way you expected. Check your email; you'll find the acknowledgement you received confirming that the data was imported.

After receiving this confirmation, we suggest you run and compare the Profit & Loss report, the Balance Sheet, Accounts Receivable, Accounts Payable, GST Liability and, if appropriate, Payroll Liability reports. Be sure you run these reports using the Accrual basis, with the dates set to All. Use the Accrual basis because reports run in both products using the Cash basis might not match.

PAYROLL AND DATA CONVERSION

In Chapter 9 we spoke about the Payroll feature in QBO coming from a third party software provider called KeyPay. Although this is the case, when you opt to have your file converted, some payroll data will come across via journal entry, such as current payroll expense and liability balances. You will need to do some housekeeping and set up opening balances for each employee, especially if your migration took place in the middle of the financial year, because you must ensure that the employees' Payment Summary values will be correct when lodged. For further details on setting up employees, refer to Chapter 9.

Starting Again

Need a do-over? During the first 90 days of a subscription, you get a 'do-over', which enables you to wipe the entire file clean and begin again. If this is something you need to do and you're feeling confident, simply follow these steps:

1. **Open the client's file.**

2. **In the address bar after you see the word 'APP', type 'PURGECOMPANY' as follows:** `https://sg.qbo.intuit.com/app/purgecompany`.

   You will see a screen similar to that shown in Figure 14-21.

FIGURE 14-21:
The screen that appears when you are purging a file.

3. **On the far bottom right side of the screen, type the word 'YES'.**

4. **In the next screen, select the button Wipe Data.**

Switching between Client QBO Companies

As you've worked through the previous chapter and this one, you might have noticed that client QBO companies don't, by default, open in a separate tab in your browser. So, what do you do when you want to stop working in one client's books and start working in another client's books?

Well, you can click the Accountant button on the QBOA toolbar at any time to redisplay the QBOA interface and your list of clients. From there, you can click the QuickBooks logo beside any client's name to open that client QBO company.

But you really don't need to take two steps to switch between client QBO companies; instead, take advantage of the Go to Client's QuickBooks list box on the QBOA toolbar.

When you're working in a client QBO company, the name of that company appears in the Go to Client's QuickBooks list box; if you click the company name, a list of all your client QBO companies appears. Just click the name of the company you want to open. No need to worry about saving work; QBO automatically saves as you work.

Chapter **15**

Exploring a Client's Company from QBOA

A client's QBO company looks a little different when viewed using QBOA. This chapter explores the interface you see when you open a client QBO company from QBOA. It also covers some facets of a client QBO company you might want to review for your client to make sure things flow smoothly for both of you.

Opening a Client's Company

You can open a client's company in QBOA from the Client List page; on the client's line in the list, click the QuickBooks logo (the circle with the letters *q* and *b* in it). Alternatively, you can use the Go to Client's QuickBooks list on the QBOA toolbar, which remains visible at all times, making it easy for you to switch from one client QBO company to another. Simply open the list and select the name of the company you want to open (see Figure 15-1).

You don't need to take any special action to close a client QBO company; you can simply open another client QBO company (see Figure 15-2), or you can sign out of QBOA from the Gear menu on the QBOA toolbar. If you want to return to your QBOA screen, select the Accountant button on the top left of your screen.

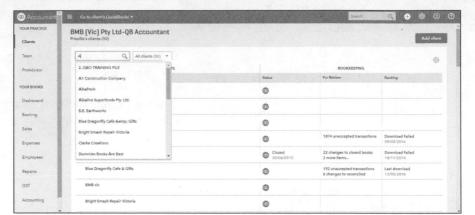

FIGURE 15-1:
You can click the QuickBooks logo or use the list on the QBOA toolbar to open a client's QBO company.

FIGURE 15-2:
Switching between client companies.

TIP

To access two different companies simultaneously, you can't just open another browser tab and sign in to QBOA. Instead, you need to use separate browsers. Or, if you're using Chrome, you can sign into Chrome as a different user. See Chapter 18 for details on Chrome users.

Reviewing a Client QBO Company

You'll probably want to review the company setup information for client QBO companies to make sure that things are set up properly for your client. In particular, you'll want to review the settings, the Chart of Accounts and the lists of client QBO companies.

TIP

The first time you open a client QBO company that you have created, a wizard walks you through establishing basic setup information. But you can review and change that information at any time.

Examining company setup information

You review company setup information to make sure that the client QBO company uses the correct accounting method and legal business entity. To review company settings, follow these steps:

1. **Open the client QBO company you want to review.**

You can click the QuickBooks logo on the Client List page of QBOA, or you can use the list of clients in the QBOA toolbar.

2. **Click the Gear button on the right side of the QBOA toolbar to display the Gear menu (see Figure 15-3).**

FIGURE 15-3:
The Gear menu.

3. **From the Settings group on the left side of the Gear menu, click Company Settings.**

The Company tab (selected on the left side of the Settings dialog box) appears (see Figure 15-4).

4. **Review the settings.**

In particular, set or correct the Company Name and Legal Name.

To make changes, click any setting. QBO makes the setting options available; make your changes and click Save.

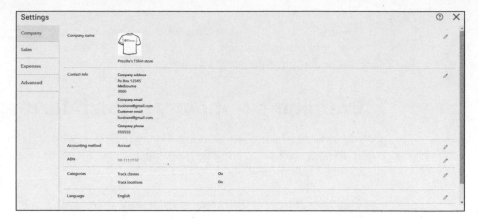

FIGURE 15-4:
The Company
Settings dialog
box for a client
QBO company.

5. **Click Advanced on the left side of the Company Settings dialog box.**

   The settings on the Advanced page of the Company Settings dialog box appear
   (see Figure 15-5).

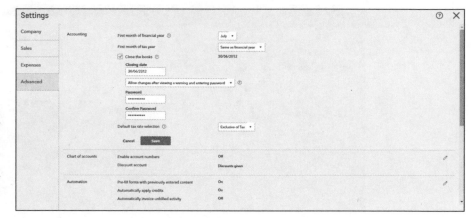

FIGURE 15-5:
Review and, if
necessary, make
changes to
settings on the
Advanced tab of
the Settings
dialog box.

6. **Review the settings.**

   In particular, set or correct the following:

   - The settings in the Accounting section, which include tax year information
     as well as the QBO company's accounting method

   - The settings in the Chart of Accounts section

   - The settings in the Other Preferences section, which includes displaying
     warnings when duplicate cheque numbers and bill numbers are used

7. **Click Done to save your changes.**

QBO displays a message at the top of the screen indicating that your changes were saved.

Taking a look at the Chart of Accounts

In addition to checking company settings, you should review your client's Chart of Accounts to make sure it looks the way you want. In the client QBO company, click the Accountant Tools button and choose Chart of Accounts (see Figure 15-6) to display the Chart of Accounts page shown in Figure 15-7.

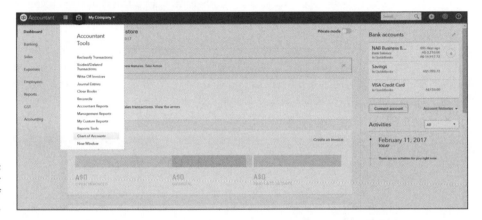

FIGURE 15-6: Accessing your client's Chart of Accounts.

FIGURE 15-7: From the Chart of Accounts page, you can add and edit accounts.

TIP

You could also access the Chart of Accounts for your client via the Accounting section of the Navigation menu or via the Gear icon on the top right of your screen, under the Settings heading. (All roads lead to Rome.)

If you chose to enable the option to use account numbers while you were reviewing the Advanced company settings (refer to Figure 15-5), the Chart of Accounts page displays a column for account numbers at the left edge of the Chart of Accounts page and the Batch Edit button in the upper right corner. You can use the Batch Edit button to add account numbers, as described later in this chapter in the section 'Adding account numbers'.

Editing or adding accounts

You might need to edit an account to change an account's Category Type or its name, and you use the Account window to make the change.

TIP

If you decide to add account numbers to the Chart of Accounts, you can add an account number in the Account window, but there's a much easier way, which we show you in the next section.

To display the Account window, click the down arrow in the Action column at the right side of the account and, from the menu that appears, click Edit (see Figure 15-8).

FIGURE 15-8:
To edit an account, use the down arrow in the Action column.

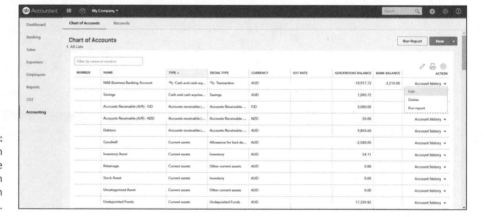

Or, if you need to create a new account, click the New button above the list. The window you see when creating a new account looks just like the one you see when you edit an existing account.

TIP

If you double-click an Asset, Liability or Equity account, QBO displays the account's ledger (except Retained Earnings, which displays a report). If you double-click an Income or Expense account, QBO displays a QuickReport for the account. You also can click the Account Activity and Report links in the Action column to display a ledger or a report.

Adding account numbers

In the preceding sections, we promised we'd show you an easy way to add account numbers to a QBO company Chart of Accounts. First, make sure you enable the setting on the Advanced tab of the Settings dialog box (in the Chart of Accounts section) shown previously in Figure 15-5.

Then, on the Chart of Accounts page, click the Batch Edit button (the one that looks like a pencil on the right side of the table above the table headings) to display the page shown in Figure 15-9.

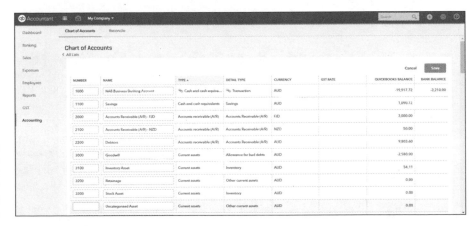

FIGURE 15-9:
Use this page to set up account numbers for the Chart of Accounts.

Type account numbers in the Number column. Save buttons appear at the top- and bottom-right corners of the page; click either button after you finish entering the account numbers.

TIP

Because a QBOA session times out by default after 60 minutes of non-use, you might want to save periodically as you enter account numbers.

TIP

After you enter account numbers, you can sort the Chart of Accounts in account number order by clicking Number in the column headings on the Chart of Accounts page.

Reviewing list information

You can review list information for your client QBO companies. Using the links in the Navigation bar, you can view overview information about customers, suppliers and employees. In Figure 15-10 we look at the Sales tab.

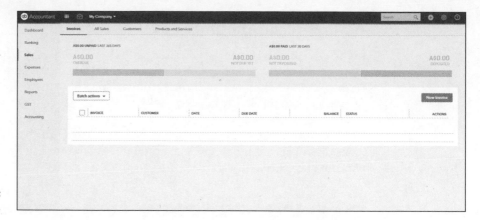

FIGURE 15-10:
The Sales tab.

From the tabs at the top of the Sales tab, you can view a recent list of invoices, sales and payments, customers, and a list of your client's products and services. You can also filter the list to view a particular subset of the list. For example, you can filter the list of customers on the Customers page to view only those customers with overdue invoices. And you can use the Batch Actions button (just below the filter bar) to perform, well, batch actions, such as sending statements to a batch of customers. If your list is long, use the text box beside the Batch Actions button to search for a particular list entry. You also can sort the list by name or by open balance; just click the appropriate heading below the Batch Actions button.

TIP

You can import names into a people list. For more information, refer to Chapter 4.

To review other lists, click the Gear button in the QBOA toolbar. In the Lists section of the Gear menu that appears, you can opt to view any of three common lists (the Currencies list, the Recurring Transactions list or the Attachments list). Or you can click All Lists at the top of the Lists section to display the Lists page shown in Figure 15-11, which you can use to navigate to any list other than a people-oriented list, including Location and Class lists.

For more extensive details on working with lists, refer to Chapter 4.

Exporting and importing bank feed rules

When your client takes advantage of bank feeds and downloads transactions from the bank to their QBO company, you can help ensure that the transactions post properly. In many cases, the rules used by one client can apply to another so, rather than re-creating rules, export them from one client and import them to another.

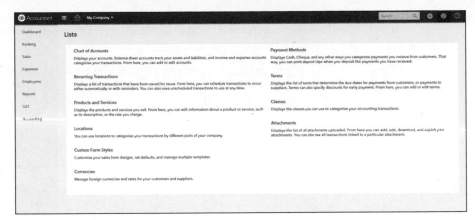

FIGURE 15-11:
Use this page to open any list other than the Customers or Suppliers lists.

When you export rules, QBO exports all the rules in the client's company. You can then selectively import rules.

To export rules from a client company, open that company and follow these steps:

1. **Choose the Banking link in the Navigation Menu.**

2. **On the Bank and Credit Cards page, click the down arrow beside the File Upload button in the upper right corner of the page.**

3. **Click Manage Rules.**

QBO displays the Rules page (see Figure 15-12).

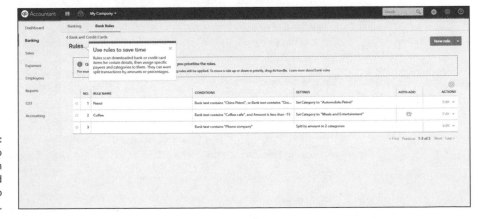

FIGURE 15-12:
Use this page to export rules from one client and import them to another.

4. **Click the down arrow beside the New Rule button and choose Export Rules.**

   QBO creates an Excel file containing the rules and stores it in your Downloads folder. The name of the file includes the name of the client whose rules you exported and the words 'Bank_Feed_Rules'.

   QBO displays the directions for what you do next — which we outline in the following steps. Click Close in the QBO message.

5. **Switch to the company to which you want to import these rules.**

6. **Repeat the preceding Steps 1 to 4; in Step 4, choose Import Rules.**

   QBO starts a wizard that helps you import the rules (see Figure 15-13).

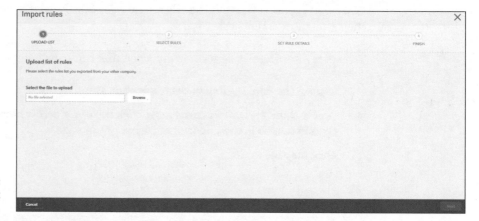

FIGURE 15-13:
The Import
Rules wizard.

7. **On the first Import Rules wizard screen, select the file you created in Step 4 and click Next.**

8. **On the second wizard screen, select the rules you want to import and click Next.**

9. **On the third wizard screen, you have the option to select categories for the rules that match the Chart of Accounts of the client to which you are importing the rules. Make any changes and, when you finish, click Import.**

   QBO tells you how many rules imported successfully.

10. **Click Finish.**

    QBO redisplays the Rules page for the client you opened in Step 5, where you can verify that the rules you wanted to import appear.

For more detail on working with rules, refer to Chapter 8.

Chapter **16**

Working in a Client's Company

You work in a client's QBO company in much the same way your client does; refer to Chapters 4 to 11 for detailed information. In this chapter, we focus on ways you can navigate easily using shortcuts, and search for and review transactions.

Making Navigation Easy

Much of mouse navigation is obvious; click here and click there. But you can use a few not-so-obvious tricks to navigate easily, including some keyboard shortcuts. Some common navigation techniques are specific to Chrome; see Chapters 18 and 19 for more information.

Using keyboard shortcuts

Hidden away in QBO companies are keyboard shortcuts that you might want to use. We show them here in Figure 16-1, and you also can find them on this book's cheat sheet.

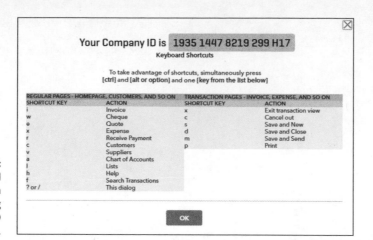

Your Company ID is 1935 1447 8219 299 H17

Keyboard Shortcuts

To take advantage of shortcuts, simultaneously press
[ctrl] and [alt or option] and one [key from the list below]

REGULAR PAGES - HOMEPAGE, CUSTOMERS, AND SO ON		TRANSACTION PAGES - INVOICE, EXPENSE, AND SO ON	
SHORTCUT KEY	ACTION	SHORTCUT KEY	ACTION
i	Invoice	x	Exit transaction view
w	Cheque	c	Cancel out
e	Quote	s	Save and New
x	Expense	d	Save and Close
r	Receive Payment	m	Save and Send
c	Customers	p	Print
v	Suppliers		
a	Chart of Accounts		
l	Lists		
h	Help		
f	Search Transactions		
? or /	This dialog		

OK

FIGURE 16-1:
Keyboard shortcuts you can use while working in a client QBO company.

TIP

To get this cheat sheet, simply go to www.dummies.com and search for 'QuickBooks Online For Dummies Cheat Sheet' in the Search box.

To view these shortcuts (and the current client QBO Company ID), press and hold Ctrl+Alt and then press the forward slash (/) key. Mac users, substitute Option for Alt here and in the next paragraph. If you press Ctrl+Alt+/ without opening a client QBO company, the Company ID you see is your own.

To use any of these shortcuts, press and hold Ctrl+Alt and then press the appropriate key to perform its associated action. For example, to open the Invoice window, press Ctrl+Alt+I.

Opening multiple windows

Many times, accountants want to work with multiple windows, and you can do that in QBO. Within the same QBO company, you can duplicate a browser tab using the New Window command on the Accountant Tools menu on the QBOA toolbar (see Figure 16-2). You can read more about the other commands on the Accountant Tools menu in Chapter 17.

TIP

If you're using Chrome, you also can duplicate a browser tab by right-clicking the tab and choosing Duplicate. In Firefox, you can duplicate a browser tab by clicking in the address bar and pressing Alt+Enter.

When you click the New Window command, QBO opens a new browser tab and displays the same information that appears in the original browser tab. But, from that point, you can display different information for the same company in each browser tab. And, if you're working in Chrome on multiple monitors, you can split the tabs onto different monitors. Drag the tab you want to place on a different monitor in a downward direction, and it splits away from the browser. You can immediately drag it to another monitor or you can release the mouse button, in which case a second instance of Chrome appears. You can then drag either instance to a different monitor.

FIGURE 16-2:
Use the New Window command while working in a QBO company to duplicate the window you're viewing.

TIP

The same technique works in Firefox; drag a Firefox tab downward and release the mouse button. The tab splits away and appears in a second instance of Firefox. You can then drag either instance to a different monitor.

Working in two companies simultaneously

Suppose that you're done working with one client and want to open a different client. As described in Chapter 14, you can click the Go to Client's QuickBooks button on the QBOA toolbar and select a new client. Or you can click the Accountant button in the upper left corner of the QBOA interface to redisplay the Client List page and then click the QuickBooks icon for the client QBO company you now want to open. Either way, QBOA displays the information for the newly selected client.

That brings up the question, 'How do I work in two different companies simultaneously?' Well, you can open a different browser, sign in to QBOA and open a second client QBO company. For example, if you're working in Chrome, you could open Firefox using the same QBOA login information. You can then open two different companies, as we show in Figure 16-3.

If you're working in Chrome, you also can take advantage of Chrome users and open Chrome as a different user. You'd have, effectively, two instances of Chrome running simultaneously. See Chapter 18 for more information on Chrome users.

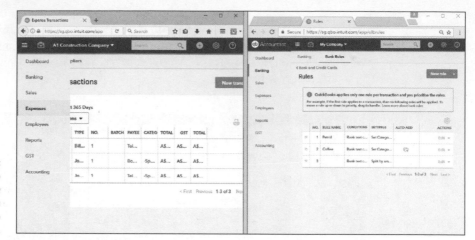

FIGURE 16-3:
To work in two companies at the same time, you can use two browsers.

Examining Available Transaction Types

In Chapters 5 to 9, we cover transactions in some detail, so we're not going to repeat that information here. But you can see the available transactions by opening a client QBO company and then clicking the Create menu (the plus sign) shown in Figure 16-4. Available transactions are organised on the menu by the type of people to which they pertain. And the Create menu contains an 'Other' category for transactions that don't pertain to particular types of people — like bank deposits.

REMEMBER

Before you open the Create menu, its button appears as a plus sign (+), but after you open it, as we did in Figure 16-4, the button changes to an X.

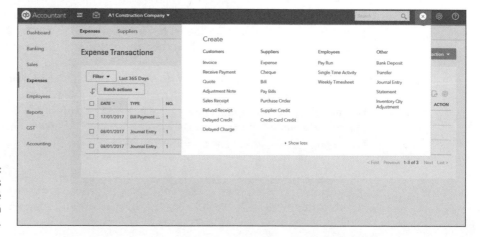

FIGURE 16-4:
The transactions you can create while working in a QBO company.

If you want to view only the more commonly used transactions, click the Show Less link at the bottom of the Create menu. The link changes to the Show More link so that you can redisplay all types of transactions.

Searching for Transactions

More often than not, you'll be searching for transactions in a client QBO company rather than creating them. You can search for transactions using the Search box on the QBOA toolbar at the top of the client QBO company window (see Figure 16-5). When you click in the Search box, QBO displays a list of recent transactions and reports.

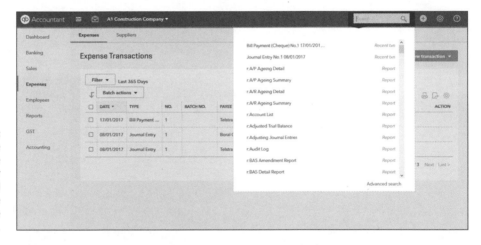

FIGURE 16-5:
Type any phrase you want to use as a search filter or click Advanced Search at the bottom of the Search list.

If you see the result you want, you can click it to open it in the appropriate window. If you *don't* see the result you want, you have a couple of options.

First, you can type in the Search box, and QBO responds with sample results. If you still don't see the result you want, try your second option: Click Advanced Search in the lower right corner of the menu, and QBO displays the Search page (see Figure 16-6).

You can limit the search to a particular transaction type, choose to search for any of several types of data, and specify whether the search should contain, not contain, be equal to or not be equal to the search criteria.

TIP

From any transaction window, you can view recent transactions of that type by simply clicking in the search field without typing anything.

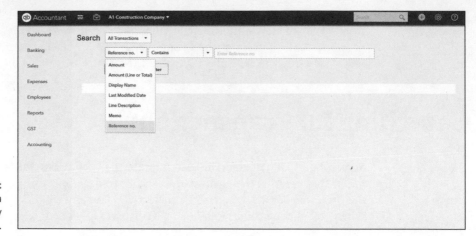

FIGURE 16-6:
Set criteria for a more specifically defined search.

Chapter **17**

Using Accountant Tools

A ccountant Tools are available to anybody who opens a client QBO company from QBOA. You can become a user in a QBO company in one of two ways:

» As described in Chapter 14, your client can invite you to be the Accountant user on her account. But each QBO company can have only two Accountant users.

» As described in Chapter 13, the Master Administrator of the QBOA account can set up users.

This chapter takes you through using the Accountant Tools to make your life a lot easier.

Facilitating Accountant Activities

Accountants often need to reclassify transactions, examine voided and deleted transactions, write off invoices and perform other activities. QBOA contains tools to make performing these activities easy.

The Accountant Tools menu contains a few tools that make an accountant's life easier, such as the Reconcile page; from this page, you can opt to reconcile an account you select, or you can review existing reconciliation reports.

Also from the Accountant Tools menu, you can choose Journal Entries to display the Journal Entry window, or Chart of Accounts to display the Chart of Accounts window. You also can use the New Window command to quickly open a new window in QBOA.

To view and use the tools QBOA makes available to accountants, open any client QBO company. Then, on the QBOA toolbar, click the Accountant Tools button (the one that contains the icon that looks like a suitcase). QBOA displays the Accountant Tools menu, shown in Figure 17-1.

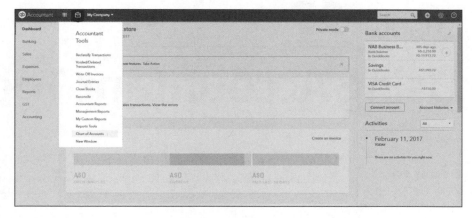

FIGURE 17-1:
The Accountant Tools menu contains commands specifically designed to aid the accountant.

Running through Accountant Tools

In this section, we take you through some of the Accountant Tools you'll likely find most useful.

Using Reports Tools

The Reports Tools feature found in the Accountants Tools list allows the accountant or bookkeeper to set default report dates, lock (close) the books and view a list of accounts along with their reconciliation status (see Figure 17-2).

Reclassifying transactions

When you choose Reclassify Transactions from the Accountant Tools menu, the Reclassify Transactions page appears (see Figure 17-3). You can use this page to reclassify transactions without worrying about the company's closing date.

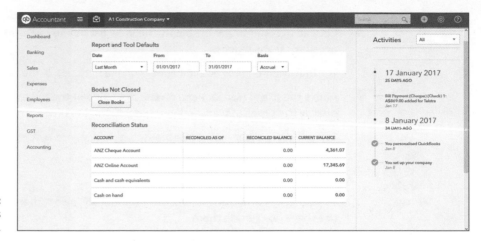

FIGURE 17-2:
The Reports Tools screen.

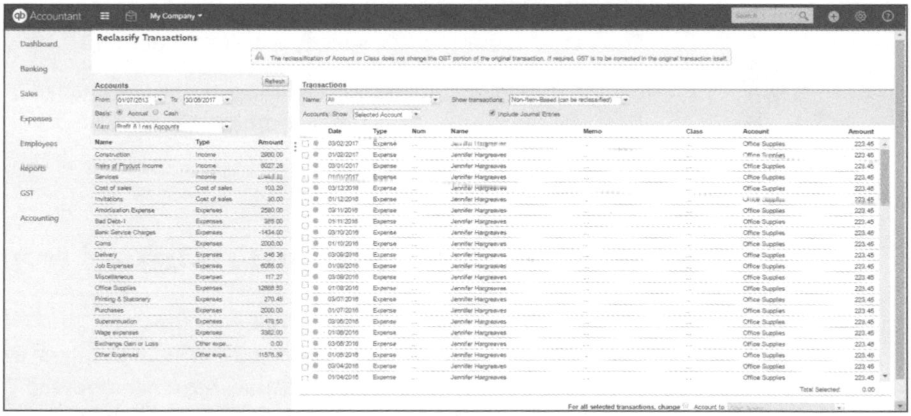

FIGURE 17-3:
Use this page to reclassify transactions.

You use the information in the grey areas of the Accounts section on the left side of the page and the Transactions section on the right side of the page to filter for the date range and type of accounts (Profit and Loss or Balance Sheet) you want to consider. You then select an account on the left side of the page, and QBOA displays transactions that meet the criteria on the right side of the page. You can reclassify, individually or as a group, transactions that display a green circle.

Follow these steps to reclassify transactions:

1. On the left side of the page, set the date range you want to consider, along with the accounting basis.

2. From the View list box, select the type of accounts you want to consider — Profit & Loss accounts or Balance Sheet accounts.

3. **Click an account in the list below the View list box to examine that account's transactions.**

   The transactions in the account appear on the right side of the page.

4. **Above the list of transactions on the right side of the page, set filters to display the types of transactions that you might consider reclassifying.**

   You can make changes to transactions that display green circles.

   You can click a transaction to open it in its transaction window and then make changes to it.

5. **To change several transactions simultaneously, select them by clicking the check box beside them.**

6. **Below the list of transactions, select the For All Selected Transactions, Change check box.**

7. **From the Account To list, specify a different account.**

   If Class Tracking is turned on, you'll also see a field to change the assigned class, the same way you can change an Account.

8. **Click the Reclassify button.**

Examining voided and deleted transactions

You can click Voided/Deleted Transactions on the Accountant Tools menu to display the Audit Log. The default view of the Audit Log (see Figure 17-4), shows information about those transactions that have been voided or deleted. But you can click the Filter button to set a variety of different filters to view other types of transactions and events.

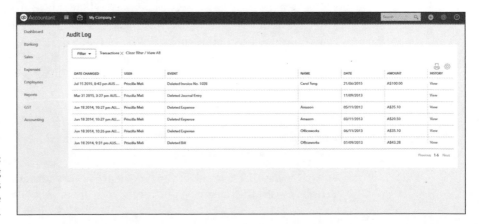

FIGURE 17-4:
Use the Audit Log to view all kinds of activity in the QBO company.

Writing off invoices

Choosing Write Off Invoices from the Accountant Tools menu displays the Write Off Invoices page, which enables you to view invoices you might want to write off, and then write them off to an account of your choice. *Note:* This does not currently take the GST component into consideration.

At the top of the page, you set filters to display the invoices you want to review. Select the age of the invoices to view those

>> Greater than 180 days

>> Greater than 120 days

>> In the current accounting period

>> In a custom date range you set

You also can set a balance limit.

As you can see in Figure 17-5, QBOA displays the date, age, invoice number, customer name, original invoice amount, and the amount still due on the invoice. To write off any invoices, click the check box beside them. Then, at the bottom of the page, select the account you want to use to write off the invoices and click the Preview and Write Off button.

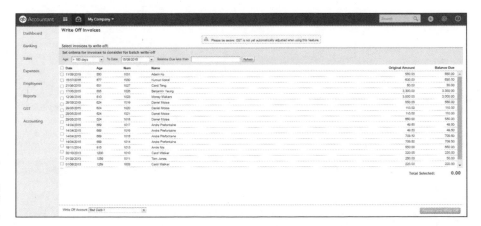

FIGURE 17-5:
Writing off
invoices.

QBOA displays the Confirm Write Off dialog box shown in Figure 17-6. If the information in the dialog box is correct, click Write Off. Otherwise, click Cancel.

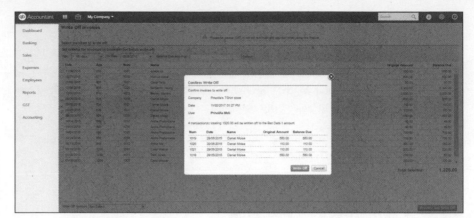

FIGURE 17-6:
Confirm that you
want to write off
the selected
invoices.

Closing the books

You use the Close Books command on the Accountant Tools menu to display the
Advanced page of the QBO company's Settings dialog box, shown in Figure 17-7.
You can click anywhere in the Accounting section to edit the fields in that section,
which include the closing date for the books.

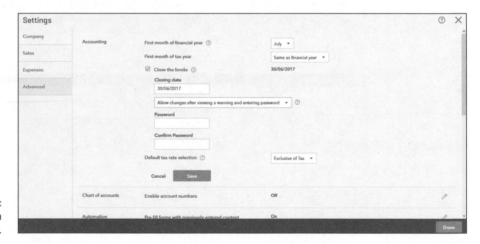

FIGURE 17-7:
Setting a
closing date.

You can set a closing date and then allow changes after the closing date after QBO
issues a warning, or you can require a password to enter changes after the closing
date. Click Done to save your changes.

Reviewing reports

Reports in QBOA work the same way as reports in QBO; refer to Chapter 11 for details.

But QBOA contains some reports of particular interest to accountants. If you open a client QBO company and then, from the Accountant Tools menu, click Accountant Reports, the Reports page appears. The Accountant Reports tab spotlights the reports available to QBOA users, as shown in Figure 17-8.

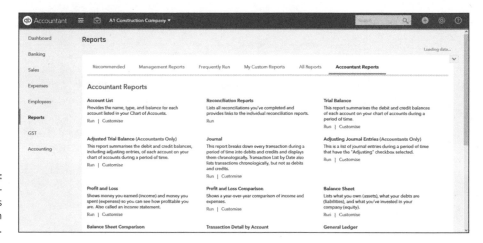

FIGURE 17-8:
Accountant-
oriented reports
available in
QBOA.

If you choose Management Reports from the Accountant Tools menu (or if you click the Management Reports tab that appears on the Reports page shown in Figure 17-9), QBOA displays two customised management-style reports: Expanded Company Financials and Basic Company Financials. Both reports display a collection of reports, complete with an elegant cover page and a table of contents.

The Expanded Company Financials report contains the Profit and Loss, Balance Sheet, Statement of Cash Flows, and the A/R Ageing Detail and A/P Ageing Detail reports. The Basic Company Financials report contains all reports except the Ageing Detail reports. Using the Edit link in the Action column, you can edit either report package to add or delete reports and modify the appearance of pages in the report, including determining whether pages such as the table of contents appear in the report. Using the down arrow that appears in the Action column, you can print these reports, send them via email, export the information to .PDF files or .DOCX files, and make copies of them so that you can make your own set of management reports.

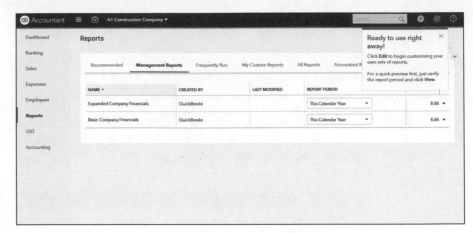

FIGURE 17-9:
Management reports exclusive to QBOA.

TIP

Copying one of these reports before you change it is a great idea; that way, you keep the original report intact but create your own version of it as well.

If you choose My Custom Reports from the Accountant Tools menu or from the Reports page, reports you have customised and saved appear.

The Part of Tens

IN THIS CHAPTER

» **Becoming familiar with Chrome users**

» **Working with Chrome windows and tabs**

» **Getting to know the Omnibox**

» **Understanding the star**

» **Learning about the Chrome Menu**

» **Signing in to and out of Chrome**

» **Using the Chrome Web Store**

Chapter **18**

Almost Ten Things about the Chrome Browser Interface

C hrome — officially Google Chrome — is the free web browser created by Google, Inc., the American-based multinational corporation that focuses on Internet-related products and services, such as Gmail for email, Google Maps and Google Docs, just to name a few. Most of Google's profits come from online advertising technologies.

You can use QuickBooks Online (QBO) and QuickBooks Online Accountant (QBOA) in the Chrome, Firefox, Safari and Internet Explorer browsers (at the time of writing, you could use Microsoft Edge, but not to export to the QuickBooks desktop product). In our experience, we find that QBO and QBOA work best in Chrome. If you're not familiar with Chrome or haven't worked much in it, this chapter and Chapter 19 are designed to help you become adept at using Chrome with QBO and QBOA. This chapter focuses on helping you become familiar with the Chrome interface and make use of it. Figure 18-1 shows you how Chrome looks shortly after you install and open it; don't forget to refer back to this figure as you read the chapter.

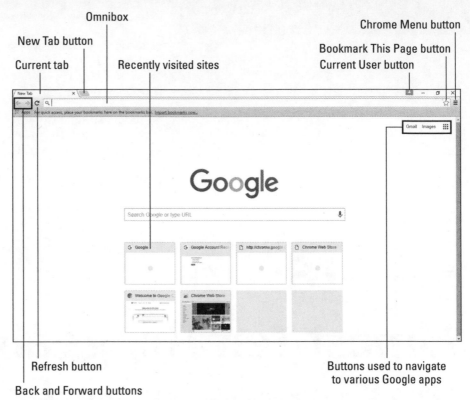

Omnibox

New Tab button

Current tab

Recently visited sites

Chrome Menu button

Bookmark This Page button

Current User button

FIGURE 18-1:
Reviewing the
Chrome interface.

Refresh button

Back and Forward buttons

Buttons used to navigate
to various Google apps

Google and the Google logo are registered trademarks of Google Inc., used with permission.

TIP

If you don't already have Chrome installed on your computer, you can visit www.google.com/chrome/browser/. From this web page, you can download and install Chrome.

Understanding Users

The Current User button in the top right corner of the screen represents a Chrome user. The icon may appear generically, as you see it in Figure 18-1, or it may display your name or email address. In Chrome, you can set up multiple users, each of whom can have different Chrome settings. In this way, each person using Chrome on a single computer can customise the program, saving his or her own bookmarks, passwords and more. See Chapter 19 to learn how to create a Chrome user.

Windows and Tabs

You can open Chrome more than once to view multiple web pages — a process called *opening a new window*.

To open a new window, first open Chrome. Then press Ctrl+N, and a second instance of the Chrome browser appears. In Figure 18-2, we've resized Chrome's second window so that you can see both instances of Chrome. Also notice that two buttons for Chrome appear in the Windows taskbar.

Two instances of Chrome

FIGURE 18-2:
When you open a new Chrome window, two instances of Chrome run simultaneously.

Two Chrome icons appear on the task bar.

But in most cases, you don't need to open multiple instances of Chrome; you can use Chrome's tabs to display multiple web pages while you work.

Tabs appear at the top of the Chrome window and initially display the same short-cuts you see when you open a new window. You can add a tab by clicking the New Tab button, which appears just beside the last open tab (refer back to Figure 18-1). And, you can close any tab by clicking the X that appears in the tab. You also can reposition tabs in the Chrome window by dragging a tab's title.

In either a new window or a new tab, you navigate to a new website using the Omnibox (read on).

Using the Omnibox to Visit a Web Page

You've probably heard of the *address bar* in other browsers; Chrome refers to the text box at the top of the browser as the *Omnibox* because it's a multi-purpose box.

To visit a web page, type the address of the web page into the Omnibox and either press Enter or click the Refresh button. After you've visited a few websites, you can click the Back and Forward buttons to revisit pages you have recently visited in the order you visited them.

TIP

If you right-click or click and hold either the Back button or the Forward button, you can view a historical list of the websites you have visited. You can left-click one to return to it.

Using the Omnibox to Search the Web

Chrome uses the Omnibox to combine the functions of navigating to websites and searching the Internet; as you might expect, Chrome uses Google's search engine by default. You can type a search term into the Omnibox and, as you type, suggestions driven by Google's search technology appear. You can then click a suggestion to navigate to the associated Google search page or web page.

A grey icon appears to the left of each suggestion in the Omnibox; the icon indicates the type of suggestion:

>> A piece of paper represents a page you've viewed previously or a website related to what you're typing.

>> A magnifying glass indicates that the suggestion is a potential search term.

>> A star identifies a suggestion as one of your existing bookmarks (see the next section for more on bookmarks).

What's the Star?

You can easily save the web address of a site you visit frequently so that you don't have to type the address each time you want to visit the site. In Chrome, saving a web address is called *bookmarking*, and you click the star icon to create a bookmark for the web page you are currently viewing. You can read more about working with bookmarks, including managing bookmarks, in Chapter 19.

Examining the Chrome Menu

You can click the Chrome Menu button (see Figure 18-3) to view a series of commands that help you work in Chrome.

Chrome Menu button

Chrome Menu

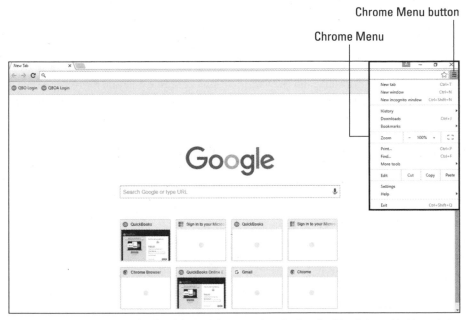

FIGURE 18-3:
The Google
Chrome Menu.

Using options on the Chrome Menu, you can

>> Work with bookmarks (described in Chapter 19)

>> Reopen recently closed tabs

>> Copy and paste text

>> Save a web page

>> Clear browsing data

>> Find text on a web page

>> Print a web page

>> View files you have downloaded

>> Make changes to Chrome's settings

The options available to you on the Chrome Menu aren't limited to the ones we've listed — there are too many for us to list them all. But, for example, if you want to see how your web browsing affects your computer's use of memory, you can choose Chrome Menu ⇨ More Tools ⇨ Task Manager.

About Signing in to (and out of) Chrome

We're going to repeat ourselves in this section because it's important for you to understand the ramifications of signing in and signing out of Chrome. Let us start by saying — emphasising, in fact — that you don't have to sign in to use Chrome. In particular, you don't need to sign in to Chrome to use QBO or QBOA.

That said, why sign in? If you sign in, bookmarks and passwords you save, browsing history and settings are saved to the cloud. You can then sign in to Chrome on a different computer and use all your settings from that computer or any computer.

The act of signing in can result in some negative side effects. Even though you sign out of Chrome, Chrome can still remember some of your information, making it visible to anyone who uses Chrome on the same computer. And, on a public computer, leaving traces of your activity could result in others gaining access to your personal information, email and saved passwords.

WARNING

We strongly urge you to avoid signing in to Chrome if you are using a public computer. Remember, you don't need to sign in to Chrome to use QBO or QBOA. And, we'll be repeating this warning again in this chapter (editors, take note) because it's important to the security of your financial data.

If you want to sign in to Chrome, you need a Google account. If you have a Gmail email address, you already have an account, and you can skip the next section.

Creating a Google account

If you don't have a Google account, you can easily create one; creating a Google account automatically creates a Gmail email address and a Google+ profile. Once you have a Google account, you can use Google services such as Gmail, Google Docs and Google Calendar.

REMEMBER

If you already have a Gmail email address, you already have a Google account. Skip the following steps and continue in the next section.

Follow these steps to create a Google account:

1. **Navigate to** www.google.com.

2. **Click the Sign In button in the top right corner of the page.**

3. **On the page that appears, click the Create Account link.**

   The link appears below the box where you would ordinarily provide your email address.

4. **Provide the requested information.**

   The requested information includes your name, a username, which is a proposed Gmail email address and associated password, birth date, gender, mobile phone number, current email address and the country in which you live. Note that your mobile phone number is actually optional.

5. **Click the Prove You're Not a Robot check box and provide the verification information.**

6. **Check the I agree to the Google Terms of Service and Privacy Policy box.**

   You can click the links for Terms of Service and Privacy Policy to review the statements.

7. **Click Next Step.**

   At this point, you will probably be prompted to verify your account using either a text message or a voice call; select a method and, when you receive the verification information, provide it onscreen.

8. **On the Create Your Profile page, you can add a photo to your Google+ profile.** If you don't want to set a profile photo at this time, click Continue.

   Google creates your account.

Signing in to Chrome

If you sign in to the Chrome browser, bookmarks and passwords you save, browsing history and settings are available to you from any computer.

WARNING

Avoid signing in to Chrome if you are using a public computer, because signing out might not remove all your information, leaving it visible to anyone who uses Chrome on the computer.

To sign in to Chrome, follow these steps:

1. **Click the User icon in the top right corner of the browser.**

2. **Click Sign in to Chrome.**

   The sign-in form appears, requesting your Google Account email.

3. **Type your email address and click Next.**

4. **Type your password and click Next.**

   A message appears, letting you know you are signed in to Chrome (see Figure 18-4).

5. **Click OK, GOT IT.**

   The Current User button changes to reflect either your name or your email address — an indication that you are signed in to Chrome.

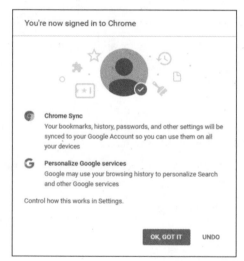

FIGURE 18-4: Once you've signed in to Chrome, this message appears.

Google and the Google logo are registered trademarks of Google Inc., used with permission.

Signing out of Chrome

You should sign out of your Google account when you finish using Chrome, or when you no longer want changes you make on your computer saved to your Google account and synced to Google Chrome on your other devices. Signing out also can help if you think an error with Chrome's synchronisation has occurred, and you want to try to fix the error by signing out and then signing in again.

REMEMBER

By default, when you sign out of your Google account in the browser window, you leave behind traces of yourself. On a public computer, it's possible that other people might gain access to your personal information, email and saved passwords.

An option appears during the sign-out process that you can select to eliminate all traces of you on the computer. The option deletes saved information on the local computer about the Chrome user who signed in.

WARNING

On your own private computer, deleting all traces of the user who signed in, including the user profile, might be a bit more drastic than you want. You can opt to clear history separately and less drastically; see Chapter 19 for details on clearing history. But if you're working on a public computer, you should delete the user as well as the user's settings.

Follow these steps to sign out of Chrome:

1. **Click the Chrome Menu button to open the Chrome Menu.**

2. **Click Settings.**

   The Chrome Settings page appears (see Figure 18-5).

3. **In the Sign In section at the top of the page, click Disconnect your Google Account.**

   A confirmation dialog box appears (see Figure 18-6).

4. **Select the Also Clear Your History, Bookmarks, Settings, and Other Chrome Data Stored on This Device check box if you want to eliminate all traces on the computer of the user who signed in to Chrome.**

WARNING

   Checking this box deletes everything on the computer associated with the user — your account history, bookmarks, settings and other Chrome data saved on the computer. We can't repeat this mantra often enough: If you are working on a public computer, you should safeguard your privacy and check this box. However, if you're working on a private computer, you can safely keep the user and optionally clear history. To keep the user, do not check this box; see Chapter 19 for details on clearing history.

5. **Click Disconnect Account.**

    Google signs you out of your Google account and Chrome. The appearance of the Current User button returns to a generic form.

Using the Chrome Web Store

You can enhance the capabilities of Chrome using web apps, plug-ins, and extensions such as calculators, ad blockers or password managers. These browser-capable enhancers work like software you install on your computer, phone or tablet, but they typically function within Chrome.

WEB APPS AND PLUG-INS AND EXTENSIONS, OH MY!

So what exactly is a web app and how does it differ from a plug-in or extension? Honestly, for the purposes of this book, you probably don't care. But, for better or for worse, here are some simple definitions:

- Web apps run inside your browser with their own dedicated user interface.

- Extensions, unlike web apps, do not typically have a user interface. Instead, they extend the functionality of Chrome and the websites you view using Chrome.

- Plug-ins are similar to extensions in that they extend functionality by helping Chrome process special types of web content, but a plug-in affects only the specific web page that contains it.

So, as you can see, each has a technical definition that distinguishes it from the others but, for most of us, the bottom line is this: All of them enhance the capabilities of a browser by providing some functionality that the browser does not, inherently, provide.

You can obtain web apps, plug-ins and extensions from the Chrome Web Store found at chrome.google.com/webstore. The Chrome Web Store provides tools you can use to search for web apps, plug-ins and extensions.

Web apps you install should appear on the New Tab page, from which you can launch them. You also can remove a web app by right-clicking it on the New Tab page and then clicking Remove from Chrome.

Extensions run by default when you open Chrome. You can view a list of installed extensions from the Settings page. Choose Chrome Menu ⇨ Settings. Then, on the left side of the Settings page, click Extensions (see Figure 18-7).

FIGURE 18-7:
You can view and enable or disable extensions from the Settings page.

Click here to view installed extensions.

You might want to disable an extension if you suspect it is causing a conflict as you work; uncheck the Enabled check box beside the extension. If the extension proves to be the source of your problem, you can delete it by clicking the trash can icon beside it.

TIP

If you click the Get More Extensions link at the bottom of the Settings page where you view an extension, Chrome opens a new tab and takes you to the Chrome Web Store, where it displays, by default, available extensions.

Plug-ins enable certain types of web content that browsers can't process. When Chrome encounters a plug-in on a web page, Chrome allows the plug-in to perform its function. Learn more about managing plug-ins in Chapter 19.

Selecting a Theme

You can use *themes* to change the appearance of Chrome. Themes can change the colour of the Chrome window, or they can add background pictures to the entire browser. The idea here is to provide some interest to the browser page background.

You can find available themes in the Chrome Web Store; in the Navigation pane that runs down the left side of the Chrome Web Store page, click Themes to pre-view available themes.

If you install a theme and then later change your mind about using it, choose Chrome Menu ⇨ Settings. On the Settings page, in the Appearance section, click Reset to Default Theme.

Chapter **19**

Ten Ways to Use Chrome Effectively

C hapter 18 helps you understand and work with the Chrome interface. This chapter introduces some browser tips and tricks that can make using Chrome easier and more effective — both in general, and specifically with QBO and QBOA.

Setting a Home Page

Many browsers sport a button that you can click to return to your *Home page* — the page that appears when you open the browser. When you open Chrome, by default, the New Tab page appears. Although Chrome doesn't show the Home page button by default, you can display it and also set a page that will appear when you click the Home page button. *Note:* Chrome doesn't display the page you set as the Home page when you open the browser; instead, the Home page appears when you click the Home page button.

Before you begin the following steps, make sure you know the web address of the page you want to set as your Home page:

1. **Choose Chrome Menu ⇨ Settings.**

   The Settings tab appears.

2. **In the Appearance section, click the Show Home button check box.**

   The Home button appears between the Refresh button and the Omnibox (see Figure 19-1). At this point, Chrome opens the New Tab page whenever you click the Home button.

Home button

Google and the Google logo are registered trademarks of Google Inc., used with permission.

FIGURE 19-1: Adding the Home button and setting a Home page.

Show Home Button check box   Click here to set a Home page address.

3. **Click Change.**

   The Home page dialog box appears (see Figure 19-2).

4. **Select the Open This Page option and type a web address.**

5. **Click OK.**

   When you click the Home button, Chrome displays the page you set as your Home page.

FIGURE 19-2:
Use this dialog
box to type the
web address of
your Home page.

*Google and the Google logo are registered trademarks of
Google Inc., used with permission.*

TIP

If you open certain sites every time you start Chrome, you can pin each page as a tab. See the section 'Duplicating and Pinning Tabs'.

Chrome and Security

Chrome includes several tools that help to keep you safe online. As you are no doubt aware, bad things can happen as you browse the Internet. You can run into *phishing* schemes, where someone tries to trick you into sharing personal or sensitive information, usually through a fake website, some of which look extremely genuine. You also can run into websites that have been hacked and contain *malware* that tries to install itself on your computer, often without your knowledge; malware usually tries to harm you and your computer in some way, from simply messing up your computer's behaviour to trying to steal information.

Chrome includes technology, enabled by default, that helps protect you from phishing schemes and malware, displaying a warning whenever you visit a potentially dangerous page.

Chrome also uses a technique called *sandboxing* to open websites. Sandboxing isolates computer processes from anything else happening on the machine. If a sandboxed process crashes or becomes infected with malware, the rest of your computer remains unaffected. Each tab in Chrome opens as a separate process, completely independent of other tabs. If a website contains malware, the sandboxing technique isolates the malware to that browser tab; the malware can't jump to another Chrome tab or to your computer. You eliminate the malware threat when you close the infected website's browser tab.

REMEMBER

A third method hackers can use to gain access to your computer is by the use of plug-ins. *Plug-ins* are small add-on programs for browsers. Because they are add-on programs, plug-ins can become out-of-date and hackers can use them to try to introduce malware onto your computer. Adobe Flash Player is one of the most popular browser plug-ins; it is used most often to view video content. Out-of-date versions of Adobe Flash Player are also notorious for introducing malware into computers. Chrome reduces the threat that Adobe Flash Player poses by directly integrating it into Chrome. Because of this integration, updates for Adobe Flash Player are included in Chrome updates.

Chrome also regularly checks for the latest security update without any action on your part. By integrating Adobe Flash Player and regularly checking for security updates, Chrome greatly reduces the danger of malware infection.

To view the default security measures, you can follow the next steps:

WARNING

1. **Choose Chrome Menu ⇨ Settings.**

   Don't change security settings unless you really know what you're doing.

2. **Scroll to the bottom of the page and click Show Advanced Settings.**

   - In the Privacy section, the Protect You and Your Device from Dangerous Sites option warns you if Chrome detects that the site you're trying to visit might contain phishing or other malware.

   - From the HTTPS/SSL section, you can manage your SSL certificates and settings.

Chrome and Privacy

Chrome enables you to control the information you share online. For example, you can change your privacy settings, delete your browsing history and browse in Incognito mode. To adjust privacy settings, follow these steps:

1. **Choose Chrome Menu ⇨ Settings.**

2. **Scroll to the bottom of the Settings page and click Show Advanced Settings.**

3. **In the Privacy section, click Content Settings.**

   From the Content Settings dialog box, you can make a variety of changes.

In the following sections, we list the settings you might be most likely to change. If we don't cover a setting you want to change, you can search for help on that setting at support.google.com/chrome.

Handling cookies

You can control how Chrome handles cookies. In most cases, websites you visit place *cookies* on your computer for the purpose of recognising your specific browser/computer combination if you return to the site. Chrome allows cookies by default, because they are typically harmless, but cookies can allow sites to track your navigation during your visit to those sites.

TIP

Third-party cookies are cookies placed on your computer by one website for some other website. To increase privacy, most people block third-party cookies to prevent sharing information with parties not directly associated with the sites they visit.

Chrome and JavaScript

You can control whether Chrome runs JavaScript, which web developers often use to make their sites more interactive. If you disable JavaScript, you might find that some sites don't work properly.

Allowing plug-ins

Plug-ins appear on specific websites and are used by website developers to process web content that browsers can't inherently handle. For example, Adobe Flash Player processes content that web browsers don't inherently process. Chrome allows plug-ins to run by default, and if you disable this feature, various websites might not function as expected.

Working in Incognito mode

If you work in *Incognito mode*, you can browse the web without recording a history of the websites you have visited and without storing cookies. Using Incognito mode doesn't make Chrome more secure; it simply enhances your privacy by preventing Chrome from keeping a record of the sites you have visited during that particular browsing session. Even in Incognito mode, you shouldn't visit websites that you wouldn't feel safe viewing in a regular Chrome window.

To use Incognito mode, choose Chrome Menu⇨New Incognito Window. A new instance of Chrome opens; notice that two buttons for Chrome appear on the Windows taskbar. The new Chrome instance displays an incognito window like the one shown in Figure 19-3, and the Incognito icon appears in the upper left corner of the browser window, immediately to the left of the New Tab tab. You use an Incognito window the same way that you use the regular Chrome window; while you work, Chrome doesn't record a history of the sites you visit nor does Chrome allow sites to store cookies on your computer.

To stop browsing incognito, you must close the instance of Chrome that's running incognito.

Incognito icon

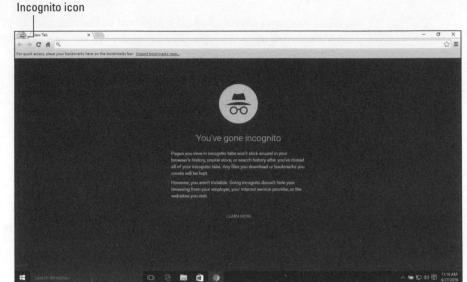

FIGURE 19-3:
An Incognito
window.

Google and the Google logo are registered trademarks of Google Inc., used with permission.

Deleting browsing history

Like all browsers, if you work in a regular Chrome window (rather than an Incognito window), Chrome keeps track of the websites you have visited during each browsing session. Browsers save your browsing history, among other reasons, to decrease the time you wait to see a web page that you have previously visited. And browser history can help you return to a website you visited previously even though you can't remember the website's address.

To view your browsing history, choose Chrome Menu➪History➪History. A page similar to the one shown in Figure 19-4 appears; your browsing history is organised by date and time, with the most recent sites you visited appearing first. You can click any entry to redisplay that web page.

You also can delete all or only part of your browsing history, typically to maintain your privacy. From the History page, click Clear Browsing Data. The dialog box shown in Figure 19-5 appears; you can choose the type of data you want to delete and the timeframe over which to delete that data.

REMEMBER

If you delete all of your cookies, you might need to re-identify yourself at websites where you were previously 'known', such as your bank's website. The process involves getting a code from the website and entering it, typically along with your password at that site, so that you can verify that you are, indeed, the user the website thinks you are.

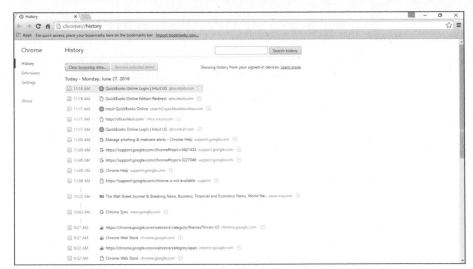

FIGURE 19-4:
Use your browsing history to revisit a web page you visited previously.

Google and the Google logo are registered trademarks of Google Inc., used with permission.

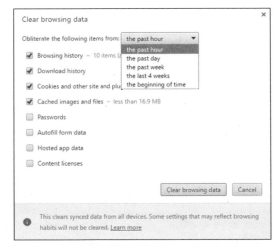

FIGURE 19-5:
Use this dialog box to delete browsing history.

Google and the Google logo are registered trademarks of
Google Inc., used with permission.

TIP

To delete a single browsing history entry, display the History page (shown previously in Figure 19-4) and hover the mouse pointer over the entry you want to delete. Select the check box to the left of the entry and, if appropriate, select additional entries to delete. Then click the Remove Selected Items button that becomes clickable at the top of the History page.

Reviewing miscellaneous privacy settings

In addition to the settings previously described in this section, you can control the way Chrome handles the following situations; the following descriptions describe Chrome's default behaviour:

>> Chrome asks for permission whenever a website wants to use your location information.

>> Chrome asks for permission whenever a site wants to automatically show notifications on your computer desktop.

>> Chrome asks for permission whenever sites or apps such as games want to disable your mouse pointer.

>> Chrome asks for permission whenever websites request access to your computer's camera and microphone.

>> Chrome asks for permission if a website wants to bypass Chrome's sandbox technology and directly access your computer.

>> Chrome blocks pop-ups from appearing and cluttering your screen.

To use Chrome effectively with QBO and QBOA, you can't block *all* pop-ups. By default, Chrome blocks all pop-ups. If you try to use QBO or QBOA while pop-ups are blocked, you'll see a screen similar to the one shown in Figure 19-6.

Click this button to display options for handling pop-ups on a particular website.

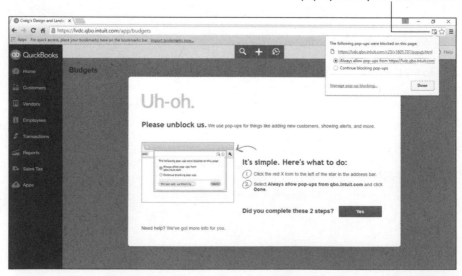

FIGURE 19-6:
When all pop-ups are blocked, you can't access QBO or QBOA.

Google and the Google logo are registered trademarks of Google Inc., used with permission.

Note the pop-up blocker icon at the right edge of the Omnibox. Click it to display the message shown in Figure 19-6, and then select the first option to allow QBO and QBOA pop-ups.

You can turn on pop-ups selectively for any website. Follow these steps:

1. **Click Chrome Menu ⇨ Settings.**

2. **Click Show Advanced Settings.**

3. **In the Privacy section, click the Content Settings button.**

4. **In the Content Settings dialog box, scroll down to the Pop-ups section and click Manage Exceptions (see Figure 19-7).**

5. **In the Pop-up Exceptions dialog box that appears, type the name of the website for which you want to manage pop-ups.**

6. **From the Behavior list box beside the web address, choose Allow or Block.**

Using Google tools to manage privacy

Although Google can collect a lot of information about you, you can control just how much information Google collects using Google's privacy management tools. Visit myaccount.google.com/intro; from this website, you can, for example, use the Ads Settings to log in to your Google account and adjust the ads Chrome shows you.

Using Bookmarks in Chrome

Bookmarks enable you to save a web page address so that you can easily return to it. In this section, you learn to

>> Create a bookmark

>> Use a bookmark to display its associated web page

>> Display the Bookmarks bar in Chrome to make bookmarks more accessible

>> Organise bookmarks by renaming them, placing them into folders, changing the order in which they appear when you view bookmarks, and deleting bookmarks you no longer need

Creating a bookmark

Creating a bookmark is easy. First, navigate to the web page you want to bookmark. For example, you might want to bookmark the QBO or QBOA sign-in page. Then click the Bookmark This Page button (the one that looks like a star) at the right edge of the Omnibox, press Ctrl+D or choose Chrome Menu➪Bookmarks➪Bookmark This Page. The Bookmark Added! dialog box appears (see Figure 19-8).

You can change the bookmark's name (we shortened ours) and the folder in which Chrome stores it. By default, Chrome offers two folders:

>> The Bookmarks bar folder

>> The Other Bookmarks folder

Choose one of these folders, click Done, and Chrome saves your bookmark. All bookmarks you create appear at the bottom of the Bookmarks menu; choose Chrome Menu➪Bookmarks to see them.

If you place the bookmarks you use most often on the Bookmarks bar, they can be easily visible and available for use, as you'll see in the next section.

So, logically, because you're an organised human being, you want to know if you can create your own folders and organise your bookmarks using your organisational style. Yes, you can, using the Bookmark Manager, and you can read more about the Bookmark Manager later in this chapter in the section 'Managing bookmarks'.

Bookmarks can 'break' and display 'page not found' messages (error code 404). If this happens, manually navigate to the page and save the bookmark again, overwriting the original bookmark.

Displaying the Bookmarks bar

By default, Chrome saves your bookmarks to the Bookmarks bar, which appears just below the Omnibox every time you open the New Tab page. The Bookmarks bar makes using bookmarks faster and easier because bookmarks are always visible. You can simply click the appropriate bookmark on the Bookmarks bar to display its associated web page.

To take full advantage of the Bookmarks bar, you should display it on all Chrome tabs (instead of just the New Tab tab). Press Ctrl+Shift+B or choose Chrome Menu ⇨ Bookmarks ⇨ Show Bookmarks bar. Chrome displays as many bookmarks as possible on the Bookmarks bar, based on the names you give to your bookmarks: The shorter the name, the more bookmarks Chrome can display. But you can easily get to the bookmarks you can't see by clicking the small button containing two right-pointing arrows at the right edge of the Bookmarks bar (see Figure 19-9).

Bookmarks bar   Click here to display additional bookmarks.

FIGURE 19-9:
Take advantage of the Bookmarks bar.

Google and the Google logo are registered trademarks of Google Inc., used with permission.

Importing bookmarks

If you've been working in a different browser and want to copy your bookmarks from that browser to Chrome, no problem. Choose Chrome Menu ⇨ Bookmarks ⇨

Import Bookmarks and Settings. The Import Bookmarks and Settings dialog box appears (see Figure 19-10).

FIGURE 19-10: Use this dialog box to identify what you want to import.

Select the browser from which to import them and select or deselect the check boxes beside the items you want to import; different browsers offer different importing options. Then, click Import, and Chrome imports the information. The imported bookmarks appear in a folder on the Bookmarks bar, and you can use the Bookmark Manager, described in the next section, to reorganise these bookmarks.

Managing bookmarks

If you're like us, you'll learn to love bookmarks — perhaps to your detriment. As you accumulate bookmarks, finding them to be able to use them becomes a project. You have a few avenues available to you:

>> You can organise your bookmarks by repositioning them on the Bookmarks bar and on the list of bookmarks on the Bookmarks menu (choose Chrome Menu ⇨ Bookmarks).

>> You can create folders for your bookmarks and place bookmarks in the appropriate folder.

>> You can search for a bookmark.

To reposition bookmarks, you can drag them on the Bookmarks bar or on the list of bookmarks (either the list that appears when you click the button at the right edge of the Bookmarks bar, or the list of bookmarks that appears at the bottom of the Bookmarks menu). A black line (vertical if you're dragging on the Bookmarks bar or horizontal if you're dragging on either list of bookmarks) helps you locate the new position for the bookmark; simply release the mouse button when the bookmark appears where you want it to appear.

You also can use the Bookmark Manager to reorder bookmarks; in addition, using the Bookmark Manager, you can create folders and organise bookmarks into those folders, delete bookmarks and folders you no longer need, rename bookmarks and search for bookmarks.

To open the Bookmark Manager, choose Chrome Menu⇨Bookmarks⇨Bookmark Manager. A tab like the one shown in Figure 19-11 appears.

Bookmark Manager Organize menu   Bookmarks search box

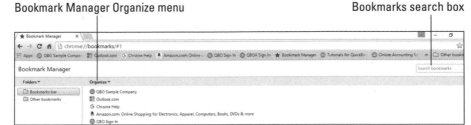

Google and the Google logo are registered trademarks of Google Inc., used with permission.

FIGURE 19-11:
The Bookmark Manager.

TIP

The Bookmark Manager window works the same way that Windows Explorer and File Explorer work; if you're familiar with Windows Explorer or File Explorer, you already know many of the techniques you use to organise bookmarks.

The left pane displays existing folders and the right pane shows the bookmarks in each folder you select in the left pane. You use the Organize button just above the left pane to make organisation changes.

TIP

To delete any bookmark or folder except the Bookmarks bar folder and the Other Bookmarks folder, click the bookmark or folder and then press the Delete key on your keyboard. Nope, you can't delete the Bookmarks bar folder or the Other Bookmarks folder.

You can use folders to organise bookmarks; for example, you can organise bookmarks by subject. Although you can add new folders to the Other Bookmarks folder at the bottom of the list on the left, we suggest that you confine your organisation to the Bookmarks bar folder. You can compare keeping all your bookmarks on the Bookmarks bar to owning only one file cabinet. The cabinet has multiple drawers (folders, in this analogy), but you need to search only one cabinet to find what you need. Finding a particular bookmark will be easier if you use only the Bookmarks bar folder.

To create a new folder on the Bookmarks bar, choose Organise⇨Add Folder. Type a name for the new folder and press Enter.

When you create a new bookmark that you want to place in this folder, select this folder in the Folder list box of the Bookmark Added! dialog box (refer back to Figure 19-8).

To add an existing bookmark to a folder, click the bookmark on the right side of the Bookmark Manager window and drag it to the appropriate folder on the left side of the Bookmark Manager window.

To reorder bookmarks or folders, drag the bookmark or folder up or down in the list on either side of the Bookmark Manager window. That is, you can drag folders in the left side of the window and bookmarks or folders in the right side of the window. A horizontal black line appears as you drag and helps you locate the new position for the bookmark or folder; release the mouse button when the bookmark or folder's black line appears at the correct location in the list.

To rename any folder or bookmark, right-click it and choose Edit from the menu that appears. Then, type a new name and press Enter.

Suppose that, after this wonderful organising you've done, you can't remember where you put a particular bookmark. No problem. Use the Bookmarks search box (refer to Figure 19-11). Type an address or search term into the search box and press Enter. Chrome displays any bookmarks that match the address or search term. To cancel the search and redisplay all your bookmarks, click the X that appears in the search box.

When you finish working in the Bookmark Manager window, click the X that appears in the tab's name.

Duplicating and Pinning Tabs

Chapter 18 describes how to open multiple tabs as you browse in Chrome and how to reposition tabs within the Chrome window.

At times, you might find it useful to duplicate a QuickBooks company tab you've already opened so that you have that tab open twice — or so that you can open two different tabs for the same company simultaneously. To duplicate any tab, right-click the tab and choose Duplicate from the shortcut menu that appears (see Figure 19-12). Chrome automatically opens another tab using the web address of the duplicated tab. You can then work on the tabs independently of each other, switching to different tabs in the same company.

FIGURE 19-12:
Duplicate a
browser tab in
Chrome.

*Google and the
Google logo are
registered trademarks
of Google Inc., used
with permission.*

You might also find it useful to *pin* a particular Chrome tab; pinned tabs open automatically whenever you start Chrome. To pin a tab, right-click the tab and choose Pin Tab from the shortcut menu that appears (refer to Figure 19-12).

TIP

If you decide you no longer want a pinned tab to appear each time you open Chrome, right-click the pinned tab and click Unpin Tab from the menu that appears. Be aware that the Unpin tab command appears only if you previously pinned the tab.

Using Chrome on Multiple Monitors

Here's another tab-related trick: If you have more than one monitor, you can pull one tab out of the Chrome window and drag it to your other monitor so that you can work in QBO/QBOA on multiple screens. Again, because tabs in Chrome function independently, the work you do in each window is independent of the other.

To pull a tab, click and drag the tab; a preview of the new window appears. Release the mouse button and the tab appears in a new window onscreen. If you didn't drag the tab to a different monitor, no problem. Just drag the new window by its title bar to your second monitor. (Yes, if you have three monitors, you can repeat this process.)

Setting Up Chrome Users

In Chapter 18, we explain that you can set up multiple users, each of whom can have different Chrome settings. At that time, we promised that we'd show you how to set up multiple Chrome users — and, here we are.

If you want to log in to two different QBO companies from a single QBO account, you can use different Chrome users. To create a user, choose Chrome Menu➪ Settings to display the Settings tab. In the People section, click Add Person to display the Add Person dialog box (see Figure 19-13).

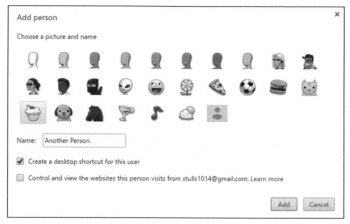

FIGURE 19-13:
The Add Person dialog box.

Google and the Google logo are registered trademarks of Google Inc., used with permission.

Select an icon for the new user and enter a name for the user; the name will appear in the Current User button, and the icon will appear when you click the Current User button in the upper right corner of the Chrome window. Optionally, you can create a desktop shortcut for the user so that the user can quickly and easily open his or her own version of Chrome. Then click Add.

Another instance of Chrome opens and you'll see two buttons on the Windows taskbar. You can identify the current user by looking at the Current User button in the upper right corner of the browser, and you can easily switch from one user to another. Let's assume that you have opened only one instance of Chrome, so only one button appears on the Windows taskbar. To switch users, click Current User➪ Switch Person, as shown in Figure 19-14.

Chrome displays a window listing the currently defined users (see Figure 19-15); click one or click the Add Person button to go through the process of creating a new user.

Assuming you select an existing user, Chrome opens a new browser window. If you don't maximise Chrome, you can easily see the open windows.

TIP

To shortcut the process of switching users, you can right-click the Current User button; a list of available users appears and you can click the one you want.

FIGURE 19-14:
To initiate switching users, use the Current User button.

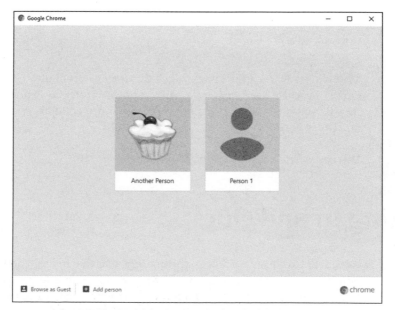

FIGURE 19-15:
Select a different user.

You can use the menu that appears when you click the Current User button to easily change a user's name or icon. To change a user's icon, click the Current User button and then click the picture currently displayed (see Figure 19-16). Chrome opens the Edit version of the dialog box you saw earlier in Figure 19-13. Just select a different icon. And you can change the user's name here, too.

Click here to change
the icon, user name, or both.

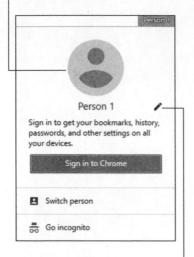

FIGURE 19-16:
Edit a user's icon,
name or both.

Click here to edit the user's name.

To change only the user's name, click the Current User button and slide the mouse cursor over the user's name; a pencil appears (refer to Figure 19-16). Click the pencil, and the text for the user's name becomes editable. Just type a new name and press Enter.

REMEMBER

You can delete a user from the Chrome Settings tab.

Zooming In and Out

At times, tired eyes need help; fortunately, you can zoom in and out of Chrome's windows easily. Press Ctrl++ (plus sign) to make the information in the window larger (known as *zooming in*) and Ctrl+- (minus sign) to reduce the size of the information in the window (you guessed it: *Zooming out*).

WARNING

Be aware that, while zooming in is great for enlarging text, zooming can also alter how web pages appear, even to the point of hiding content that would otherwise be visible. So, if something seems to be missing, try resetting the zoom factor to 100%.

Downloading Files

Chrome can display many different types of documents, media and other files, such as PDF and MP3 files. But you might need to save a file to your computer.

Instead of clicking the file's link — which is always tempting — right-click the link and, from the menu that appears, click Save Link As. Then, in the dialog box that appears, navigate to the folder on your computer where you want to save the file, give the file a name you'll recognise and click Save. The file downloads and you can monitor the download progress in the lower left corner of the Chrome browser window.

REMEMBER

If you click a link to a file, it might download automatically or it might open within the Chrome browser. To prevent a file from opening in Chrome, make sure that you right-click the link.

To view and open any downloaded file, use the Downloads tab (see Figure 19-17). Choose Chrome Menu ⇨ Downloads. From this tab, you can

- **»** Open downloaded files by clicking them
- **»** Open the Downloads folder by clicking the Show in Folder link below any downloaded file, or by clicking the Open Downloads Folder link above the list of downloads and below the Bookmarks bar
- **»** Search for downloads using the search box by clicking the magnifying glass in the upper right corner of the screen, just below the Bookmarks bar
- **»** Clear the Downloads list using the Clear All link above the list of downloads and below the Bookmarks bar

FIGURE 19-17:
The Downloads tab.

Google and the Google logo are registered trademarks of Google Inc., used with permission.

Chrome on Mobile Devices

You can use the Chrome browser on mobile devices as well as on desktop computers (of course you can!). Chrome works on both iOS and Android, and the Chrome app is typically preinstalled on Android devices because Android and Chrome are both Google products. Chrome on a mobile device functions pretty much the same way that Chrome on a desktop computer functions. One important note: The Chrome menu button looks like three vertically aligned dots instead of the bars you see in the desktop version of Chrome.

Appendix

QBO, QuickBooks Desktop and Data Conversion

Although you can import most data from Xero, MYOB and Reckon software as well as a QuickBooks desktop company into QBO, not everything converts. In some cases, some things convert completely or have counterparts in QBO. And some things convert partially or have simply been replaced by QBO features. But in some cases, things don't convert and no QBO substitute feature exists.

This appendix explores data conversion and gives you a sense of what you can expect if you convert a QuickBooks desktop company to QBO.

General Limitations of Importing Desktop QuickBooks Data into QuickBooks Online

When you convert a desktop QuickBooks company to QuickBooks Online (QBO), some data fully converts, some partially converts, and some doesn't convert at all. In addition, QBO contains comparable features for some desktop QuickBooks features and doesn't contain comparable features for others.

As you'd expect, you might bump up against limitations while trying to import your desktop QuickBooks data into QBO. Detailed information about those limitations can be found in this appendix.

TIP

For more information, visit the QuickBooks FAQ, 'Why some data doesn't come over from QuickBooks desktop'.

The tables provide detailed information; generally, here's a list of what doesn't convert:

>> Subtotal items, tax items and other group items

>> Memorised transactions and reports

>> Some payroll items

>> Customer and supplier accounts, types, contact information, credit card and limit information, and sales reps

>> Customer, supplier, employee and item custom field information

>> Attached documents

>> Price levels

>> Sales form templates

>> Pending transactions

>> Reconciliation reports

Note: Budgets are available only in QuickBooks Online Plus.

Also, inventory items do convert. However, if you have hundreds of items, you might opt not to convert inventory and then do some clean-up and setup work to balance things in your QBO company, as described in the online video at `www.screencast.com/t/0hgpGl2MJJwf`.

How QuickBooks Desktop Lists Convert to QuickBooks Online

When you work with some desktop QuickBooks company lists, some fields convert into QuickBooks Online (QBO) but others don't. This section is organised by desktop QuickBooks list. Also included is some information about how inventory works in QBO.

Customer and Job List

When it comes to conversion, the fields in the Customer:Job list of the desktop QuickBooks product fall into three categories:

>> Fields that convert include Customer, Company Name, Mr./Ms./?, First Name, Middle Initial, Last Name, Phone, Fax, Alternate Phone, Email, Resale No., Terms, and Is Taxable check box.

>> Fields that convert with exceptions include Bill to Address (except Note), Ship To Address (except Note), Preferred Payment Method (except from QuickBooks 2003 or later), Credit Card Information (except from QuickBooks 2003 or later), and Note (up to 4,000 characters).

>> Fields that don't convert include Contact, Alt. Contact, Customer Type, Rep, Price Level, Tax Item, Custom Fields, Account, and Credit Limit. Also note that inactive status customers convert as active.

TIP

After conversion, you can edit customers to make them inactive.

In addition, these Pro Only fields don't convert: Job Status, Start Date, Projected End, End Date, Job Description, and Job Type.

Item List

In transactions, subtotal items appear on separate lines, with text in the Memo field indicating they are a subtotal.

Group items don't convert; instead, each item in the group appears on a detail line, and zero-amount lines appear at the start and end of the group to identify the items that were part of the group. The top line shows the group name, and the bottom line shows the group description.

Tax group items don't convert, but you can set up combined tax items in QBO.

Employee List

The information in the desktop QuickBooks edition Employee List converts to QuickBooks Online, but QBO retains only the following information:

>> Mr/Ms

>> First name

>> Middle initial

>> Last name

>> Address

>> Print As

>> Phone

>> Tax File Number

>> Email address

>> Hire date

>> Release date

Supplier List

The following Supplier List fields don't convert:

>> Contact

>> Alternate contact

>> Note

>> Inactive

>> Supplier Type

>> Credit Limit

>> Tax ID

>> Custom fields

A look at inventory . . .

QBO supports basic inventory needs; if you run a service business or sell finished goods, QBO should be able to support your inventory needs. Inventory items convert as two-sided items in QBO with prices and costs but no quantities. Here's how QuickBooks Online converts inventory parts and transactions:

» QBO creates new sub-items called Inventory Asset and COGS for each inventory item used on a transaction. Although the names of these sub-items imply that they are accounts, they aren't. These items contain the same description as their parent item, but have, respectively, the inventory asset account and COGS account associated with them. Conversion uses them to ensure that reports are correct after conversion.

» After each inventory line on converted invoices, sales receipts, credit memos, and on some bills, cheques, and credit card transactions that contained inventory items, QBO creates two new detail lines using the new sub-items that represent the inventory asset and COGS amounts.

For unpaid or partially paid transactions that contain inventory items, cash basis reports with a COGS amount in QBO will be different from cash basis reports with a COGS amount in desktop QuickBooks. Cash basis reports for fully paid inventory transactions or non-inventory transactions will be the same in QBO and desktop QuickBooks.

After you convert inventory from a QuickBooks desktop company to QBO, you can't just start using inventory in QBO. You need to go through a clean-up process. You can find excellent details on the clean-up process in the 'How to Resolve Post Conversion Inventory Issues in QBO' video. Following is a general description of the clean-up process.

Generally, conversion creates the new sub-items as a temporary measure for the sole purpose of making sure that your reports are correct. After conversion, you find, in the Chart of Accounts, an Inventory account converted from your QuickBooks desktop company. Then, when you turn on inventory and quantity-on-hand tracking in QBO, QBO creates *another* Inventory account — the one that you use going forward as you work in QBO. To establish the correct inventory dollar valuation in the Inventory account created by QBO and to make your inventory items update the correct Inventory account going forward — the one created by QBO — you need to edit each inventory item (not the sub-items created during conversion) and fill in the correct quantity on hand. This process results in doubling your inventory value by displaying it in both the Inventory account created from your QuickBooks desktop company during conversion and in the Inventory account QBO creates. To correct the overstatement, you use a journal entry that removes the dollars from the QuickBooks desktop Inventory account.

But before you correct the inventory value and after you've edited every item, you can and should delete the sub-items created during conversion.

Because you need to do the clean-up process on an item-by-item basis, if you have hundreds of inventory items, you might find all of this overwhelming. As an alternative, you can opt not to convert inventory and, instead, follow the instructions found in the video. The video suggests that you import the Item List but not the details for each item. Instead, set up the details of each item in QBO. For hundreds of items, importing only the list information will probably be faster and cleaner.

Importing list information only has one downside: You lose the historical data associated with your inventory items. But nothing is stopping you from keeping your QBO desktop company around for the times when you might need that history.

Features That Convert Completely

The following table lists transactions and features that fully convert from a desktop QuickBooks company to a QuickBooks Online (QBO) company or have comparable features in QBO. For more information, visit the QuickBooks FAQ, 'Why some data doesn't come over from QuickBooks desktop'.

Area	Type of Data
Customers	Credit memos and refunds, invoices, sales receipts and online invoicing.
Supplier	Bills and bill payments.
Employees	Time tracking. Payroll accounts and transactions convert but the details behind the transactions, such as employee year-to-date information, do not convert. QuickBooks Online Plus provides the feature comparable to Payroll in the QuickBooks desktop product.
Banking	Credit card charges, journal entries, reconciliation, transfer funds, write cheques and make deposits.
Lists	Accounts, classes, and payment methods; see the section, 'How QuickBooks Desktop Lists Convert to QuickBooks Online' for more information
Other	Accountant's Review feature.

Transactions and Features for Which Most Information Converts in QuickBooks Online

The following table lists transactions and features for which most data converts and comparable transactions and features exist in QuickBooks Online (QBO). In some cases, exceptions exist, as described in the Notes in the following table. You can also find specific notes in the section, 'How QuickBooks Desktop Lists Convert to QuickBooks Online', earlier in this appendix. And for more information, visit the QuickBooks FAQ, 'Why some data doesn't come over from QuickBooks desktop'.

Type of Data or Feature	Notes
Receive Payments	Discounts convert to credit memos that are linked to the payment.
Statement Charges	Sales or credits that were entered directly in an A/R register are converted to invoices.
Tax	QBO supports multiple tax rates and agencies, but only transactions created in QBO appear in QBO's GST Centre.
Quotes	Quotes convert but work differently in QBO. In QuickBooks desktop, you turn an estimate into an invoice. In QBO, you add data from a quote onto an invoice and you assign each quote a status: Pending, Accepted, Closed, or Rejected. There is no progress invoicing at this time in QBO, but a workaround can be found at the Fundera blog entry, 'Job Costing QuickBooks Online with Sub-Customers'.
Registers	None.
Customers & Jobs	Some fields convert completely, some convert with exceptions, and some don't convert. Refer to the section 'How QuickBooks Desktop Lists Convert to QuickBooks Online' for details.
Items	QBO refers to items as products and services and uses three types. All item types convert (two-sided QuickBooks desktop items convert to two-sided QBO items) except for subtotal, group, and sales tax group items. Subtotals from QuickBooks desktop transactions appear on separate lines on invoices, with text in the Description field indicating that they are subtotals, but subtotal items do not convert. QBO contains a feature that enables you to add subtotals to sales transactions. Refer to the section 'How QuickBooks Desktop Lists Convert to QuickBooks Online' for details.
Employees	Essentially, employee information found on the Personal and Address & Contact tabs of the Edit Employee dialog box in desktop QuickBooks converts and is retained. Payroll information does not convert.

(continued)

(continued)

Type of Data or Feature	Notes
Other Names	QBO contains no Other Names list and converts all names on this list in your desktop QuickBooks company data file to suppliers. Checks with payees from the Other Names list might convert with the payee field deleted.
Suppliers	All suppliers convert, but some fields don't convert. Refer to the section 'How QuickBooks Desktop Lists Convert to QuickBooks Online' for details.

Features That Might Not Convert but Have Comparable Features in QuickBooks Online

In some cases, some data might not convert in QuickBooks Online (QBO). But QBO contains comparable transactions and features that you can use. The following table lists that information. For more information, visit the QuickBooks FAQ, 'Why some data doesn't come over from QuickBooks desktop'.

Type of Data or Feature	Notes
Inventory	QBO tracks inventory, but you can opt not to convert inventory and, instead, use the information found in the "How to Resolve Post Conversion Inventory Issues in QBO" video to set up inventory.
Purchase orders	QBO converts open purchases from desktop QuickBooks to open purchase orders in QBO. Received in Full or Closed desktop purchase orders convert to closed QBO purchase orders and are not linked to their corresponding bill.
Payroll items	Some but not all Payroll items convert.
Payroll data	Transactions and payroll accounts are converted so your books will balance, but details behind the transactions are not converted. Liability refunds, adjustment transactions, and opening balance transactions that affect accounts are converted to journal entries. Refer to Chapter 9 for details on handling payroll in QBO.
Customisation	No desktop QuickBooks templates convert to QBO.
Memorised transactions	Memorised transactions do not convert, but you can set them up in QBO as recurring transactions.
Audit trail	Audit trail information does not convert, but QBO uses the Activity Log to provide an audit trail.

Type of Data or Feature	Notes
Closing date and password	QBO converts closing date and associated password information and tracks new exceptions, but the Exceptions to Closing Date report in QBO doesn't show previously accumulated exceptions.
Reminders	QBO doesn't convert desktop QuickBooks reminders but does contain its own comparable feature.
Users and permissions	QBO does not convert usernames, but you can re-create them. In QBO, you can set access permissions similar to those in desktop QuickBooks, but you can't set permissions to control activity at the level of transactions.
Import/Export	QBO exports to desktop QuickBooks 2004 or later and to Microsoft Excel. QBO doesn't import from or export to other applications that use .IIF files. Transaction Pro Importer is the third party to use with QBO for importing transactions and unsupported lists from Excel or CSV.
Budgets	QBO doesn't convert desktop QuickBooks budgets, but QBO Plus does contain its own budget feature.
Memorised reports	QBO doesn't convert desktop QuickBooks memorised reports but does enable you to memorise QBO reports.
Customer messages	QBO Plus retains customer messages stored on converted desktop QuickBooks sales forms. Although you can include customer messages on sales forms in QBO, you need to enter them manually each time because QBO does not support a predefined list of customer messages.
Online banking	QBO converts desktop QuickBooks online banking accounts and their transactions, but in QBO you must set them up again for online banking.
Tax group items	Tax group items don't convert, but you can recreate them in QBO as combined rates.

Features That Don't Convert and Don't Exist in QuickBooks Online

The following table lists transactions and features that don't convert from desktop QuickBooks to QuickBooks Online (QBO) and also have no comparable feature in QBO. Although one or more of these transactions or features might be deal breakers, remember that, for many of these features, you can use workarounds.

Type of Data or Feature	Notes
Finance charges	QBO converts existing finance charge invoices with no data loss but contains no feature to automatically assess finance charges. If you used finance charges in QuickBooks desktop, the conversion process creates a QBO product or service item called Finance Charge. You can use this item to manually assess finance charges.
Receive Items	QBO doesn't support tracking items on purchases and has no comparable feature for any of the ways you receive items in desktop QuickBooks. All of these transactions convert to QBO as bills.
Item price levels	QBO doesn't convert item price levels from desktop QuickBooks and contains no feature to automatically adjust product and service prices.
Shortcut list and icon bar settings	These features don't convert from desktop QuickBooks to QBO and no comparable features exist in QBO. Keyboard shortcuts do exist; anywhere in QBO, press Ctrl+Alt+/ to see the list. For a list of handy shortcuts, see the cheat sheet article '16 Keyboard Shortcuts for QuickBooks Online and QuickBooks Online Accountant'.
Synchronise contacts	QBO does not contain any way to synchronise your contacts with other data sources.
Write letters	QBO contains no comparable feature to the desktop QuickBooks Write Letters feature.
Discounts	QBO doesn't automatically calculate terms discounts. QBO converts discounts already given to customers in desktop QuickBooks as credit memos and discounts taken from vendors as vendor credits.
Pending sales	No pending sales transactions convert from desktop QuickBooks to QBO, and QBO contains no feature comparable to the pending sale.
Progress invoices	At the time of writing, QBO doesn't support turning an estimate into a series of invoices as a project progresses. QBO converts progress invoices from a desktop QuickBooks company to invoices in QBO, but the following fields don't convert: Estimate Qty, Estimate Rate, Estimate Amount, Prior Quantity, Prior Average Quantity, Prior Average Rate, Prior Amount, Prior %, Curr %, and Total %.
To do notes	QBO doesn't convert QuickBooks desktop to do notes and doesn't contain a comparable feature.
Customer, supplier, and job types	QBO doesn't convert customer, supplier, or job types and has no corresponding feature to categorise customers, suppliers, or jobs.
Online bill payment	QBO converts accounts you use for online bill payment, but no online bill payment service is available in QBO. QBO converts cheques marked 'To be Sent' in desktop QuickBooks, but not their payment status.
Tax support	QBO doesn't convert or support tax line assignments and doesn't export information to tax preparation programs.
Fax invoices	QBO contains no feature to fax invoices, but you can email invoices.

Index

About the Authors

Priscilla Meli has provided bookkeeping services for various clients in numerous industries for the past 12 years and is the director of Bookkeeper Hero, a business that supports small- to medium-sized enterprises with all aspects of bookkeeping and business management, specialising in cloud accounting and QuickBooks Online training. Priscilla was one of the first members of the Intuit QuickBooks Online Trainer Writer Network, and has provided group training to accountants and book-keepers around Australia. Priscilla has authored other step-by-step guides to using QuickBooks Online while remaining active in her bookkeeping practice. Priscilla lives in Victoria, Australia, and enjoys qigong, meditation and self-improvement and motivational seminars.

Elaine Marmel is President of Marmel Enterprises, LLC., an organisation that specialises in technical writing and software training. Elaine has an MBA from Cornell University and has worked on projects to build financial management systems for New York City and Washington, DC, training more than 600 employees to use these systems. This prior experience provided the foundation for Marmel Enterprises, LLC., to help small businesses implement computerised accounting systems.

Elaine spends most of her time writing: She has authored and co-authored more than 90 books about software products, including Windows, QuickBooks, Quicken for Windows, Quicken for DOS, Microsoft Project, Microsoft Excel, Microsoft Word for Windows, Word for Mac, 1-2-3 for Windows, and Lotus Notes. From 1994 to 2006, she was also the contributing editor for the monthly publications *Inside Peachtree for Windows*, *Inside QuickBooks* and *Inside Timeslips*.

Elaine left her native Chicago for the warmer climes of Arizona (by way of Cincin-nati, OH; Jerusalem, Israel; Ithaca, NY; Washington, DC and Tampa, FL) where she basks in the sun with her PC and her dog, Jack, and cross-stitches.

Authors' Acknowledgements

From Priscilla: A special thanks to our Aussie team who helped take the US manual and localise it, painstakingly, page by page, to give the reader an accurate overview of the QuickBooks Online Australian offering. It would not have been possible without those stars in our Melbourne and Sydney QBO support team and to Alison Ball, the glue that binds us all together. It was a pleasure working with you all on this amazing project. It was a pleasure working with you all on this amazing project.

From Elaine: Because a book is not just the work of the authors, I'd like to acknowledge and thank all the folks who made this book possible. Thanks to the Wiley team in the US, especially Katie Mohr for the opportunity to write this book. Thank you, Le'Darien Diaz, for once again being a technical editor extraordinaire, for easing my way as I worked with QBO and QBOA, for ensuring that I 'told no lies', and for offering valuable suggestions along the way. Last, but certainly not least, thank you, Scott and Maureen Tullis, for the outstanding job you did to guarantee that my manuscript was understandable and to manage everything involved in producing this book; you did a great job and really made my life easy. You make a fabulous team together, T-Squared.

Publisher's Acknowledgements

We're proud of this book; please send us your comments through our online registration form located at dummies.custhelp.com.

Some of the people who helped bring this book to market include the following:

Acquisitions, Editorial and Media Development

Acquisitions Editor: Lucy Raymond

Project Editor: Charlotte Duff

Editorial Manager: Ingrid Bond

Production

Graphics: SPi

Technical Review: Intuit

Proofreader: Kerry Laundon

Indexer: Don Jordan, Antipodes Indexing

The author and publisher would like to thank the following copyright holders, organisations and individuals for their permission to reproduce copyright material in this book:

>> Cover image: © Intuit Australia Pty Ltd 2017.

>> Screen captures from QuickBooks Online used with permission. © Intuit Australia Pty Ltd 2017. QuickBooks Online and the QuickBooks Online logo are registered trademarks of Intuit Australia Pty Ltd. Any data displayed in these images is fictitious, and any similarities with any actual data, individual, or entity is purely coincidental.

>> Microsoft Excel screenshots used with permission from Microsoft.

Every effort has been made to trace the ownership of copyright material. Information that enables the publisher to rectify any error or omission in subsequent editions is welcome. In such cases, please contact the Legal Services section of John Wiley & Sons Australia, Ltd.